MW00564487

Collecting Antique
COPPER & BRASS

Collecting Antique
COPPER & BRASS

Peter Hornsby

MPC

British Library Cataloguing in Publication Data

Hornsby, Peter
    Collecting antique copper and brass.
    1. British brassware, to ca1900 — Collectors' guides
    2. British copperware, to ca1900 — Collectors'
    guides
    I. Title
    739'.52'0941

ISBN 0 86190 118 5

Cover illustrations from the MPC Picture Collection
with the grateful assistance of Spurrier-Smith (Antiques), Ashbourne

Published by;
Moorland Publishing Co Ltd,
Moor Farm Road, Ashbourne,
Derbyshire, DE6 1HD, England

Printed in the UK by:
Butler and Tanner Ltd,
Frome, Somerset

CONTENTS

1
INTRODUCTION

A few items made of brass, copper and bronze would have been found in the homes of the rich in the middle ages, but it was not until the sixteenth century that their use became widespread. Seventeenth-century inventories show a surprising quantity of brass and copper in homes, mostly used in cooking; 80 per cent of domestic objects recorded in inventories at death were for cooking and included such items as pots, pans, cauldrons and skillets. Less frequently found were candlesticks, while few other objects occur with any regularity. There are no comparable figures for later periods but it is clear that by the nineteenth century a much larger range of objects made in these metals were to be found in people's homes and that they were both for use and decoration.

At the start of the eighteenth century the industry was based on small work shops and individual craftsmen but by the end of the nineteenth century brass, especially, was produced on a large scale in factories. Until the late seventeenth century most brass and copper objects used in British homes were imported from Holland and Germany, but gradually local production increased. By 1750 Britain was self-sufficient, and exported large quantities of finished goods. By the 1850s Birmingham dominated the scene as the largest centre of brass production in the world.

What was started as a strategic move to provide cannon for Queen Elizabeth's ships and army ended as a major British industry supplying the world. This did not all come about by chance. Many areas of Britain were rich in copper and zinc. There was the water power, and later the steam power, to drive the hammers and engines and the coal to smelt the ores and make

the brass. At first imported skills had to be relied on, but gradually Briton's acquired the technology for themselves.

Although brass and copper are no longer widely used in the home, their appeal is undiminished. Antique and modern brass and copper are found widely as decoration, where its soft glow helps to enrich our lives.

Each age tends to produce a dominant material. Pewter was pre-eminent in the seventeenth century and plastic and stainless steel overwhelm our kitchens today. In the same way brass, copper and bronze had a special importance in the domestic scene in the eighteenth and nineteenth centuries. Many other materials found their way into our homes and each played their role. Above all copper, brass and bronze dominated kitchens, provided lighting and decorated living rooms for well over two hundred years. To begin with most things were made solely for use but by the late Victorian age brass was widely used as decoration.

What little has been written on British domestic brass, copper and bronze has been directed primarily towards the earlier periods of the industry in the seventeenth century. British brass, copper and bronze from these times is rare and costly. It is hard to find and even harder to buy. Yet antique shops and auction sale rooms regularly offer a range of interesting eighteenth-and nineteenth-century copper, brass and bronze objects. The difficulty is that little is known about the products of the eighteenth and nineteenth centuries. What is lacking is a systematic study of the kind of British copper, brass and bronze which can still be found and which does not cost a small fortune. This book aims to fill this gap.

This book examines the main domestic items

made in brass, copper and bronze in Britain, with occasional examples from the Continent for comparison, but inevitably there will be some items which have been omitted as the range of goods made by 1850 is amazing. Examples of the more important forms are illustrated, but as there were over 100,000 different designs in the nineteenth century alone, only a small percentage of objects can be shown. It is one of the pleasures of this field of study that the last word will never be written, for we are learning every month of new forms which have come to light or which are recognised for what they are for the first time. The study of British brass, copper and bronze is still in a fluid state.

Some definitions are necessary. However we will see later that the clear cut distinctions of the text books are often blurred in reality. Brass is made from copper and zinc. Bronze is an alloy of copper and tin but sometimes contains lead. Copper, a naturally occuring element, was also used on its own, without deliberate additives.

As might be expected most alloys are not so simple. Trace elements were left in the refining of copper and contribute something to the alloys made. There are many combinations of copper, tin, lead and zinc which have proved useful.

Brass is brittle and is not easy to hammer into shape while the softer material, copper, is difficult to cast but hammers out well. Bronze was only cast.

The first chapters are devoted to an outline history of the industry, to the techniques used in the manufacture of domestic objects and to the ways of identifying and authenticating antiques made in these metals. The main categories of brass copper and bronze domestic objects are then examined in detail.

As photographs are the most useful means of showing different types and styles, examples of most major types of objects are illustrated in this book for each group or category. It is inevitable that in a book of a limited size not all minor variations can be shown. Variations of most major forms must be expected. Examples with different lids, knops, stems and bases and so on must be anticipated.

Where a piece can be closely dated the caption will record when we believe that it was made. However, in some cases it is only possible to make rather broad judgements. When dating antiques it is too easy to speak glibly of an item being about 1670 or 1780 and so on. Such precision, even within ten years, is hard to achieve.

ACKNOWLEDGEMENTS

Over ten years of research have gone into the preparation of this book and a large number of sources have been tapped, some consciously, other perhaps unconsciously.

I owe a great debt to those who have gone before me and this is gratefully acknowledged. Most of the books, manuscripts and other sources used are listed on pages 279-80.

I also acknowledge a debt to the many people and individuals who have helped in other ways, especially The Winterthur Museum, Delaware, USA; Birmingham Local History Library; The Bodleian Library, Oxford; Local History Library, Somerset, Landesgewerbeanstalt, Bayern, Nuremberg, Germany; Manchester Polytechnic; The British Library, London; Bristol Museum and Art Gallery; The Castle Museum, York; County of Avon Reference Library, Bristol; Leicestershire County Council, Museums, Art Galleries and Records Services, Leicester; Devon County Library, Exeter; Cheshire County Council Records Office, Chester; Nottingham County Council, Leisure Services Dept, Nottingham; Oxfordshire County Council Archives, Oxford; Somerset County Council Records Office, Taunton; Local History Library, Taunton; City of London Guildhall Library; Jack Baggott; Pat Barrett; Dr Roger Brownsword; Mike and Ray Casimir; Pat Kydd; David Rosa; Christopher Sykes; The Business Archives Council; Surrey Industrial History Group; Staffordshire Industrial Archaelogy Society; William Salt Library, Stafford; Peerage of Birmingham Ltd; Robert W. Skinner Inc; Worshipful Company of Armourers and Brasiers Company; Worshipful Company of Founders; Davis Gelatine Ltd; Leeds Castle Foundation; Harrods; The Rushlight Society.

Individual acknowledgements for the photographs used are given in each case after the captions.

I know that on many occasions my wife and I created havoc when invading people's shops and homes to photograph antiques and I can only hope that those who suffered in this way will be mollified by the final results.

2
HISTORY OF THE BRASS, COPPER AND BRONZE INDUSTRY

THE EARLY PERIOD

Historians of the brass industry are agreed that no brass was made in Britain before the Elizabethan period. Hamilton opens his *The English Brass and Copper Industries to 1800* with the words 'Until the reign of Elizabeth no brass had been made in England'. Joan Day in her book *Bristol Brass. The History of the Industry* makes a similar claim 'brass, ... was not produced in this country until the end of the sixteenth century'. Gentle and Field in their *English Domestic Brass* are in agreement 'no brass was made in England until the end of the sixteenth century'.

In the face of such unanimity can we accept that our story starts with Queen Elizabeth?

It depends on what you mean by the making of brass! If brass making means the manufacture of brass metal from copper and calamine (zinc) ores mined in Britain, then without doubt brass can be dated to the sixteenth century and not before. Virtually no calamine or copper were being mined in Britain and by definition therefore there could be no British brass.

This does not mean that no brass alloy objects were being made in England prior to 1500. On the contrary there is considerable evidence that both in London and the provinces, domestic items were being cast from imported ores which contained both zinc and copper. Harrison, a contemporary observer writes in 1577, 'of brass bell metal and such as are brought over for merchandising from other countries' and continues 'and yet I cannot but say that there is some brass found also in England but so small in the quantity that it is not greatly to be esteemed.'

Another sixteenth-century writer, Stowe in his *Survey of London*, records of Lothbery that 'This streete is possessed for the most part by Founders that cast candlesticks, chaffing dishes, spice mortars and such like copper and laten[1] works'.

There is evidence that craftsmen in London were making brazen[2] objects much earlier, for as early at 1365, a petition mentions 'Candlesticks, Laver pots and other things' in terms of their local manufacture.

The Worshipful Company of Founders was active in the fourteenth century and its existence confirms that sufficient copper was being imported into Britain for its members to make bronze castings. The guild membership of between seventy-six and one hundred in the sixteenth century would have needed substantial quantities of copper even if some was melted down and re-used.

In 1504 the Pewterers petitioned the king, Henry VII, regarding the sale of brass and pewter of poor quality outside London. They were trying to curb the activities of hawkers or chapmen, ie door-to-door salesmen. The petition asked that nobody other than pewterers and brasiers 'shall sell or chaunge eny Pewter or brasse newe or old at eny place ... but only in opyn fayres or Markettes or in their owne duellying Houses'. It asked for standards of quality to be established and that no one should 'cast or werk eny pewter vessell or brasse ... but that it is as gode fyne metall as is the pewter and brasse caste or wrought' in the City of London. This all provides further evidence that brass was widely

---

1   Laten or latten, from the french *laiton*, was a form of brass, especially that beaten into sheets.
2   'Brazen' means items made from copper alloys which have been brazed or heated in manufacture.

worked and sold in the early sixteenth century.

In 1599, partial records show that copper worth £87 and latten sheet worth £282 were imported into England. In 1567, the merchant James Harvie received 17cwt of 'black latten' while John Elliots, another merchant, imported a cargo of 5cwt of shaven latten and another of $2^1/_2$cwt.[1]

It might be thought that it was only bronze that was being cast in England prior to 1500 and there is no doubt that cooking pots, mortars, church bells and other items in bronze or in a lead bronze were made in London and by provincial makers. However there is also hard evidence that objects closely akin to brass were also being produced here. An analysis of several English candlesticks, undertaken by Dr Roger Brownsword, showed that in addition to copper, tin and lead, there were substantial amounts of zinc.[2]

It is true that local manufacture was probably of little importance compared with the importation of finished goods from Holland and Germany. Most of the craftsmen would have been in business in a small way. It is not possible to estimate the number of braziers and founders using zinc in their alloys or the amount of brass being made in Britain prior to 1500. Harrison is probably correct that it was of little significance.

The pitfalls of linking together three separate enterprises all under the one heading of brass making can easily be appreciated. Each element: the mining of copper ore and its refining to make copper metal, the making of brass and finally the manufacture of brass objects all need to be independently examined.

SIXTEENTH-CENTURY DEVELOPMENTS

The existence of copper in Cornwall and Cumberland was known in the Middle Ages but it was not until the sixteenth century that any large-scale copper mining in Britain was undertaken.

The turbulent times of the sixteenth century had convinced Queen Elizabeth and her advisers of the need to have a home based supply of copper for the casting of bronze cannons and this lead to efforts to develop copper mining here. A German engineer Höchstetter, in association with Haug & Co, came over to England in 1564 and sank test shafts at the site of an old thirteenth-century mine in Cumberland. In 1568 this new venture was incorporated as the 'Mynes Royal' and large scale mining began at Keswick in Cumberland. In spite of the restrictions on bringing foreign workers into England the strategic value of the new enterprise was sufficiently important to allow them to recruit 400 German miners. In 1569 63 tons of copper was mined near Keswick, and at its peak, 4,000 workers are said to have been employed. Growth was slow, for the demand for copper was limited by cheap imports and by high transport costs. Mining also commenced in Devon and Cornwall, but substantial losses were made in those counties.

In 1568 another state-based monopoly was created when the 'Society of Mineral and Battery Works' was incorporated, once more with German assistance. This company was to establish the manufacture of brass wire and other brass objects and as a first step the company sought a supply of calamine, a zinc ore essential for brass making. This was found in the Mendip hills of Somerset.

A smelting plant was established at Tintern on the River Wye, between Monmouth and Chepstow, to make brass from the local calamine and from copper brought by sea from Cumberland. At first they experienced considerable difficulties in making a brass of a satisfactory quality. In the face of these problems interest was soon lost in brass-making and Tintern turned to more profitable iron working.

In 1582 the right to make brass was leased to John Brode and two other men, who started a brass-making works at Iselworth, near the River Thames, west of London. Brode's efforts, although technically more successful, were frustrated by financial disputes with his partners and with the Mineral and Battery Company and the works had ceased to operate by 1597.

In 1596-8 some Dutchmen created a brass-

---

1 'Black latten' was unfinished latten sheet and 'shaven latten' was brass sheet which had been cleaned off to rid it of the tarnish that developed in its manufacture.
2 Until the eighteenth century English craftsmen used zinc ore (calamine) rather than metallic zinc.

1 The Arms of the Society of the Mines Royal granted in 1568. From a seventeenth-century engraving. (*Photograph by Eric Adkins*)

2 The arms of the Society for the Mineral and Battery works from the same source. (*Photograph by Eric Adkins*)

making works at Rotherhithe on the eastern side of London. Both at Rotherhithe and Tintern brass was made from copper, and calamine but the production of brass objects was undertaken by out-workers rather than in the company's own workshops. Out workers were freelance craftsmen working on their own account.

Thus at the end of the sixteenth century copper was being mined in England, the first British brass was being made and turned into brass utensils and wire cards[1] for the wool trade. All these operations were still on a small scale.

We have already seen that in London the Founder's Company was well established in the sixteenth century and there were also braziers at work although their activities were not regulated by a guild in the same way as those of the founders and armourers. Outside London individual craftsmen continued to cast bells, mortars, cooking pots, candlesticks and other utensils.

All the English makers faced competition

from imported goods and many probably augmented their stocks with imports from Flanders. The imports of 'battery' ware, that is wrought copper and brass utensils that had been made by beating or battering, was valued at over £6,000 in 1558 and at £3,600 in 1565. At a price of £2 per cwt this meant that in London alone some 150 tons of battery ware were being imported in 1558.

We have some idea of the kind of objects being imported from the cargo lists of English-owned boats in 1567-8. In that year 5cwt of frying pans, seven dozen brass bed pans and $1\frac{1}{2}$cwt of copper bed pans, twenty-four dozen candlesticks, twenty 'middle' candlesticks, ninety-two pair of andirons and creepers,[2] and three gross of latten andirons, 20lb of copper pans and one dozen warming pans were imported from Antwerp. In addition there were substantial cargos of battery. Merchants like Roger Knight and John Lambe were recorded as each importing between 15 and 20cwt of wrought objects.

THE SEVENTEENTH CENTURY

Mining continued at Keswick but little else was done by the Mines Royal to expand mining in

Britain. A new mine was opened a few miles away at Coniston in Lancashire in the early years

---

1 Wire cards were used in the preparation of the wool for spinning, lining up the threads and were vital

to that industry, then the most important in England.
2 Andirons and creepers were fire dogs.

of the seventeenth century and although at first successful, it was in trouble by 1627 and probably ceased work before the Civil War broke out.

During the Civil War Keswick was sacked by Scottish troops, many German miners were killed and mining operations ceased. By the 1670s little of the small town of smelting houses, miners' cottages and the watermills remained.

There was considerable development in the field of brass making. Work recommenced at Isleworth and Tintern during the century and it continued at Rotherhithe. New works were begun at Nottingham, where Sir John Pettus, writing in 1670, suggests 4,000 workers were employed in all aspects of the operation. There were also works at Chilworth near Southampton which were operated by the Mineral and Battery Company after 1606, and at the Ember Hill, Thames Ditton, following a lease of rights in 1634. It must not be assumed that brass-making was undertaken primarily to produce the raw material to make domestic items. Behind the development of brass was an effort to replace imports of carding wire from Europe with British-made wire. To encourage local manufacture a duty on imported wire was imposed for a time and in 1638 the Government banned the import of foreign brass wire. However the Civil War interrupted brass production, and what was made during that period was used by both sides to cast cannon and virtually all domestic production came to an end.

After the war the Mines Royal and the Mineral and Battery Company, which were Royalist in persuasion, were restricted in what they could do and during the interregnum other entrepreneurs were able to operate outside the control of the companies. Two foreigners, Daniel Demetrius and Jacob Momma opened a works at Esher in Surrey around 1649, using Swedish copper. Initially they prospered but in 1658 they were embroiled in disputes as to their right to operate with the Mineral and Battery Company. Momma opened the Ecton mine in Staffordshire and a nearby copper works in 1665 to avoid the restrictions of the Mineral and Battery Company, but the venture lost money and he was dead by 1680.

The lease of Esher Mills was taken up by a company headed by William Dockwra in 1691.

John Houghton, writing in 1679 in *Husbandry and Trade Improved* comments on the manufacture at Esher of 'battery such as kettles and since as more profitable for the Kingdom, the manufacture of wire for the great trade of pin making.' He suggests that 'they were the only brass wire works in England'. The company was in difficulties by 1696 and was eventually to be linked to the Bristol Brass Company in 1708-9.

Following the return of Charles II in 1660 the Mines Royal and the Mineral and Battery Company were restored to their former status and both attempted to regain their monopoly positions. It was quickly realised that the two companies might operate more effectively if combined and in 1668 they were joined to form the 'United Society'. At the same time the Crown gave up its monopoly rights over copper and calamine mining and thus opened the way for private ventures outside the control of the United Society.

By 1697 160 tons of copper were being produced in Britain, even though Keswick was never re-opened. There were still large scale imports, especially from Sweden. Although the United Society continued to exist for many years and made attempts to restore its primacy, by the first decade of the eighteenth century it was a spent force, although copper smelting continued under its auspicies for some years.

Other brass works were opened at Wandsworth, where 'Kettles and frying pans' were amongst objects made in brass. Associated small workshops operated at Keele in Staffordshire, Newcastle under Lyme, Coalbrookdale and in Birmingham.

The imports of copper and latten had risen from £499 in value in 1608-9 to £2,412 in 1639-40 and although figures are not available for the last years of the century, other evidence suggests that the levels of imports rose steeply. Likewise imported finished goods had risen in value from £1,472 in 1608-09 to £5,525 prior to the Civil War.

In the last two decades of the seventeenth century the high levels of brass imports and the low production of copper and brass at home lead to a virtual collapse of brass making. Sir John Pettus, writing in 1670, says of the works in London and Nottingham 'But these latten and brass works are decayed'.

3 A seventeenth-century engraving of Comsumloch Hill, a copper mine in Cardiganshire. Also called 'Come Some Luck' mine in Sir John Pettus's study (see Fig 4). (*Photograph by Eric Adkins*)

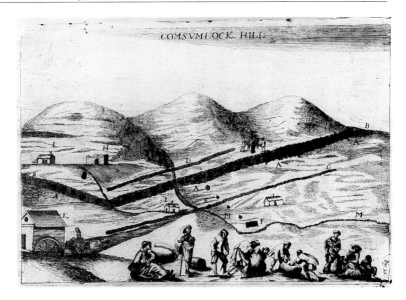

To some extent London escaped the worst of the problems faced elsewhere. Reliable figures for membership of the Founder's Company are not available for much of the century but based on the number of apprenticeships and admissions of freemen, it is probable that in 1691-1700 there were around 200 members. This was twice the size of the guild in the sixteenth century.

In 1613 the Founders Company had reclaimed their traditional authority over 'all masters and workers of molten Brasses and copper' in the 'city and three miles compass of the same'. One element of this control was exercised by their right of search, seeking low quality products. In 1652, for example, several shops were examined and two traders, Abell Hodges and Evan Evans, were found to have poor quality stock. Seizures were made in 1653 from fourteen shops.

By the end of the century the number of people seeking admission to the Founders Company as freemen was declining. In 1681 there were twenty-three admissions, in 1691 twenty-two admissions and in 1700 only twelve.

The membership of the Armourers Company can be estimated at 170 at the end of the century. The armourers did not make copper or brass domestic objects, but their membership by now did include some braziers. Their apprenticeship records reflect a degree of stability. In 1663 there were twenty-three apprenticeships, in 1670 twenty-six, in 1680 twenty-eight and in 1690 twenty-seven.

The authority of the Founders was seriously undermined in the second half of the century and something very similar probably occurred with the Armourers. The problem caused by the Parliamentary victory, and the subsequent exclusion of Royalists from the guild, the breakdown of trade in the Civil War, the effects of the Great Fire of London and the Dutch War as well as internal disputes meant that by 1670 the responsibilities of the company 'hath been of late very much neglected and omitted'.

Outside London many small founders were active. Most are known to us today for their casting of church bells but many did make mortars, cooking pots, candlesticks and other copper alloy items. There were guilds of hammermen to be found in other towns including Ludlow and Salisbury, for example. The Salisbury guild had a variety of craftsmen as members including armourers, cutlers, pewterers, braziers, iron workers, watchmakers, wire makers, saddlers, and pin makers.

Amongst founders there were four members of the Knight family who worked at Reading and four Beldales who operated from Gloucestershire and Wiltshire. In Bristol William Purdue cast bells, thirty-nine of which still survive in Gloucestershire churches. The Bagleys of Northamptonshire worked from 1632 to 1779. They are known for their church bells, of which 128 are

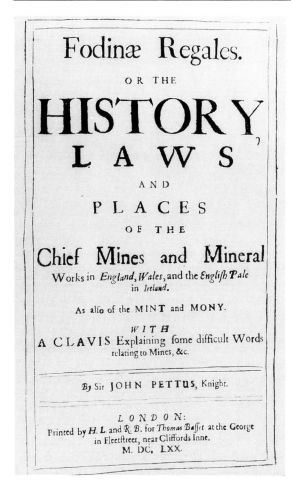

Fodinæ Regales.

OR THE

HISTORY,

LAWS

AND

PLACES

OF THE

Chief Mines and Mineral

Works in *England*, *Wales*, and the *English Pale*
in *Ireland*.

As also of the MINT and MONY.

WITH

A CLAVIS Explaining some difficult Words
relating to Mines, &c.

By Sir JOHN PETTUS, Knight.

LONDON:
Printed by *H. L* and *R. B.* for *Thomas Basset* at the George
in Fleetstreet, near Cliffords Inne.
M. DC. LXX.

4   The front piece of the first major study of British copper and brass, written by Sir John Pettus in 1670. (*Photograph by Eric Adkins*)

5   A mortar by John Palmer (or Palmar) of Canterbury, a founder who cast bells, mortars and other domestic items in the first half of the seventeenth century. (*Robin Bellamy Ltd*)

6   The founder's mark of Edward Neale of Burford, dated 1659. (*Robin Bellamy Ltd*)

still in Northamptonshire churches, 89 in Oxfordshire, 95 in Warwickshire, and 57 in Gloucestershire; a total of 354 bells which have survived.

In Salisbury the Tosiers worked from 1679 to 1730. Keane of Woodstock, James Smith of York, William Oldfield of the same city, Thomas Bartlett of Durham, The Palmers, father and son, of Canterbury, Edward Neale and his son of Burford were amongst other founders.

Alongside the traditional founders many small local brazier's workshops appeared. The term 'brazier' is, from this time on, applied to all metalworkers or hammermen and not just to people who worked in brass.

We are fortunate to have the wills and inventories of some seventeenth-century braziers including, Richard Parshouse of Worcester, Henry Hayley of Tuxford, John Gilbert of Uttoxeter and William Morris of Mansfield.

On his death in 1681 Morris had more than 4cwt of kettles and brewing pans in stock and more than 3cwt of old brass for re-use. Hayley had in his shop in 1688 nine brass frying pans, four pairs of candlesticks, three copper pots, one brass mortar, two warming pans, other pans and kettles and quantities of tinware and pewter.

Gilbert who died in 1660-1 had 175 different items in his 'shopp' including hops, iron, saws and rope. Clearly he sold things other than brass but he did have five pairs of Garter buckles, worth 3d, as well as three pairs of brass scales and a pair of brass 'trymmers' in stock.

Parshouse was in business on a larger scale and had milled brass, bell brass, yellow brass, and old brass objects to a total value of £67. He also had 'raw' (ie unfinished) kettles, valued at £52 19s 0d. and his working tools and moulds were worth £13 13s 0d. In addition he had for sale andirons, skillets, ladles, kettles, pots and pans, warming pans, chaffing dishes, frying pans and stew pans. Among his stock were also recorded £28 3s 0d of 'Flanders' pots, possibly imports from Holland.

THE EIGHTEENTH CENTURY

Until the early eightteenth century the making of brass was in the hands of a few small companies while the manufacture of brass objects was undertaken by numerous individual craftsmen. The century saw a radical change in the structure of the industry. For the first time larger companies were established to make brass and several centres developed. The divisions between mining and refining and the making of brass, which had existed since the formation of the monopolies in the sixteenth century became blurred. The new larger companies worked in all fields.

Copper Mining and Smelting During the eighteenth century Cornish copper production rose sharply. In 1726-35 it stood at around 6,000 tons of unrefined ore per year yielding between 400 and 800 tons of refined copper. By 1770 more than 30,000 tons of unrefined ore was being extracted with a net production of perhaps 3,000 tons of metal and by the end of the century Cornwall was producing more than 45,000 tons of ore which yielded about 5,000 tons of refined copper. In 1787 more than 7,000 miners were employed in mining copper, while two companies employed more than 1,000 men each.

The Parys mine in Anglesey was opened in the 1770s and at its peak, from 1773 to 1785, produced large quantities of ore and dominated the copper trade. It employed more than 1,200 workers, but by 1791 the mine's production was declining. During the same period the Ecton mine in North Staffordshire was producing large quantities of very high grade ore, but was virtually exhausted by the early nineteenth century.

In spite of the rise in production of copper in the eighteenth century there were difficulties. Demand was uneven, for some years there was over-production, the mining companies were at the mercy of one great customer, the East India Company, which bought a substantial part of their ore for export. The purchases by the East India Company confirm the increase both in demand and production. In 1731 they bought 205 tons of copper. Between 1751 and 1772 they acquired an average of 721 tons annually, while for the years 1774-1791 the average annual purchases were over 1,500 tons. Price changes and attempts at a cartel all created uncertainties.

The overall increase in the demand for copper in Bristol underlines the rapid development of the trade. The average annual purchases of copper for the main companies recorded rose from 2,820 tons per year in 1733-37 to 9,722 in 1765-70 — a rise of over 350 per cent.

Imports of refined copper from Europe continued throughout the eighteenth century but there was a steady decline after 1730 as British production expanded. In 1730 2,479 tons of unworked ore were imported. By 1740 this had declined to 1,290 tons and by 1770 imports were only 322 tons a year.

The bulk of copper was smelted in South Wales at Swansea and Neath although the largest eighteenth century smelting companies were the English Copper Company and Freeman & Co both based in Bristol. Bristol also smelted copper and in the 1690s at Conham, near Bristol, copper smelting works were established with three 'melting' houses. A second smelting works was opened at Crewe's Hole and by 1712 Bristol refiners was using some twenty-five furnaces and producing about 200 tons of copper a year. It is estimated that by 1720 this had risen to between 400 and 500 tons.

In Warrington the works opened about 1719, described at the time as 'a very large works for the refining of copper'. New smelting works were opened in 1771-2 but these were in decline by 1786.

In Cheadle, Staffordshire, copper smelting commenced around 1768 and was still being undertaken in the area into the twentieth century. The copper was brought on the backs of horses, on waggons and by canal. At its peak Cheadle had thirty-six copper smelting furnaces.

Brass Making Calamine, the other essential ingredient for brass, was originally mined in the Mendips but substantial additional sources were soon discovered and it was also produced in Cornwall, Derbyshire, Yorkshire and Staffordshire. The volume of calamine mined was sufficient for the export of quantities to Sweden and to Holland, where it was turned into brass and re-imported to compete with our own developing brass industry. The increase of calamine production can be illustrated by the production figures for Derbyshire which rose from 40 tons a year in 1746 to over 500 tons in 1796.

William Champion at Warmley near Bristol was the first person to develop metallic zinc in Britain for making brass. Calamine was smelted in four furnaces and by 1738 the company was making 200 tons of 'spelter' (zinc metal) annually. In the early 1700s Abraham Darby and partners, including a vintner, a cidermaker and a pewterer, established the Baptist Mill at Keynsham near Bristol for making brass. A deed of 1706 says that these men 'had for several years then past jointly carried out ... the art of making brass or battery'. Darby soon turned his attention to the casting of iron but the Bristol Brass Wire Company continued to operate. Other works developed in the valley of the Avon along the banks of the rivers Frome, Boyd, Chew and the Warnley Brook. According to a Swedish observer there were thirty-six furnaces in Bristol by 1729 and the city was 'the principal place where English brass is made'. Some 300 tons being produced annually.

In 1709 the troubled works at Esher in Surrey were incorporated with the Bristol Brass Wire Company. The making of brass at Esher continued until the 1750s when the mill reverted to the grinding of corn.

William Champion was the leading spirit behind the formation of the Warmley works in 1741. By 1754 there were seventeen copper furnaces, twelve brass furnaces and four for calamine smelting and by 1761 there were five spelter furnaces, fifteen for brass and twenty-two for copper. At its peak Warmley employed 800 men. There was a battery mill, a kettle mill and a rolling mill for the manufacture of brass plates. The works flourished between 1746 and 1761. In 1767 their sales are estimated to have been worth £94,000 per year. The works were extended in 1761-4 and in 1767 two steam engines were introduced but after 1765 financial difficulties struck the company. It was bought by the Bristol Brass Co in 1769 and in 1832 the works were sold.

By the end of the century Bristol had already lost its pre-eminent position. The site at Conham was sold in 1794. Crew's Hole, owned by the Bristol Brass Co, was leased to other operators in 1780 and was sold up in 1828. The Bristol Brass Co became a property company in 1833.

Thomas Patten, in partnership with others, opened a works for brass-making at Cheadle in 1734. The company prospered and copper refining works with which it was associated at Warrington, Cheadle and South Wales, kept it supplied with refined ore. In 1755 the company took control of a battery works at Greenfield, Flint where copper sheet and rolled copper were made and as well as vessels 'of any kind or size'. Brass wire was made at Alton, brass and copper sheet produced at Oakamoor and Brookhouse. The Brookhouse works had furnaces but brass-making was transferred to Oakamoor in 1830. In 1852 the Cheadle Company was sold to Thomas Bolton, Birmingham manufacturer.

Warrington was another centre. Thomas Patten opened works there around 1717 and at one stage there were twelve furnaces working.

At Macclesfield Charles Roe established a mill in 1758 where copper was smelted and turned into brass. It is reported that the works 'made brass pans, Kettles and brass battery ware'. The names of the streets around the mill reflect its importance. Close to where the works stood are Calamine Street, Copper Street and Brasshouse Street. By 1766 there were six watermills in operation and the company was concentrating on the manufacture of copper and brass products. After Roe's death the smelting of copper was moved to Neath and by 1806 the brass side of the works had ceased.

Some brass had been worked at Birmingham in the seventeenth century. At this stage Birmingham makers mostly produced small items such as locks, thimbles, buckles, buttons and toys. Scrap was widely used for these tasks as there was no local brass-making works.

Metal working was well established in the town by 1683 when there were 178 smith's 'hearths' operating. There was a steady expansion of brass working in the early eighteenth century but progress was held back by the poor communications and the need to bring in brass.

One of these problems was overcome in 1740, when Turner opened a brass-making works at Coleshill, although brass was still bought in from Bristol, Cheadle and other areas. By 1754 Turner was producing 300 tons of brass annually. At that time there were nine brass furnaces in the city and this had risen by 1791 to nineteen. In 1769 the opening of the canal led to an improvement in communications and Birmingham rapidly expanded. In 1781 a major-brass-making company was established at Birmingham.

The manufacture of items in brass and copper was undertaken by individual craftsmen. In spite of the progress in the trade, there were frequent changes of partnership and bankruptcies were common. To give two examples, the partnership between Thomas Horton and J. Jarvis was disolved in 1775 while that of Thomas Dowler and Isaac Anderson ended in 1788.

The names of 136 braziers are contained in the town's local newspaper in the eighteenth century. Of these 100 worked within the city walls, the others being from nearby towns. Many craftsmen worked in more than one metal. John Pridgeon, for example, opened his shop at 119 Digbeth Street in 1760 to sell both brass and pewter. Edward Durnell, had his shop at the 'Bell and Two Candlesticks' near the Bear in Bull Street where he sold 'all sorts of brass, copper, pewter and cast iron goods'. Most braziers had small workshops with a few apprentices and journeymen. Only a handful of enterprises would have employed more than twenty people.

During the period of rapid expansion there was a ready market for experienced workers. For example James Hudson was advertising for 'a hammerman' in 1784 and Edward Durnall wanted a 'Journeyman brazier' in 1766. Property was also regularly advertised for use as workshops. One house was offered for sale in 1762 as 'suitable for brazier' and another to let in 1756 as 'fit for a brazier'.

A wide range of brass ware was made in the city. Grove, Wood, and Lee, for example, were candlestick specialists. Durnall is one of seven Birmingham makers whose marks have been found on candlesticks. He advertised, that he had made 'an entire new sett of brass candlesticks of the most elegant pattern'. He also sold jacks, Dutch ovens, and French stew pans. Sam White made candlesticks but also sold 'peppers, flour boxes and snuffers.' John Darbyshire sold kettles and pewter dishes, Bayley offered brass and iron jacks, grates, fenders, fire shovels, lamps and other household furniture in brass and iron. Baker made fenders. Frying pan manufacturers included Massey, Oram, Phillips, Rand, Round, Tandy, Terrell and Wills.

The London guilds continued to control founding and brazing within that city. The Armourers Company was extended in 1708 to include braziers. This amalgamation, combined with the general advance in brass working, lead to a rise in the number of freemen being admitted to membership in the early years of the eighteenth century. Freedom admissions[1] rose from 114 over ten years from 1700-9 to 141 by 1720-30, but after 1740 there was a decline and by 1750-60 there were only sixty-nine admissions. Fewer apprenticeships were also entered into. In 1690 twenty-seven apprenticeships were undertaken and this level was maintained until 1730 when there were twenty-three admissions. The average annual entry in the 1740s was only twelve and while there was a small rally in the 1770s and 1780s, by 1800 the average was only ten.

The Founders Company also faced difficulties. Admissions to the freemen's roles totalled 144 for the years 1700-1709, and remained relatively high until 1750-9. A decline occurred with membership admissions of eighty-four in the

---

1 When admitted to the membership of a guild the applicant received the 'Freedom' of the corporation. Hence the term 'Freedom' admissions.

7 An early eighteenth-century bell of the type cast by many bell founders. (*Robin Bellamy Ltd*)

1760s, sixty-eight in the 1770s and eighty-three for the 1790s. Apprenticeships records partly confirm this trend. There was an average of eighteen admissions per year in the 1700s, rising to thirty-two per year in 1710-19. A period of stability followed until the 1790s when only fifteen admissions on average occurred annually.

In 1767 the Founders Company admitted a draper to membership following the path of several other guilds letting in people without trade connections. In 1785 the guild finances were in difficulty and by 1795 the guild was inactive. By 1811 workers in brass were complaining that many untrained people were being admitted to membership and by the early nineteenth century it's role was minimal.

Individual founders remained at work in other areas. Bridgewater for example was another small centre of the trade. By 1797 there were between 200 and 300 people working in the brass trade. The town had several foundries including one run by Thomas Bayley, a maker of candle-sticks and bells. Bayley was in partnership with Street, another Bridgewater founder, about 1750. In 1785 Thomas Pyke was making skillets and bells and he too had a partnership with Street. It was Street and Pyke who offered 10,000 sets of weights for sale in Exeter in 1775 and they even made clock movements. Pyke was mayor of the town in 1791 and 1811.

The Tosiers of Salisbury, the Bagley's of Chalcombe, the Smiths of York and other established family workshops were joined by other craftsmen including Stephen of Norwich, Gardiner of the same city, Borroughs of Devizes, Henry Pennington of Peterborough, the Newcombes of Leicester, and William Sellars of York.

Some founders were clearly very active over a wide catchment area. Thomas and William Bilbie, a Devonshire family, made bells between 1742 and 1793 and there are 352 bells of theirs in Devonshire churches. Thomas Pennington has left 480 bells in Devon churches while the Ruddalls, perhaps the most active family of all cast 4,521 bells between 1694 and 1826.

The Cors of Aldbourne in Wiltshire were followed at the same foundry by John Stares and later by Edward Read. Eighty-eight of Cors' bells are extant. The Wells of Aldbourne are survived by 260 bells. They also made other domestic items and advertised in the *Marlborough Journal* of 1772 'Likewise Mill Brasses Cast and sold at Lowest prices'.

There were also individual braziers at work up and down the country. Many repaired pots and pans, or turned their hand to anything required of them, but others would have filled some part of the local demand for brass and copper ware. Some idea of how these small braziers operated can be gained by an examination of the inventories of three Nottingham makers. George Cecille had pewter and brass including £46 worth of kettles, coppers, warming pans, cast frying pans, a candlestick and chamber pots in stock at his death in 1705. Amos Torr, who died in 1744, had kettles, wired pans, bed pans and bright pans and Thomas Leaper, dead in 1700, had pewter and thirty ring chaffing dishes, salts, battery, sadware[1] and holloware[2] in brass and copper in his shop. In comparison William Seney of Walsall, about 1716-18, was in business on a

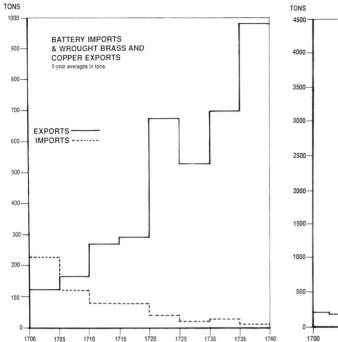

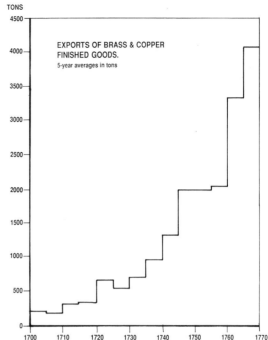

larger scale, with fifty-five outworkers.

The eighteenth century saw a rapid development of brass-making and of the manufacturing of brass goods and copper battery ware. The extent of this change can be measured in by the imports and exports of brass and copper ware.

Between 1700 and 1710 imports of battery were still larger than exports but as can be seen from the graph, exports rose fast and imports declined. After 1725 imports were insignificant. As the second graph indicates exports continued to rise throughout the century.

THE NINETEENTH CENTURY

The production of copper metal reached an apex in 1835 at over 150,000 tons but this was insufficient to meet the demand from the copper and brass-makers. Imports rose, especially from South America. By 1865 Chile was selling more than 40,000 tons of copper to Britain. In 1865 Birmingham itself needed 19,000 tons of refined copper of which 7,800 tons was from old metal which was melted down. The refining of copper and the manufacture of brass was, by the 1850s, in the hands of a few large undertakings.

In the nineteenth century the demand for brass and copper increased considerably. Several factors were at work, and one of the main

causes behind the rapid expansion of the brass trade was technological change.

The introduction of the railways in the 1830s created a demand for copper tubing for steam engines. The development of gas lighting meant that many miles of copper and brass pipes were required to bring gas into people's homes and its popularity lead to a massive demand for copper and brass gas fittings. One major Birmingham manufacturer of brass tube was making 100,000ft a year. There were dozens of companies making gas fittings and one, Faraday & Co, about 1836, offered in their catalogue twenty-four types of wall gas fittings and twenty standing lamps.

The development of oil lamps and the use of mineral oil as a fuel created a demand for brass lamps. Many hundreds of thousands of lamps were made. In 1860 there were few lamp makers but by 1865 there were sixty-three firms manu-

---

1 Sadware is the term for flat plates and dishes in contrast to holloware.
2 Holloware is the term for items made to hold food or drink.

facturing them. Later, at the end of the century, electricity was beginning to be installed and there was a demand for electric fittings many of which were made in brass.

Other new products also led to expansion. Brass bedsteads became popular in the 1840s and whereas there were four or five makers in Birmingham in 1849, this had increased to forty-two by 1892. There were only three other bedstead works in Britain.

Whereas most domestic brass and copper items were made for family use up to 1870, by the 1890s much was being produced for display or ornament. Warming pans, jardinieres (or planters) chestnut roasters, door stops and andirons were made for display around the hearth or in living rooms.

In the 1830s and 1840s taste underwent a sudden shift and very elaborate styles were briefly in demand. Many older domestic items were therefore replaced by objects of 'high fashion'.

The rise in the population and increasing national wealth also fueled the demand for brass and copper products in the home.

The other main changes in the century were the growth of larger firms in brass manufacturing and the concentration of the industry in Birmingham. Many small firms continued to produce domestic brass and copper ware but increasingly the production was in the hands of middle sized companies. One Birmingham factory, Winfield, for example, with 100 employees in 1830 had expanded to 433 by 1849, to 700 in 1852 and to over 800 in 1869. W.C. Aitkin in his history of brass and brass manufacture in Birmingham suggests that the average size of firms at the start of the century was sixty to eighty people and that this average had grown to between 200 and 300 by the 1860s. This may have been true of the few larger firms but G.C. Allen in his *Industrial Development of Birmingham and the Black Country* holds that in 1800 'with two or three exceptions the workplaces consisted of a dwelling house' and that by 1860 the average firm size was still only twenty to thirty workers.

What had actually occurred was that many smaller companies continued to operate on a limited basis employing a few workers each, while at the same time some undertakings had grown considerably and had become larger employers.

The total number of people employed in the city in these industries rose very fast. The following table estimates the number of people employed in the brass industry in Birmingham during the nineteenth century.

Year	Numbers
1831	1800
1841	3400
1851	6700
1861	8300
1871	11000
1881	19000
1886	22000
1911	32000

In 1851 it is suggested that there were only about 300 to 500 candlestick makers in the city. This traditional side of brass-making was in some decline but the newer areas were growing fast. There were, for example, about 5,000 people employed in brass bedstead-making in 1865 and this had expanded several times over by 1886.

Other areas of Birmingham's trade were in decline in the 1860s due to higher wages, higher costs and lower demand but the development of the brass industry was virtually unchecked.

Birmingham became the dominant centre for the making of brass and copper ware. In 1800 there were some fifty undertakings in the city concerned with brass and copper. By 1830 this had increased to 160 and by 1865 it had risen to 216. The nature of the work undertaken by these firms also changed considerably:

Type	1800	1830	1865
Foundry & stamping	28	144	176
Plumbing & cocks	6	32	39
Candlesticks	6	17	14
Rolled brass & wire	5	17	31
Gas lamps & fittings	0	34	88
Tubes	0	12	20
Others	5	24	49

By no means was all Birmingham brass production related to the domestic market. Of the copper used in 1865, 11,000 tons went for sheathing for the hulls of wooden ships, bolts, railway engines, engineering, boilers, wire and other industrial purposes. 2,000 tons were made into rolled brass and perhaps 4,000 tons went to all other fields including domestic production.

Some idea of the diversity of larger firms can be illustrated by the activities of R.W. Winfield, founded in 1827, who in 1887 rolled metal, made brass and copper tubes, drew wire, made chandeliers, gas fittings, electroliers (electric light fittings), bedsteads and carried out art work and general foundry.

There was a steady demand in the city for skilled labour as exemplified by advertisements in the local press. In 1807, for example, J. Boulton at Prince Street required two or three journeymen who 'would have constant employ' and in 1838 a notice to brass founders called for 'a person who has been accustomed to a brass foundry rough warehouse'.

Property was regularly advertised as suitable for foundry work including an 1850 notice offering a room 75ft by 9ft at Bridge Street Mill, Broad Street. Equipment was also regularly offered for sale including a 'large pair of furnace bellows, good as new' in 1807 and a set of 'patterns for Tea Kettle knobs, Button Moulds, Turning lathes etc and about 1800 lead button patterns, books and patten cards' were all offered in the same year by Mr J. Peeven, brass founder and button maker.

With larger companies came an increased use of steam power but the extent and speed with which this source of power was adopted must not be over-emphasised. Even in 1865 the use of steam power was limited to a few companies. For example a 'two horse Mill, erected on the most improved principals... with three sets of rollers' was advertised for sale in 1807. Steam power was increasingly available. In 1850 one offer made in the local press, 'to be sold cheap' was for five steam engines between 12 horse power and 25 horse power.

It is only in the last thirty years of the century that steam power was widely used, belt driven machines were universally adopted and that large factories gradually drove out the small workshops from many areas of production.

The last three decades of the nineteenth century saw the decline in the use of cast brass and the increasing use of die stamping, piercing and spinning for producing of domestic brass ware.

The other important eighteenth-century brass-making centres were in decline. John Aitkin in his *England Delineated*, published in 1788, wrote of Bristol that 'the copper and brass manufacturers were of capital importance but are now much declined in consequence of monopoly'. The monopoly referred to was that of the city of Birmingham.

In Bristol this decline was dramatic. Companies such as Ellis & Tyndall with rolling mills at Woodland, Mead & Champion and Anderson New & Co all ceased operations by 1820. Only two major undertakings survived well into the nineteenth century. These were John Freeman & Co at Swinford on the River Chew and Hartford & the Bristol Brass Co at Saltford and Keynsham. The former was sold up in 1838, the latter in 1859. Two mills at Avon and Saltford did continue to produce battery products into the 1880s.

The role of the two City companies, the Founders and the Armourers & Brasiers was virtually at an end in the nineteenth century although they continued their ceremonial and charitable functions. London continued to house some small and middle-size braziers and founders.

Thomas Mears who became Master of the Founders Company in 1828, operated the old Whitechapel Foundry and was succeeded by two members of his family. Among smaller companies operating were the Warners, who revived the Cripplegate Foundry in 1850, and who made many skillets which have survived, as well as other domestic items. There were many other smaller firms at work including Clark & Co of Houndsditch who offered 'the greatest Price given for old Metals', and Hayward Taylor, who about 1835 advertised his 'lift pumps, beer engines, water closets and cocks'.

In *Artisan and Politics in early Nineteenth century London* it is recorded that there were 2,000 people employed in the brass and copper trades in the city in 1831 and that by 1841 this had declined to 1,500 people. It is likely that the level of employment continued to decline for the rest of the century. These figures should be compared with employment levels in Birmingham.

Most country areas retained one or more braziers and a few founders continued to operate throughout the nineteenth century, but by 1900 Birmingham was the most important centre of brass production in the world.

3

THE MANUFACTURE OF COPPER, BRONZE AND BRASS AND THE MARKETING OF PRODUCTS

MANUFACTURE

In 1700 brass, copper and bronze items were still made by hand by craftsmen. The concept of the division of labour did not exist and each man would produce a finished article. Workshops were small, the master employing perhaps one or two journeymen and an apprentice who spent seven years learning his trade. Some use was made of out-workers for repetitive tasks such as the casting of handles.

In the eighteenth century larger companies were mostly involved with the refining of copper and the making of brass, but the changes introduced by the industrial revolution were slow to spread to the copper and brass trades. Even as late as 1860 steam power was a rarity. It was only in the later part of the nineteenth century that small workshops were replaced by factories and production lines appeared, with workers under-

8 A rare survival: an early sixteenth-century copper ingot from a wreck off Cornwall. This is the form ingots took when the molten copper was run off from the smelting and refining ovens.

taking one task on a repetitive basis before passing the object on to the next stage of production. Many tasks previously carried out by skilled men could be done cheaper and quicker when aided by machines. Factories became larger and production rose sharply.

All generalisations are dangerous in such a complex story, but as a guide to understand the developments one can divide the manufacture of brass and copper objects into three phases:
1 from 1700 to 1750, was the period when individual craftsmen made each object by hand using hand tools and a few machines driven by water power.
2 from 1750 to 1850, saw the introduction of fretting, cutting and embossing machines, the increased use of tilt hammers and the slow development of larger factory units.
3 from 1850 onwards, was the time of factory production, with steam-powered machines and a method of production based on the division of labour.

Refining Copper
We know from the analysis of sixteenth-century copper ingots that German craftsmen had the ability to produce a pure copper free of most trace elements, but early British attempts to make a similar quality copper failed. For most of the seventeenth and eighteenth centuries smelters were experimenting with ways of eliminating impurities such as sulphur and arsenic.

Initially copper was smelted in ovens with charcoal and the copper poured off. From the 1680s coal was more generally used for smelting.

The basic process was for the ore to be heated

22

to just below melting point over several days, then for it to be crushed and stamped. Lime was then added to the crushed ore to act as a flux and the mixture was then placed in ovens and heated to high temperatures for a few hours. Any slag would be taken off and the melted copper poured into small round moulds. This process was repeated several times, each yielding a higher grade copper. By 1800 refined British copper was as good as that from any other source.

Refining of Calamine/Zinc

After it had been washed and sorted calmine ore was baked in small ovens for four to five hours. The calcined ore[1] was then laid out and beaten with iron hammers and then 'picked' over a second time for the removal of alien materials. The refining of zinc was a comparatively simple process and high grade *Lapis Calamine* was readily available by the seventeenth century.

Making Bronze

Bronze was made by melting copper and adding the other elements such as lead and tin. In the period prior to the mining of copper in Britain, only imported copper was available. Lead was added to help the alloy sustain sudden blows as a tin-copper bronze can be brittle. Such a lead bronze alloy was especially suitable for bells, mortars and cooking pots.

Making Brass

Brass was initially made from calamine and copper. The process by which this was accomplished was known as the 'cementation' method.

The first attempts by British brass-makers were not too successful. An eighteenth-century report spoke of brass from Bristol as being 'hard, flawry and scurfy', and this is one of the reasons that British-made brass was slow to succeed in the 1680-1720 period. By the second quarter of the century however quality brass was made in Britain.

In the cementation process the two metals were mixed with charcoal or later with coal and then fired in circular ovens lined with fire bricks.

The exact proportions of copper, calamine and coal varied from brass-maker to brass-maker.

One recorded formula was for 40lb of copper to be added to 56lb of calamine. This mixture yielded 56lb of brass; an alloy of 72 per cent copper and 28 per cent zinc. The Cheadle Brass Co used 40lb of coal or charcoal, 100lb of calamine and 66lb of copper shot. The mixture was fired for 10 to 12 hours. At Esher they used two parts of copper, four parts of calamine and one part of shruff or old brass. Another report suggests that from 16cwt of copper and 36cwt of calamine some 25cwt of brass could be obtained: a ratio of just over two to one of calamine to copper.

The loss by evaporation or from impurities was as high as 50 per cent. The average brass made contained around 15-20 per zinc. Greater amounts of zinc could not be added to the copper as the calamine simply burned off in the process.

A way to make use of metallic zinc had been discovered in Germany in the early eighteenth century but it was not until William Champion of Bristol returned from Europe that this process was introduced here. The idea was to make mineral zinc or spelter by a separate process and use this with copper in the making of brass. Champion patented his process in 1738. He used granulated copper which absorbed zinc more easily than did the crushed ore but the method used in smelting remained similar to that used in the cementation method. From the 'granulation' method a brass of 66.6 per cent copper and 33.3 per cent zinc could be made.

It was not until 1781 that a process which enabled copper and zinc to be mixed directly was evolved by Emmerson of Bristol. There did not appear to be a great financial incentive to adopt the new process as the cost of metallic zinc in the 1780s was £40 per ton while the cost of calcined calamine was only between £6 and £8. Even allowing for the greater quantities of calamine needed compared with zinc, the net cost of the calamine in the cementation process was only £24 per ton.

The new process involved the use of zinc shot and copper shot, both made by water cooling the molten metals in a shot tower. A typical formula was for 54lb of shot copper, 10lb of calcined

---

1 Calcined means heated or roasted.

9   A scene from the White-chapel bell foundry, in the nineteenth century. Where clay moulds were used the outer cover could be in the form of a cope. This shows the finishing of the cope. (*Guildhall Museum, City of London*)

10   This nineteenth-century drawing shows the cope being lowered into position in a bell foundry. Notice the furnace for melting the metal in the background. (*Guildhall Museum, City of London*)

calamine and 32lb of zinc shot to be melted in the ovens. Initially the brass made by the new process was inferior, but eventually its quality improved so that a commentator of the time wrote of it as more 'malleable' and 'free of knots'.

Some brass-makers in many areas continued to use the old cementation process into the nineteenth century as it worked well and was less costly if slower. For instance the Cheadle Company, which was noted for the high quality of its brass did not abandon the cementation process until 1830 when their original works were closed.

Casting
It is not always clear as to what type of mould was used with cast objects.

Large hollow objects such as bells, mortars and cooking pots were usually made in clay or sand moulds. The clay mould method was to make an inner core of clay in the shape of the object to be cast. This was dried and covered by a layer of a suitable powder, to ease separation, and another layer of clay of an even thickness, was applied. Any inscription or decoration would be carefully modelled in this clay cover. This would, in turn, be covered with the separating powder and a final cover of clay would then be applied. The outer cover would be cut away in two parts and dried. The middle moist clay covering would be removed and the outer cover would be returned to cover the inner clay core, leaving a gap into which the molten bronze would be poured.

If the casting was well done the lines of the outer clay joint would hardly be seen and could be easily removed by scrapping and polishing. But where the object being made was of less consequence, the joint was often left as it was. If the base of a cast pot of the seventeenth century is examined it will be seen that there is a small protruding lump of metal in the centre of the base where the molten bronze was originally poured into the mould and which was then cut off to remove the surplus casting.

The advantage of this method was that large objects with complex shapes could be made. If the inner core was constructed using a wooden or stone model then other copies could be made.

Another method of casting known as the 'lost wax' method was used for fine castings but was seldom employed for domestic ware. With this method a clay core the shape of the object required was modelled and an even wax coat applied, of a thickness equal to the thickness of the casting required. Fine detail would be worked into this wax coat. This was then covered in a clay outer core. Holes were made through which the wax could escape and the metal enter and the mould was heated and the molten metal poured in. The mould was then broken open and the hollow casting removed.

Brass was mostly cast in sand moulds. For this system two boxes were needed, both made with sides only. The first box was packed with casting sand. A special dry sand[1] was needed which would impact well and it had to be hard packed. A model or pattern of the object to be made was then pressed into it, leaving half of the object above the surface. This surface was then dusted with a separating powder such as red brick dust, charcoal powder or bean flour and the other box, also filled with casting sand placed on top. This would transfer the remainder of the pattern into the surface of the sand in the top box. The two boxes would be taken apart and the pattern removed. The two halves of the mould were then clamped together and the alloy was poured into the mould through a hole cut for the purpose. Channels would also have been cut to allow the escape of air.

1 Other materials including horse hair and dung could be added to the sand.

11 An eighteenth-century founder casting in a sand mould using an iron ladle. The melting furnace is of the earlier 'cupola' type. (*BBC Hulton Picture Library*)

Simple objects could be made in one casting. With hollow objects two similar castings had to be made and the two halves brazed together. This was done by binding the two parts together, spreading brass filings over the join and firing the object. With the melting point of the solder and the body so close, many castings must have been lost in the process.

The use of sand moulds meant that for many objects, such as candlesticks, several castings could be made at one pour.

In the seventeenth century founders were able to cast hollow objects such as candlesticks using an inner core which was fastened with pins between the impressions made in the top and bottom boxes. The core, shaped like the object itself but smaller, prevented the molten metal from filling the impression made by the pattern

13 The top (left) and bottom
(right) of a sand mould. The
outer cover is bronze. Such a
small flask could be used for
badges, buckles and the like.
Sixteenth century. (*Robin Bellamy
Ltd*)

and thus gave a hollow casting. This skill seems
not to have been understood by braziers until
later in the eighteenth century when core casting
again appeared. It is likely that the founders kept
their technique secret from the braziers, who
were challenging them in their established markets.

Moulds of stone, clay, wood and plaster of
paris were also employed. Clay and plaster
moulds would have been made by wrapping the
materials round a pattern of the object and then
cutting the outer cover away in two sections. This
method produced solid castings. Wooden and
stone moulds were made by carving. All four
materials were normally used only for small
objects and wood, clay and plaster could be used
only once.

Iron or bronze moulds were employed for
casting pewter but the melting point of copper
and brass was too close to that of iron or bronze

for such moulds to be used with these materials.

Henry Hamilton in his history of the industry
suggests that the casting method was seldom
used by brass-makers prior to 1700. The existence of many trumpet-based candlesticks of the
previous fifty years and other British cast brass-bronze items makes this unlikely. Founders were
certainly using the first two methods in the
Middle Ages and there is evidence from the
pewterer's craft that metal moulds were in use
for flatware and holloware from the fifteenth
century. Casting was a skilled task and the timing and execution of the casting needed great
experience. The craftsmen had no temperature
gauges to guide them; too hot and the metal
would bubble and steam off leaving many casting faults, too cool and it would simply not run
throughout the mould. Even as late as 1913
craftsmen were casting by 'eye' or experience
rather than using a thermometer.

14 *(right)* An iron mould, probably used for casting pewter spoons, but which might also have served for brass castings. *(Robin Bellamy Ltd)*

15 *(below)* A brass mould used for casting pewter buttons. The melting point of such moulds was too close to the alloy used for it to be used for brass casting *(Robin Bellamy Ltd)*

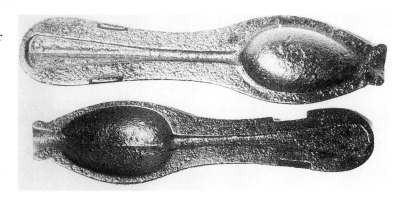

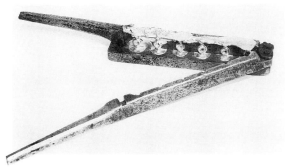

The pattern-maker's skill was also crucial. Pattern and mould makers were much in demand. There are several Birmingham advertisements of the eighteenth century confirming this; for example a 'good set of brass founders patterns consisting of sconces' were offered for sale in 1758, while Cooke White of Derby was selling brass moulds for dishes and plates in 1780.

Making Sheet Metal

Copper did not cast well and most copper items were made by hammering or 'battering' them into shape. It was impossible to take a bar or block of copper and turn it directly into an object. First a copper sheet had to be created. Sixteenth century craftsmen did this by hammering by hand. Metal sheet could also be made by hammering the copper bars under large wooden hammers tipped with steel, powered by water. Monster 500lb hammers are known to have been employed but most hammers were smaller. The hammers were driven by a waterwheel, turned by the flow of the mill stream. Hammers remained in widespread use until the nineteenth century.

Tilt hammers, worked on ratchets, could strike up to 360 blows a minute and the hammer

heads moved perhaps $2^1/_2$ to 5in at each blow. These hammers were used for shaping sheet metal into the round and for other hammer work once undertaken by a craftsman and his hand hammer. Heavy drop hammers were employed for making brass and copper sheet. They provided even, powerful and regular blows and made the task of making sheet much easier.

By the end of the seventeenth century however the first 'rolling' mills were developed. One is recorded at Esher and rolled sheet copper was produced by Coster & Co of Bristol at several works in the 1708-20 period. Rollers were driven by water power and the thick copper sheet, perhaps initially hammered by hand, was fed through between them. Initially the rollers were probably made of wood mounted with iron but later they were constructed of iron or steel. The harder the rollers and the greater the power employed, the thinner were the sheets produced. However with poor grade brass the sheets tended to split and crack if rolled very thin. Certain items, such as brass plates for clock dials

16 A metal worker's hammer with iron head and turned wooden handle. Late eighteenth century. The basic tool used by all hammermen. *(Robin Bellamy Ltd)*

17 A late seventeenth-century engraving of a copper smith forming a pail or kettle, while outside a massive vat is being shaped. (*Braunschweig State Library*)

18 A copper smith's workshops, 1698 (*Braunschweig State Library*)

and movements, were made by casting sheets about $1/_8$in thick, then laboriously filing them flat, not by rolling.

At Warmley, Bristol, in 1761 there were three 'rowling' mills producing sheets between 24 and 48in wide. There were also five battery mills driven by water power.

By the early eighteenth century rolling mills were widely used. Rolling mills were advertised often in the local Birmingham press in the mid-eighteenth century for sale or to let at Kings Norton, Cheadle, Tipton, Tamworth, Duddlestone, Wigan, and Witton.

After hammering or rolling, sheet metal had to be cleaned. This was done in sulphuric acid, which was then washed off with water.

Raising from Sheet Metal

This sheet metal was made into objects by craftsmen who cut the sheet into suitable sizes and then shaped it by hammering over wooden patterns or forms. Either hand shears or trip hammers were used to cut the sheet. When the parts such as the sides and base, were ready they were joined together by brazing or by seaming. Pans, kettles and cooking pots are among the most widely made objects by this battery method.

Water powered hammers were also used in making battery brass and copper. Up to twenty different hammer shapes and sizes might be employed in making an object. More than one item could be hammered at a time and a stack of nine frying pans, each slightly smaller than the last, are known to have been hammered in one series of operations. The shape was first cut out, each potential pan being slightly smaller than the next. The sheets were stacked and the hammer brought down. At each stage the partly made pans were again stacked so that they fitted into each other.

Stamping

In the eighteenth century toy, button and buckle makers used stamps to decorate their products and towards the middle of the century they were able to cut out the outlines by using hand or powered stamps. At first this new process was limited to small items. In 1757 dies were offered for sale in Birmingham, one 'larger enough to

19 Trip hammers at work in 1698 making items of holloware. They are slow moving hammers as the drop is considerable. On the faster hammers only two or three inches of movement was possible. Note the different shapes of hammer heads. The long-nosed ones were for shaping the insides of deep pans. On the right the pans are being finished by hand. (*Braunschweig State Library*)

stamp buckles', and John Taylor was selling stamps from Lichfield Street in 1760.

One technique was for the making and decorating under a single die or punch, of small items. Another was for the making of larger objects by stamping them out under hammers from sheet metal. In 1769 Richard Ford was granted a patent to raise saucepans, warming pans, basins and kettles by stamping. However it probably took some years before the full advantages of stamping sheet metal were widely appreciated. This process was associated with the improvements of rolled metal sheet. Sheet made under trip hammers was too thick to be easily stamped.

Flat objects could be stamped out in one operation. A steel model or die was made of the item needed. This was placed on the drop hammer. Then a sheet of lead of sufficient thickness was put underneath and the die driven into the soft lead to form a 'female' base. A sheet of brass of the right shape was then placed over the lead female pattern and a hammer dropped or driven on to the sheet using the 'male' steel die. The power of the stamp or press forced the metal to adopt the model's form.

With deeper holloware several stamping operations would be needed. The first might cut and shape the sheet. Another stamping would distort it slightly, a third operation would then force it into the broad outline required and fourth and fifth stages would turn it finally into shape. At each stage the sheet would have to be annealed or heated to make it malleable.

This process was available from the 1770s onwards, but it does not seem to have been extensively used until the nineteenth century.

Seams and Rivets

Hollow objects raised from sheet metal must have joints. Some seams are brazed but this method was out of fashion by the end of the eighteenth century. Straight brazed seams regained their popularity, however, in the late nineteenth century.

Copper did not braze well and several other ways were developed for making seams. The

20 A nineteenth-century trade card from Martineau and Smith of Birmingham, brass cock founders, showing a brass worker's bench, turning lathe and examples of their products. (*Bodleian Library*, Oxford, *John Johnson Collection, Trade Cards 3*)

earliest is the dovetail seam. Here the seam consists of a series of castellations or dovetails at right angles to each other. These are matched, fitted together and the two parts hammered together and usually soldered to expand and create a waterproof join. This method was common in the eighteenth and early nineteenth century but was still used in 1900.

Another form of seaming was ·for the two parts to be joined to be bent over each other or overlapped and the joint hammered and soldered to make it watertight. This was a nineteenth-century technique and appears frequently after 1840.

To fasten separate parts of an object together rivets or screws were used. All screws were hand

cut until 1790 and there was no standardisation of screw sizes or threads until the 1850s. With some experience it is possible to tell a hand cut from a machine-made thread and the presence of the latter is a sure sign that the screw at least is of recent origin. Rivets varied from simple plugs hammered flat at each end of the required joint to beautifully worked rivets which have been carefully compacted to expand.

Spinning

In the late eighteenth century a new method of making pewter objects from sheet metal was evolved.

A model of the item to be made was carved in wood and the sheet of pewter or tin placed next to the model held in a chuck on the lathe. The shape required was formed over the wooden core by rotating the lathe and pressing against the spinning sheet so that it took up the shape of the model.

Thin copper or brass sheet was also spun and this method was used in the middle of the nineteenth century to form simple objects.

Cutting, Fretting and Decorating

Until the eighteenth century the fretting, cutting and decorating of copper and brassware was undertaken by hand or by using water-powered trip hammers. Most decoration was created by hand engraving or by the use of hand punches.

From the middle of the eighteenth century die stamps were used to decorate brass and copper ware. The stamping out of fretted patterns on such objects as fenders was no longer done manually after 1850. From then on fretting and cutting was undertaken by steam-powered presses.

Finishing

In every process the final task was to clean and polish the products. Cast items had to be trimmed off to remove the casting surplus and to give them the required smooth appearance. This was done on a lathe or with the use of scraping tools or with a chisel and hammer. Just why the undersides were so carefully cleaned off is unclear but there is no doubt that all eighteenth-century brass was carefully turned or scraped.

One suggestion is that this was done to save brass since brass was costly and labour was cheap. However the economic basis for this suggestion is not clear. Another theory suggests that a high degree of finish was dictated by customer demand and by pride in workmanship.

An object would then be burnished or polished on a wheel: in the words of a sixteenth-century writer 'to make them smooth and bright'. Ox gall, from the bladders of cattle, or some other lubricant would be used steel or agate polishing tools which were then held against the rotating object.

Lathes were an important part of any brass making workshop. In Birmingham in the eighteenth century there are many references to lathes for sale. A 'polishing' lathe was offered in 1756, fifteen lathes in 1767, six polishing lathes in 1766 and there are offers for another twenty-nine lathes, all recorded in the local press.

Some goods were laquered before sale to protect them from oxide. There is a 'wanted' advertisement in the Birmingham press, for a woman 'that lacker brass foundrry well', to confirm this.

Power

Mill streams were harnessed to supply water power to drive trip hammers and for the earlier cutting and stamping processes. The brass industry was slow to adopt steam power. Steam engines were in Bristol by 1749 and in the late eighteenth century steam engines were in use in Birmingham for the polishing of copper and brass and for the rolling of sheet metal. A battery mill at Digbeth in 1836 had four steam driven hammers, for example. But steam power was only occasionally employed in Birmingham until the 1860s, when most workshops and factories adopted this source of power.

THE MARKETING OF BRASS, COPPER AND BRONZE PRODUCTS

In the first half of the eighteenth century braziers and founders made most of the items they offered for sale in their own workshops, although some lines were purchased from other local craftsmen or bought from a nearby city. The trade was a direct one from maker to public with few wholesalers. However middlemen were employed to transport the goods to other towns and there were 'chapmen' or street salesmen, who bought their stock from local makers and hawked their goods door to door or offered them in local markets and fairs.

If you wanted to buy a brass or bronze object you would have gone first to your local brazier or founder and either bought what you were seeking, if he had it in stock, or ordered it from him to be made for you.

The only retail shops were in towns. If you lived miles from a sizeable town you might not have access to a craftsman and then you would have visited one of the local markets and done your business with a chapman. Alternatively you would have visited one of the more important local fairs. There was a network of fairs across England, each held once or twice a year, and most people were within a day's walk of at least one and often several of these fairs. For

country folk, fairs provided the main source of many things not available locally, including what we now term 'consumer durables'. For example a Thomas More, a yeoman of Canfield in Hertfordshire, left his wife in 1566 'A brass pot she bought at Stortford fair'.

Some of these fairs specialised in a particular commodity such as cattle, sheep, leather goods, toys or horses but most had booths which offered a wide range of goods. The major fairs such as Sturbridge in Cambridgeshire were small, temporary cities. Daniel Defoe paints a vivid picture of Sturbridge Fair: 'the shops are placed like rows of streets' and he continues 'scarce any trades are omitted'. He specifically names braziers as one group found at Sturbridge. It must have been a bustling scene with tents and wooden booths set in rows over a large area, the alleys and temporary streets packed with visitors mingling with chapmen and hawkers peddling their wares. Large fairs would last several days but most were of one day's duration. For as long as most founders and braziers made their wares for the local market, this system of distribution was adequate.

During the eighteenth century larger undertakings such as those found in Bristol, Cheadle and Birmingham developed and they needed new outlets for their products. Being centred in a few towns the production was much too large collectively for just the local inhabitants. The makers needed other buyers for their goods from a much larger catchment area. At first these goods were transported by sea, via canals, as and when they were built, or by road, using pack-horse trains, to London and the big cities.

How was the brass-maker in Birmingham to get to know his potential clients in York or South-ampton, Boston or Amsterdam? The first stage was to produce catalogues which could be sent by mail to possible clients. These catalogues or pattern books, illustrated with line drawings, showed the main lines the maker was producing and listed sizes and prices. Initially these pattern books were small and easily carried but later the travellers carried oak bound boxes filled with pattern cards. Few of these eighteenth-century pattern books survive but they are a fascinating source of material.

It was in the late eighteenth century that firms began to employ travelling salesmen, or as they were termed in the 1930s 'representatives'. These salesmen would travel widely seeking orders, carrying samples and their pattern books. In 1770 for example there were twenty-five chapmen and forty-three merchants listed in the Birming-ham trade directories who dealt in brass and copper and this had grown to 131 chapmen by 1797.

As business became concentrated in a few cities and production levels rose, the makers ceased to be retailers at all and were forced to use wholesalers. The coming of the railways speeded up the transport of goods, cut the cost of ship-ment and helped to open up new markets.

Competition was often considerable. A Lon-don shop keeper in 1762, for example, wrote that 'Taylor, Gimblett, Ward and Robson [all leading Birmingham brass-makers] had been with him

like many wolves for orders'. In the major cities, such as London, specialised shops appeared sell-ing a range of fashionable goods and Sophie Von La Roche in her diary in 1786 refers to 'New Fashion articles in silver or brass shops' when commenting on the London scene.

In the 1770s most Birmingham makers were still shopkeepers as well. By 1830 few large brass-makers had retail outlets although many did establish wholesale shops in London. Brassmak-ers in Bristol found it worthwhile to have a warehouse in Birmingham by 1780 for brass ingot and there was one in London by 1783 and others were established later in Dublin and Liv-erpool.

In the early eighteenth century most of the brass, copper and bronze produced was for the local British market but export sales quickly developed, as we saw in Chapter 2. Exports rose dramatically to the American Colonies, the West Indies, to Africa (often in connection with the slave trade) France, Italy, Holland and to India via the East India Company. Special export pat-tern books were produced concentrating on those goods most likely to appeal to the local taste.

Each technological development opened up new markets for brass and copper makers. The use of gas meant a massive demand for brass tubing to pipe the gas into homes. The coming of the railways created a demand for copper tubing for steam engines. The adoption of mineral oil as a domestic fuel involved the manufacture of hundreds of thousands of lamps and so on.

By the mid-nineteenth century the distribu-tive trades were organised much as we now understand them. The makers sold directly to small shops using catalogues and representa-tives, to wholesalers and through their ware-house outlets to the trade generally. Even middle-sized firms felt it necessary to have Lon-don showrooms.

4
DATING AND AUTHENTICITY

Any one with antiques wants, at some stage, to be able to date them and be assured as to their authenticity. My experience is that most people, when they first become interested in antiques, fall into one of two categories. The first group is struck with indecision; they simply do not know how to tell a fake from a genuine item and are convinced that they are surrounded by copies and forgeries. The second group quickly achieves a sense of mastery, goes happily along, ignoring all the risks, confident in their judgement, if not in their knowledge. These two schools might be seen to represent the pessimist and the optimist in us all. Both are extreme views and neither stance is a good basis for judging antiques.

The first quality we need to have is a healthy sense of scepticism. Before a start is made in identifying and authenticating antiques, it is necessary to understand just how great or small the risks are. This is not to say that all antiques are fakes or modern copies. There are many thousands of genuine items to be found. But not all are what they purport to be and many items are much later than their owners think. Optimism does tend to reign unchecked; especially when it is profitable!

There are many criteria that can be employed in the dating of brass, copper and bronze. A good point to start is with the statistical background. An understanding of why some objects survive gives us a backcloth against which we can make judgements. Obviously not every item made in the past still exists. Many go out of fashion, are replaced by more effective alternatives, wear out or are broken. Some objects, like drinking glasses, are clearly more vulnerable than others, such as bronze cooking pots. Each type of object

has its natural life expectancy.

Once initially acquired, domestic items usually remained in use until their natural life came towards its end. From this point onwards, more and more of the items would be lost, damaged or abandoned until the moment the few survivors ceased to be old, unwanted household items and became, instead, valued antiques. From then on a plateau of survival has been achieved and few will thereafter be lost. To take a practical example. With brass candlesticks made in 1700 we would expect most to have served a useful life for perhaps 30 to 40 years until fashion or wear dictated their replacement. A copper kitchen boiler, however, might well have a shorter life as it was exposed to the heat and heavily used.

Several factors influence the length of the natural life of domestic objects. These include the material used in its composition, the kind of stresses that are applied to it, the extent to which the market for the item was influenced by fashion, whether technological change made it redundant and its initial cost. In today's terms no one would expect a plastic cup to last long; it is made of easily damaged materials, is heavily used and is cheap. By the same token a silver vase might last for centuries, being made of a hard material, and suffer little stress because it is expensive and valued.

We cannot know what percentage of any group of objects will have survived as we do not know the numbers originally made, or the length of their natural life. This weakness does not undermine the importance of survival theory as a background when considering authenticity.

While we have little statistical evidence, some educated guesses can be made. From an examination of inventories of people when they died we have some idea of the frequency with which individual items were to be found in homes. Based on the known family structure at any time and the population size, a rough estimate can be made of the number of families in England. Linking these two estimates we can estimate how many items of any type were in English homes, at any given time.

Let us take pewter candlesticks as an example. Based on the population, the size of families, levels of poverty and ownership and the frequency with which candlesticks appeared in inventories an estimate can be made as to the number in peoples houses about 1700. It seems likely that the figure would have been between 700,000 and 1,000,000. Yet we know that less than 500 survive.

Had we made the same calculation in 1730, within the natural life of pewter, we would have found many and perhaps most still in use.

A similar calculation for bronze cooking pots can be made. Inventories tell us that most homes were more likely to own a cooking pot than a candlestick and we can suggest that around 2 million pots would have been in daily use in 1700. There are certainly less than 5,000 survivors. If the natural life of such a pot was 75 years then after 1775 their numbers would have declined until a plateau was achieved.

During the eighteenth and nineteenth centuries Britain's population grew rapidly. In 1700 it is estimated to have been around six million. By 1811 it was 18.5 million and by 1911 45.2 million. Despite widespread poverty, there has been a general, albeit, erratic, increase in wealth. This too lead to an increased demand for consumer goods. Thus a candlestick maker in 1700 had a much smaller market than one in say 1850.

To take a theoretical example. If every home owned two brass candlesticks in 1700-20 this could have meant a total of between 2 and 3 million brass candlesticks. If by 1840-60 families could afford four candlesticks this would suggest a total of 30-40 million candlesticks.

We know that most older candlesticks will have been thrown away and replaced. Only a small fraction of 1700-20 candlesticks will have survived so the true odds are much against any given candlestick being from an early period.

Whether these examples are statistically correct does not matter. It is not the actual numbers that matter but the principle that is important. Of any category of antiques made over a long period of time, most will be relatively new and only a small proportion old. Think too about what levels of production there might have been in recent times for similar objects. The first rule therefore is to be sceptical. Make no assumptions but recognise that most antique objects have long since been lost.

The second rule is that no amount of study or experience can actually tell us when an object was made. It is a judgement that we are making; not a decision. Our hypothesis of age may well be wrong and one should never be too definite in dating items. Caution is the bye word. After all, we were not there when it was made and all we have to go on are a few useful pieces of information gleaned by study and experience.

No book can teach you how to tell fakes from genuine items, but it can give you the techniques which have then to be applied. Judgement comes from seeing and examining hundreds of items. This judgement can not be taught but must be acquired through hard experience. There is such a thing as a 'good eye' to use a dealers term. Some people seem to have a natural instinct for quality but there are no 'diviners' in the antiques trade, whatever may be popularly believed.

The criteria that can be applied to establish the age of copper, brass and bronze objects and their authenticity include:
1. Methods of construction and techniques used
2. Style and design
3. Maker's and other marks
4. Wear
5. The material from which they are made
6. Reproductions

METHODS OF CONSTRUCTION AND THE TECHNIQUES USED

Chapter 3 on manufacturing and marketing has outlined the major changes in the way brass and copper were worked and can provide us with some useful clues which can help us date objects from their construction.

In general it is a good idea to examine any-

21 *(left)* A sixteenth-century posnet in lead bronze cast in a clay mould. The inside was cleaned off but the exterior, which was used directly in the flames, was left almost as it came out of the mould. Note the band of bronze where the two halves of the outer mould did not completely meet. (*Robin Bellamy Ltd*)

22 *(right)* In the early eighteenth century sand castings became common, the two parts of the object being cast separately and then brazed together. The lines of this brazed joint can usually be seen as at the top of this candlestick. (*Robin Bellamy Ltd*)

thing very carefully to try and find out how it was made. How many parts does it consist of and how are they brought together? Most cast items are made up of several different castings. Candlesticks, for example, have a base, and stem and there may in addition be a drip tray. Usually after a careful examination it is possible to discover how each section was made and what method was used to bring the parts together in the whole object.

Casting

We saw that large items were mostly cast in sand moulds or by the clay mould method. Where a solid brass casting was needed there will be no join between the two parts but sometimes a very thin line can be discerned where the two parts of the mould did not fit perfectly.

Hollow castings were also made for small items using two separate castings and brazing the parts together as with eighteenth century candlesticks. Look for the signs of this brazed joint. Around 1750-70 braziers again made hollow castings in one mould using a core and seams and brazing lines disappear. The core was a smaller replica of the object and was fastened between the two parts of the sand mould with pins.

Sheet Metal

Most copper items were made from hammered sheet. In the period up to 1700 most sheet copper was produced by hammering by hand or by using large wooden trip hammers driven by water power. The sheets were thick and uneven. From this time on sheet metal was often rolled out under large presses, and from 1770-90 most sheet was made in this way. Such sheets were even and thin.

It can be hard to identify an object pressed or stamped from sheet as the surface shows neither the hammerman's marks nor the casting signs. Pressed copper and brass tends to be thin and even and its edges are either turned over and hammered or bent over a wire reinforcing. Most pressed objects are from the mid to late nineteenth century or are more recent.

SEAMS, EDGES, SCREWS AND FINISHING

Seams. In Chapter 3 we saw that seams were required in the construction of many objects. The earliest form was the dovetail. Large castellated seams were used in the eighteenth century while smaller dovetails are a nineteenth-century feature. Large dovetails were hand cut, smaller examples cut out under a hand press. Overlap seams are mostly a nineteenth-century feature.

23 *(left)* Castellated or dovetailed seams were widely used, particularly with objects made out of sheet metal rather than cast. The seams were hammered tight and often, as with this example, soldered to make the join watertight. (*Robin Bellamy Ltd*)

24 *(right)* Early dovetails seams were large and wide apart but in the nineteenth century small seams, such as in this example, were used. The original wide seams were hand cut, but these narrow dovetails were cut on a machine. (*Robin Bellamy Ltd*)

25 *(below)* The overlap seam is also nineteenth century in origin and was widely used in the last half of the century. The two parts to be joined were turned back on themselves and set into each other. The seam was then hammered and often soldered. (*Robin Bellamy Ltd*)

Edges

Most objects have a thick lip rather than a thin edge which could scratch. Where an item is cast this edge is part of the mould. Where something has been raised by hammering two methods are commonly employed for rounding off the edges. One is to turn the edge back on itself and hammer it to give it an extra thickness. This method is mainly found on objects made before 1700. The other way is to turn the edge over a wire reinforcing. This method existed in the seventeenth century but is most common after 1700. An object with an edge which has not been thickened is probably a late production and is likely to have been stamped out from roller sheet metal or spun.

Screws and Rivets

Screws can supply a clue to age but they are seldom found before 1770. Most items until this time were riveted rather than screwed. There are occasional exceptions, usually for construction reasons, where a rivet could not be hammered into place.

In the eighteenth and early nineteenth cen-

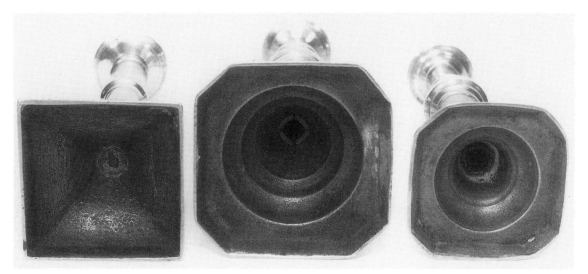

26   The bases of these three candlesticks illustrate several features. They show nineteenth-century finishing. The bases have been cleaned off, but do not show the same degree of polishing that eighteenth-century candlesticks were generally subjected to. The feet were joined to the stem with a hollow rivet. The tube, from which the rivet is formed, was inserted into the base and then expanded or opened up to make it grip the base. This was naturally easier with a tube which was split or divided, as with the central example, than with an uncut tube which can be seen on the left. (*Robin Bellamy Ltd*)

27   The candlestick base shown here illustrates the degree to which the bases were polished or turned off in the eighteenth century. The central part, which could be turned on a lathe, is well cleaned and the lathe work has been extended to the outer rim of the base but with more difficulty. The join between the base and the stem is made with a solid rivet or tine which was then hammered to expand it to grip the base. (*Robin Bellamy Ltd*)

28   The use of a lathe to turn the base was impossible where the base was oddly shaped as with this octagonal example. Here it was cleaned by using a chisel and hammer. The marks of the chisel can clearly be seen. (*Robin Bellamy Ltd*)

29 An example of the combination of turning and chiselling. The inner part of the base is turned, the other has been chiselled clean. Note also the tine. (*Robin Bellamy Ltd*)

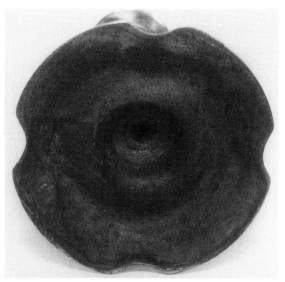

30 This base has been cleaned, but some of the marks of the sand mould can still be seen. It comes from a nineteenth-century candlestick. (*Robin Bellamy Ltd*)

31 The base has hardly been cleaned and the marks of the sand mould can easily be identified. However the solid rivet or tine, usually found on earlier candlesticks is, still present on this late nineteenth-century example. (*Robin Bellamy Ltd*)

turies screws were cut by hand and are uneven. Machine-made screws gradually replaced hand-made screws between 1790 and 1850. Hand-made screws are shorter, have thicker stems and the thread is farther apart than with machine-made examples. Machine-made screws vary in length and thickness but their threads are closer cut and are more even. Machined screws are a sure sign of late construction. Rivets however continued to be used into the twentieth century.

Finishing

If something has been cast, it comes out from the mould with a rough surface and needs finishing and then polishing. Eighteenth-and nineteenth-century makers also removed the rough impressions from the sand on the underside of objects. Makers carefully turned off the inside base of candlesticks, tankards, castors and the like. Where this was difficult because of the shape, such as with square and rectangular bases, the rough metal was cleaned off with a hammer and chisel. All eighteenth-century makers left a smooth well finished surface. By 1800 bases were still cleaned off but makers were content with removing the worst of the casting's surplus and by 1870 bases were often left uncleaned or polished and the marks of the mould are easy to see.

Decoration

Embossing Medieval craftsmen exercised great skill in decorating their work. They used patterns or forms and a hammer to create finely detailed scenes. By 1700 hand embossing had become simpler, relying more on patterns and shapes rather than figures and scenes.

With the advent of the power press, large objects could be made and decorated in one exercise. After 1850 there was a rash of thin embossed dishes and bowls made under presses with very elaborate decoration.

Engraving and Inscriptions   One way of decorating brass was to engrave its surface. There are three principal forms of engraving. The first known as 'wriggle work' is mostly found on pewter. Here a broken line is created with a series of blows with the hammer on a nail or other pointed tool; this technique dates from 1680-1720 and is occasionally found on brass.

With ordinary line engraving, the line is constant, made by a tool moved continuously across the surface. This type of engraving was practised at all periods.

Bright cutting is a method of engraving in which the cutting tool is designed so as to leave an uneven cut, deeper to one side than the other. When light reflects on this line it gives it an attractive highlight; hence its name. It is seldom found on brass or copper but is common on silver of the mid-eighteenth and early nineteenth centuries.

Inscribed items are rare but they are much prized, and for this reason, are copied. Not only are fake items given inscriptions but genuine articles sometimes have been 'gilded' with a false inscription or date to increase their value. The styles of engraving have changed much over the last 250 years. Given some familiarity with these

32   Handles and other parts of objects were usually joined by the use of rivets. Here four rivets fasten the handle to the body of this pan. Note also the vertical dovetail seam. (*Robin Bellamy Ltd*)

33 (*above*)   Decoration could be cast on the surface of objects by indenting the mould with the desired pattern. Mortars were frequently decorated in this way. Here part of a bedstead has been cast and the background then stippled with a hand tool. (*Robin Bellamy Ltd*)

34(*left*)   The quality of casting depended on the type of mould. Clay gave a better finish, but sand could produce good results. In the nineteenth century, casting tended to deteriorate and this is a poor quality casting seen on a Scandinavian candlestick. It lacks crispness and detail. (*Robin Bellamy Ltd*)

35 An example of hand embossing. This time on a nineteenth-century coal scuttle. Note also the worn kite mark at the bottom of the photograph. (*Robin Bellamy Ltd*)

36 The fretting on this fine brass fender has been carefully cut by hand (*Witney Antiques*)

37 This fretting has been machine cut and comes from a reproduction tray.

changes it is possible to roughly date inscriptions from the lettering employed.

Beware especially of objects purporting from their inscriptions to be eighteenth century where a thin and spidery script is employed, as these are modern.

38 With some experience inscriptions engraved on objects can be dated by the style of lettering and engraving used. This inscription is seventeenth century and is on a fine James II trumpet-based candlestick. (*Michael Wakelin*)

Cutting and Fretting Brass and copper were often fretted. Fretting was a form of decoration in which part of the object was cut away. In the eighteenth and early nineteenth century these frets were cut by hand and are uneven, never quite balancing perfectly. Later the frets were made under a powered stamp. Look carefully to see how the cuts were made. Hand cut frets on thick metal sheet suggests a date before 1830, while stamped patterns on thin sheet metal leads one to a date after 1850.

39 This inscription, on a clockwork spit, is typical of mid-eighteenth-century work. (*Robin Bellamy Ltd*)

STYLE AND DESIGN

Should someone without experience of antiques look at, say, a cooking pot, that is just what they would see. They would recognise it for what it was. But a collector, auctioneer or dealer in antiques would see not only a pot but would be familiar with its style or design. To the first it would be a cooking pot, but to the second group a Stuart-style pot, for instance!

For most objects there was an evolution of design. Certain styles can be found reflected in all areas of antiques. With experience it is possible to recognise the stylistic features of each period. In addition to these overall styles, there are also specific designs for particular items and these too change over time. Thus while it may not be possible to speak of a warming pan as of Georgian or Stuart style because its outline remained virtually unchanged, there are small differences in design which can help us to judge when an example might have been made.

People tend to rely very heavily on style and design. It is the easiest way to start making judgements. You will hear dealers and auctioneers blythly talking about an object being Georgian or Regency; what they actually mean is that from its style or design it seems to conform to certain established patterns which they believe to be Georgian or Regency.

Design and style are good starting points but there are risks. The first risk is that it may be a good copy made many years after the original design, not necessarily a fake but just something made in the style of yesterday. For instance Georgian-style candlesticks were being made for daily use in 1900-20.

The second danger is that it makes us think in terms of a necessary and immutable succession of designs, all neatly divided into sub-categories which can be put into a strict chronological order.

Such a view does not reflect reality. Makers altered their style or changed a design in order to sell more of what they were making. Some makers were always seeking change, others, more conservative in outlook, stuck for many years to a popular form. Thus even if you can date the moment when a new design came into popularity you can not know whether it was from the first period or made many years later. If you find a variation it is tempting to think of it as being made well after the original design but it may not be so; it could be that it was an early variation and made at the same time as the original design. The new variation may indeed have lost popularity before the first design had come to the end of its natural life.

Many brass and copper objects followed popular silver styles. The broad period styles such as those known as Stuart, William and Mary, Georgian, Chippendale, Sheraton, Regency, etc, can be found in brass but not everything made in brass and copper was capable of reflecting a particular style. A saucepan simply did not offer the scope for such design changes.

It is necessary therefore to have some familiarity with styles in other areas such as silver, porcelain and furniture. Some knowledge of design for individual objects is also required. This is harder to obtain. Old master paintings and prints are excellent sources for identifying domestic objects in European art, but there are few British interior paintings to help us.

In the eighteenth century pattern books were produced by brass-makers to sell their wares but few survive, and many of those that do are concerned with such things as handles, hinges and 'furnishing brass'. In the nineteenth century the hand-drawn catalogue or pattern book continued in use but few have survived.

MARKS

There are a number of marks that can be found on brass, copper and bronze.

Maker's Marks
Only a small minority of brass and copper pieces were marked by their makers in the eighteenth and early nineteenth centuries. It may have been

a deliberate policy not to mark their wares as this facilitated exports, especially to countries with which Britain was, or had recently been, in conflict such as France, Spain and the United States. Founders did mark mortars and skillets but cooking pots, kettles and other products were seldom marked.

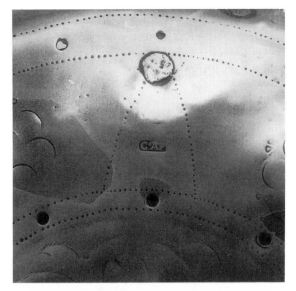

40 *(left)*   The mark in the centre of this illustration is
that of Charles Appleby of London, about 1690.
From the Marks Book of the Armourers and Brasiers
Company (Chapter 10) it is seen that he was appren-
ticed in 1683; first recorded in Court in 1720 and was
a Master in 1740. (*Robin Bellamy Ltd*)

41 *(right)*   On
the top of this
sconce is the
worn mark of a
seventeenth-
century maker.
On a trumpet-
based candle-
stick of about
1600. (*Robin
Bellamy Ltd*)

43   The mark of Joseph Wood, an eighteenth-
century Birmingham candlestick maker.

42 *(above)*   In the top left corner is the mark of
William Lee, also of Birmingham, another candlestick maker. (*Robin Bellamy Ltd*)

Some of the founders whose marks do appear
have been mentioned in chapter 2 and reference
is also made in chapter 7 to individual marks.

Some London braziers did mark their products in the 1680-1720 period and one of their
mark books is reproduced in Chapter 10. No
other region had a similar touch mark system.

A list of individual maker's marks found on
domestic metalware and check list of nineteenth-
century Birmingham workers is included in

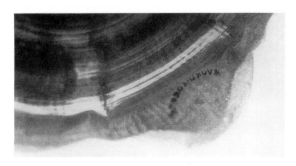

44   The mark of George Grove, one of the seven
Birmingham makers who are known to have
marked their candlesticks. (*Robin Bellamy Ltd*)

45 *(left)* The mark in the centre is that of the Army and Navy Stores, about 1900. (*Robin Bellamy Ltd*)

46 The Orb mark which is found frequently on copper and brass of the last quarter of the nineteenth century. It probably was used by a Bristol firm, John Lysaght, and was registered in 1876. (*Robin Bellamy Ltd*)

47 A typical mid- to late nineteenth-century maker's mark. This for Jones Brothers of 4 Down Street, London. (*Robin Bellamy Ltd*)

48 A mid-nineteenth-century maker's mark on a copper jelly mould. (*Robin Bellamy Ltd*)

Chapter 10.

In the later nineteenth century firms began to apply marks to their wares but it was not until the Trade Marks Acts of 1875 when designs could be registered that this became a common practice. So many trade marks were registered that it is often difficult to identify individual marks.

Where the name of a maker includes the word 'Ltd' or 'Limited' or the abbreviation '& Co' it can help us in dating the item. It was not until 1843 that companies could be easily established and the use of the '& Co' seldom pre-dates the Company's Act of that year. The use of 'Ltd' or 'Limited' indicates that the company has limited liability and this means that it was formed after 1855.

Registration and Patent Numbers

A very few objects are marked with a patent number. It is possible to identify when such a patent was issued but this can only tell us the earliest date at which an object could have been made.

Patents were only issued to inventions and thus design changes alone were not involved until the nineteenth century. Most patents involving brass or copper are for the construction of objects such as candlesticks. A typical patent might be that registered by James Barlow of Birmingham, No 8049, in 1839, which patented a way of holding the candle in the sconce and a method of fastening the stem to the base of the candleholder.

In 1842 a system of registration was introduced to give three years' protection to new designs. From then to 1883 a 'kite' or 'diamond' shaped mark was adopted with a coded reference to the date the design was registered, and the category of goods involved.

From 1842 to 1867 the year letter was at the top of the diamond but below the class letter which was outside the kite. From 1868 to 1883 the year letter was at the right-hand side. Where the marks are clear this enables us at once to know which year a design was registered. With worn marks this can be more difficult as there can be problems in identifying from which, of the two periods, a kite mark dates. However if there is a number in the bottom segment then it is a mark registered before 1868 and if it is a letter there, then it comes from the second period. The year letters are set out below:

49 A kite mark found on a bedstead. This example comes from the second series.

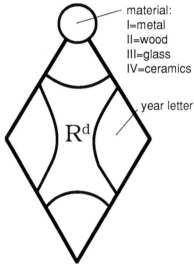

material:
I=metal
II=wood
III=glass
IV=ceramics

year letter

The registration mark. The other segments include codes for the day, month, etc, but are of less use to the collector

First Series

1842	X	1851	P	1860	Z or K
1843	H	1852	D	1861	R
1844	C	1853	Y	1862	O
1845	A	1854	J	1863	G
1846	I	1855	E	1864	N
1847	F	1856	L	1865	W
1848	U	1857	K or R	2866	Q
1849	S	1858	B	1867	T
1850	V	1859	M		

Second Series

1868	X	1874	U	1879	Y
1869	H	1875	S	1880	J
1870	C	1876	V	1881	E
1871	A	1877	P	1882	L
1872	I	1878	D	1883	K
1873	F				

The diamond mark tended to remain on designs for rather longer than the three years in which it was protected but seldom survived beyond 7 or 8 years. Its presence on an item can thus help us to date items to within that time span.

After 1883 a new system of marking was adopted. A registered number was stamped on the item. These numbers enable us to date when an object was registered. The sequences were as follows:

Registered Numbers

1884	1	to	19753		1893	205240	to	224719
1885	19754	to	40479		1894	224720	to	246974
1886	40480	to	64519		1895	246975	to	268391
1887	64520	to	90482		1986	268392	to	291240
1888	90483	to	116647		1897	291241	to	311657
1889	116648	to	141272		1898	311658	to	331706
1890	141273	to	163766		1899	331707	to	351201
1891	163767	to	185712		1900	351202	to	368153
1892	185713	to	205239		1901	368154	onwards	

In 1891 a new tariff law was introduced in the United States of America which required imports to carry the name of the country of origin. Companies exporting to the USA thus had to mark their goods and often found it easier to mark all goods rather than try and especially mark exports bound for the USA. Companies with little export trade did not immediately follow this practice but by about 1900 the stamping of a country of origin on goods was widespread.

Initially the word 'England' was required on exports and items with this mark date from 1891 to about 1909. From 1910 the words employed were 'Made in England' and after World War I the term 'Made in Britain' was also employed. However 'English' or 'Made in England' still occurred.

Other numbers and letters can be found on objects and these usually refer to pattern numbers or relate to aspects of production and are of little help in dating.

Weights and Measures Marks

From the middle ages measures to be used for the sale of liquids or grain had to be checked and conform to the standards established by the state. The standards adopted during the reign of William and Mary continued in use until 1826. Although some objects are found marked with 'AR' or 'GR' to identify Queen Anne and the three Georges, in most areas the William III 'WR' capacity mark continued in use. 'WR IV' refers to William IV and 'GR IV' to George IV. If any of these marks are found on an object then they must at least be as old as the reign involved except with 'WR' which covered such a wide period.

In 1826 the standards for liquid measure were changed and from then on several systems of capacity marking were used.

Victorian capacity marks included a 'VR' and town or county mark until 1878 when a new form of marking was introduced, which included a coded number for the locality. Edward VII and George V continued this same system.

50 An early Victorian capacity mark struck around 1840-50 on a brass mug. (*Robin Bellamy Ltd*)

51 A group of Victorian and Edwardian capacity marks on a copper baluster Scotish measure. (*Robin Bellamy Ltd*)

Few domestic items have capacity marks but where they do exist they can provide a useful method of dating. Mugs in use over a long period may carry several capacity marks but some measures were stamped on a lead seal and these may have been over-stamped, obliterating earlier marks.

THE ALLOYS

Judgements as to what an alloy is made of are frequently made on the basis of its colour. In fact you cannot tell its composition just by looking at it. For years people have spoken of 'bell metal' and 'bronze' mortars on the basis of their colour. We now know from analysis that mortars are not made of either alloy but are lead bronzes.

Most collectors will be unable to analyse the alloys from which an object is made. This can be done professionally and from very small samples of metal an object's composition can be determined. If there is a dispute about the age of an object such an analysis can sometimes help to establish the truth or falsity of an attribution.

This is because there are certain landmarks in manufacturing which have been identified by research. For example before 1400 brass was made from a fine quality copper and zinc but some of the slag left over from the copper refining process was added as a hardener. Brass thus made includes some trace elements which enable one to identify its period.

Brass made from the cementation process could not include more than 30 per cent zinc and in practice normally had a much lower level. Thus no item made before the mid-eighteenth century will contain more than this level of zinc. After 1781 much higher levels of zinc were possible. Modern brass is made from a pure alloy of copper and zinc and levels of well over 35 per cent of zinc are common.

The relationship between the amounts of lead, tin, and zinc in an alloy can also point to a possible origin. These metals were not available equally freely to makers in different parts of Europe. Zinc was easily at hand in Holland and Germany but tin was scarce. In Britain, prior to 1550, there was little zinc but tin was plentiful and cheap. The composition of an object prior to 1700 may well suggest its origin and period.

Only a few grains of material need be removed for modern analysis which is usually done by 'X-ray florescence', but it is not easy to obtain access to such facilities.

WEAR

Domestic brass and copper was made to stand heavy use. If an object is old then almost by definition it should show signs of wear. It is always possible that you will find an unused item in its original wrappings but the odds are against it. Look for signs of wear. Edges are smoothed off by use and sharp edges usually imply modern manufacture.

It is as well to run one's hands over an object. Our hands can often tell something about a piece which our eyes will not see.

Fakers try to add wear to their products. Small repairs are also no guarantee of age. Cracks and splits can be created. Wear too can be simulated by scratching. Think about the ways an object was used and work out where you would expect to see the wear or damage. In my experience fake wear is put on where it is easiest to add and it is not where it would have naturally occurred. For example with candlesticks, wear should be around the candleholder, where the candle has had to be prized out of the socket. Dents and bumps occur on the stem and on the base. Its easy to add dents with a hammer, but by and large the faker makes them too even and too sharp. Ask yourself if the wear is consistent with the kind of use the object would have received. When cop-per and brass were in daily use they were generally kept polished although items used in the hearth would have been black outside and clean within. Once set aside both metals quickly oxide. Traces of genuine oxide are thus a confirmation that an object is not new. But oxide can build up over fifty years and its existence is no guarantee of great age.

It is as well too to look for signs of original tinning on the inside of copper pots and pans as they are nearly always made this way to prevent poisoning. Many early items in brass were originally silvered and signs of this finish are a useful guide to age. Its presence does not diminish an early item but beware of electro-plated or Sheffield-plated brass and copper as this is not valued in the same way.

One problem that has to be faced is distinguishing British from other European products. By and large British collectors prefer British work, although many fine pieces of brass, bronze and copper were made in Europe. In some cases the design is so different that there is little difficulty in telling the twotrends apart, but in others similar patterns were popular everywhere. It is hard indeed to tell a Dutch or a German from a British late eighteenth-century candlestick.

Some general rules can be helpful. On balance, European brass and copper is more often decorated and embossing is very frequent. Although embossed decoration is found on British work it is not common until the late nineteenth century. European designs are often more complex, although we do seem to have shared a common taste for the simpler things with the Dutch.

If you wish to try and authenticate an object you must apply to it in turn every one of the criteria we have examined. Where they all suggest a similar period of manufacture then you may well be able to say with some confidence that this is when it was made. More often one or two criteria will conflict, each suggesting a different date and judgement has thrn to be exercised.

Remember what you are trying to do is to establish a hypothesis as to when something was made and that there is no final correct solution available to you. You may be right and you can well be wrong. Even the most experienced collector or dealer makes mistakes. Dating is not an exact science!

FAKES AND REPRODUCTIONS

Fakes are made to deliberately deceive. Reproductions are simply copies of early forms made for people to use to decorate their homes. The faker exercises great skill and aims to make a large illicit profit, Reproduction makers tried to create good, cheap copies.

Of course reproductions made fifty years ago can be aged to make them appear similar to antique examples and this has been widely done. Rough-cast candlesticks are carefully cleaned off under their bases to give them the look of eighteenth-century examples. Fake 'wear' or 'repairs' can be added to reproductions in the hope of fooling people. Wherever there is easy money to be made there will be unscrupulous people seeking more than their share.

There are few fakes. It is only recently that brass, copper and bronze domestic items have become valuable. Some fake alms dishes, aquamaniles and similar early objects are being made, possibly in Italy but as yet fakes are not a serious threat.

Reproductions are much more dangerous. From the 1890s manufacturers, in Birmingham especially, have been making copies of early forms for sale in gift shops and markets. Some of the designs they made between the 1890s and today are based on antique forms but most were not. Each firm employed their own designers and created objects in brass and copper which they thought they could sell as cheap decorations. Examples of the work of major reproduction houses are to be found in many antique shops. If you ask their date you will be probably be told that they are 'Victorian' or 'late nineteenth century' and many dealers do believe this thesis. The truth is that many will be from the 1920s or later.

Reproductions are hard to date. The metal they are made of, the patterns followed and the way they are made is largely unchanged from 1890 unto today. 'Peerage' of Birmingham still use a stamp press made around 1900 and some of the dies employed are also from that period. Each item is still made with skilled labour, using sheet brass and the methods of cutting, hammering, shaping and seaming are those employed in 1900. The finish is not so good as in the past and the sheet metal is a little thinner but it is still not easy to tell an 1890 copy from a 1930 copy.

It ought not to matter as neither are yet antique or valuable, but if people either believe or accept that the 1890s copies are actually from the 1850s then it is easy to see that so-called antiques of that period may even be less than fifty years old.

Pearson Page, the makers of 'Peerage' first appear in the Birmingham Trade Directory in 1898. It is therefore unlikely that any of their range of goods can date before that time. Indeed the company never claim to have made anything but their own work. The company chairman stated in 1974 that 'We never make anything that pretends to be "genuine" something else. All we make is genuine "Peerage" '.

They were taken over in the 1930s by another company, Jewsbury, who also incorporated other brass and reproduction undertakings in that decade including C. Jones, F. & H. Clews and Crane Industries. There is no evidence that Jews-

SHEET METAL BRASS CARD & TEA TRAYS, etc. Section 18 Page 1

All Priced Each.

No. 2597 × 5¾ in. diameter ×
2 in. deep, as shown, 11/-
No. 2399 Ditto. 11/-
Plain Edge, not Pierced.
THE FAVOURITES.

No. 3602 Round.
9 in. across top ; 1½ in. deep.
THE DOROTHY.
12/-

No. 10504 Round.
12 in. diameter × ½ in. deep
THE MARIE.
15/-

No. 2398 Oval.
11 in. long × 8¼ in. × 2 in. deep.
THE GODIVA.
19/-

No. 2470 Round.
12¼ in. across top × 3¾ in. deep.
THE EXCELSA.
27/-

No. 10505 Oval.
16 in. × 13 in. × ½ in. deep.
THE STELLA. 19/-

No. 4387 BREAD BOAT.
13 in. × 7 in. across top.
THE CHRISTY.
9/-

No. 2598
11 in. across top × 8 in. × 2½ in. deep.
THE VICTORIA.
21/-

No. 10510 FLAT CARD TRAY.
THE SOVEREIGN.
10 in. long × 6¾ in. wide, 19/-
12 in. long × 8½ in. wide, 25/-

No. 2505
15½ in. × 10¾ in. across top × 3 in. deep.
THE WALLACE.
36/-

No. 3129
11¾ in. diameter × 1½ in. deep.
THE OAKLEY.
25/-

No. 10542 PLAIN TRAYS OR PLAQUES.
9 in. 10 in. 12 in. 14 in. 16 in. 18 in. 20 in. 22 in. 24 in. dia.
9/- 12/- 14/- 16/- 24/- 28/- 33/- 41/- 57/-
THE JACOBEAN.

No. 3055
10 in. across top × 1½ in. deep.
THE CRAWFORD.
Plain, 18/- ; Engraved, 21/-

No. 3134 22 in. × 12 in. × 1½ in. deep.
THE LINDSAY. 40/-

No. 3130 18 in. × 11½ in. × 1½ in. deep.
THE PREMIER. 39/-

No. 3133 20 in. × 12 in. × 1½ in. deep.
THE SPENCER. 39/-

No. 3704 20 in. × 14½ in. × 1½ in. deep.
THE NORWOOD.

52 *(opposite)*   A page from the 1927 catalogue of Pearson Page of Birmingham. Note the several plates and trays, similar to many that can be seen today.

53 *(right)*   Another page from the same catalogue, showing some of the standing and hanging boxes being offered in 1927 as reproductions. (*Robin Bellamy Ltd, photograph by Eric Adkins*)

bury were making reproductions before 1930. At their peak the company employed 250 people and produced close to 1,000 designs. None of these company's products pre-date 1890, most were not made until the 1920s and the bulk of all their products will have come from the 1930s rather than earlier. The use of the name 'Peerage', found stamped on many items only dates from 1945, according to the company.

It is claimed that as many reproductions were based on original designs it is always possible that those on offer are from that earlier period. This is theoretically possible but statistically unlikely. Not all designs however can possibly be based on earlier forms. For example the 'Lady in Crinoline Skirt' bell made by Cyril Jones in 1930 confirms that it is not based on 'genuine old bells'. One of Pearson Page crinoline bells does not appear in their catalogues until the 1930s. Many trivets and beehive candlesticks were also introduced by the company in the 1930s.

Many of the designs that were introduced in the 1900s were also being made years later. If you cannot tell a 1920 copy from a 1930 copy and an 1890 copy from a 1920 copy then how can you tell the earliest from the latest? How to date, for example, skimmers design No 1739 which was made from 1926 to 1967. Chestnut roasters Nos 1989 and 1990 continued in manufacture over the same period, as did twist candlesticks No 1861 and 11787.

The truth is that only some of the reproductions of the 1900s were copies of earlier examples. Many were not designed until the 1920s. There were many companies making reproductions in the 1920s and 1930s and they probably made millions of copies between them.

5
LIGHTING

CANDLES

The candle was the most popular form of light over hundreds of years. The wealthy used candles made from beeswax, while most people had tallow candles. Candles were also made in the eighteenth and nineteenth centuries from spermacetti, a substance found in the head of whales, and in the 1830s, from sterine. Tallow was dominant because it was cheap; about one sixth of the cost of wax candles. Tallow is refined animal dripping, usually mutton or bullock fat since hog or pig fat stank when burned. Wicks were made from linen or other thread.

Prior to 1700 most families made their own candles but the introduction of a candle tax which lasted from 1709 to 1831, forced most people to buy from chandlers (candlesellers) duty paid. Rising living standards and a growing population caused tallow candle sales to soar, from $27\frac{1}{4}$ million pounds in weight in 1711 to over 100 million pounds by 1824.

There were three main ways of making candles. The first was to melt the fat or wax, and cast it in a thin sheet. The wick was positioned at one edge and the fat rolled round it, while it was still pliable, to form a candle. This worked best with beeswax. Candles were also cast, in wooden, pewter, iron and tin moulds. In recent years some brass candle moulds have appeared on the market, but none I have seen have convinced me that they are genuine. Again casting worked best with wax. The most widely used way to make candles was to 'dip' them. The wax or fat was melted in a deep container. A wick was then dropped into and then removed from the vat, picking up some of the hot wax. This was then allowed to cool and the operation repeated many times. At each immersion more wax was accumulated round the wick, until the candle was of the required size. Professional candle makers could dip dozens of candles in one operation using large vats.

Candlesticks

Much confusion still exists as to the dates at which various forms of candlestick first appeared. There are so many factors to be taken into consideration that in the end it becomes a 'seat of the pants' judgement, and there is little agreement among experts. If we take three leading styles and see what recent writers have given as the most likely date for the form's first manufacture we can see the extent of the confusion.

Author	Swirl Based	Cut corner Bases	Square Bases
Caspall[1]	1740	1730	1730
Gentle[2]	1755	1745	1755
Hornsby[3]	1750	1735	1760
Michaelis[4]	1735	1720	1725

1 *Making Fire and Light in the Home pre 1820*. Caspall.
2 *English Domestic Brass*. Gentle and Field.
3 For the sake of fairness the dates in my earlier book *British Pewter, Copper and Brass* are also included.
4 *Old Domestic Base Metal Candlesticks*. R. Michaelis

At first glance you might say there is some agreement but on closer examination this really is not so. For the swirl style the dates offered for its first appearance range from 1735 to 1755, for the cut corner bases from 1720 to 1745 and for the square bases from 1725 to 1760. Such a variation makes nonsense of carefully constructed classifications.

What is the truth? Basically there is no way of establishing a wholly accurate chronology. We were not there to see the first candlestick of any form cast. We do have some evidence available. As seen in chapter 4, dating is a very inexact art, but some general advice has been offered to help us make judgements. It is now necessary to look more closely at what evidence we have for candlesticks before proceeding further.

Silver forms can be most helpful as silversmiths were obliged to date their products and thus we have a reliable date for the appearance of many styles. However it is always possible that earlier dates for individual styles may not yet have been recorded. The assumption is that base metal examples came after silver forms but this may not always be true.

Maker's marks can be most helpful. Mrs Jean Burke in *Birmingham Brass Candlesticks* has identified only 144 marked eighteenth-century candlesticks made by seven Birmingham makers and while there may be other marked candlesticks yet to be discovered maker's marks are only occasionally of direct use. It can be helpful however to know that certain recorded makers were making candlesticks of a given style.

In a few cases patents can guide us but patents were generally taken out for special types of candlesticks or parts of candlesticks, such as pushers, extractors and extenders and only a few standard eighteenth-century candlesticks have these features. If you come across a candlestick with a telescopic mechanism then it probably dates after the patents issued to Eckhardt and Morton or Roberts in 1797-8. Telescopic candlesticks could be extended by pulling or turning a knob. Special grips for holding and ejecting candles from holders were the subject of several patents including those granted to Lee and King in 1841, Clive in 1842 and 1843, and Keeling in 1847. Sliding ejectors were patented by Day in 1854, Whitehead in 1854 and Manning in 1858 although there are other mechanisms to be found. One of the more interesting patents was issued to James Barlow of Birmingham in 1839 for the use of a hollow rivet to fasten the stem to the base and a candlestick with a rivet of this type dates after this time.

In the eighteenth century many brass-makers sold their wares through catalogues. These catalogues can be helpful, but they can only confirm that a particular style was in existence at a given time, rather than tell us when a style may first have appeared. In many cases we do not know for sure when the catalogues were printed.

The way candlesticks were made can be helpful. In the late seventeenth century and early eighteenth century most brass candlesticks were cast with solid or nearly solid stems as the skills for hollow sand casting did not exist. Around 1700, however, craftsmen began casting stems in two hollow sections and brazing the seams together. Less brass was used by this method and the economics of the situation soon drove out solid-stemmed candlesticks. Signs of this seam can nearly always be picked out if one breathes gently on the stem. Later in the eighteenth century, around 1760-80, stems with seamless hollow casting became possible. Core casting as it was known was much quicker than casting in two sections and seamed candlesticks were soon no longer being made.

Lastly we can look at the design of candlesticks to see what can be gleaned. There are four parts that can be helpful: the knop, sconce, stem and base. Mrs Burke has identified twelve bases and there are many other minor variations.

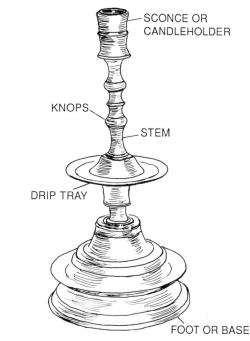

Diagram of the various parts of a candlestick

It would also be possible to trace the develop-ment of stems and sconces and build up a classi-fication based on these features. Candleholders or sconces in the first quarter of the century, were larger than those subsequently adopted, often waisted in style with thick rims at top and bot-tom. Later eighteenth-century sconces are sim-pler although shaped examples are not uncom-mon. Sconces were often separate from candle-holders in the eighteenth century. Round multi-knopped stems were popular in the first decades of the century but from around 1720 until 1780 two or three shaped knopped stems were widely popular.

The problem with using classifications based on several physical features is that it will produce many categories. Base your classification on knops, stems and bases and you have so many permutations that it can actually be unhelpful. In the end it is perhaps best to concentrate on a classification based on the shape of candlestick bases, but other classifications could be created.

So far we have been concentrating on sources of information which tell us when a style first came into manufacture. None of these criteria help us to know when it was out of fashion. It is hard to put closing dates on styles. A successful line may have been in production, unchanged, for many years. Another maker, in copying a style, may have made variations to distinguish his products from those of the initiator. Some styles may have lasted for 60-80 years. Others were short lived. To complicate the story further we know that from the late Victorian period onwards earlier styles of candlestick were once more being made. Using all the evidence avail-able a re-appraisal of candlestick styles can be attempted.

Eighteenth-Century Candlesticks

A. The Transitional Group Candlesticks with solid stems, usually with square or round bases and often with multi-knopped stems were in production from 1680 until 1730. Frequently they have high domed bases. Some later examples, about 1730 have seamed stems.

B. The Octagonal and Prism Group Candle-sticks in this group may have either solid or seamed stems. Those with octagonal bases ap-

pear from about 1700 while those with prism bases appeared around 1710. Both forms contin-ued to be made into the 1730s.

C. The Fluted, Flower and Swirl Group This group is made up of seamed candlesticks with elaborately shaped bases. It is likely that fluted bases appeared around 1735, that petal and swirl bases date from around 1750. They all continued in production into the 1770s. Examples can be found of seamless hollow stems with these bases and these must date from the 1770s.

D. The Cut Corner Group There is a large group of candlesticks with 'cut corners' on their bases. Most examples have seamed stems. The form appears around 1720 and once more lasted into the 1770s.

E. The Square Based Group Candlesticks with square bases, usually with a column stem first make an appearance in the 1750s while examples with a dished base appear about 1760. Some have hollow stems, others are seamed. They contin-ued in production for much of the nineteenth century. Those with high domed bases are proba-bly after 1780.

F. The Round Based Group Round based can-dlesticks re-appear around 1770, usually with an upward tapering stem. They are also found with 'Adam' style stems. They were made well into the nineteenth century.

Nineteenth-Century Candlesticks

If the evidence to date styles of candlesticks in the eighteenth century appears inadequate, then perhaps we may approach the next century with more confidence. However it will soon become apparent that, by and large, we are worse off for hard evidence.

In the eighteenth century brass candlesticks were so popular that pewterers gave up making pewter candlesticks. Brass candlesticks domi-nated the market for much of the century. In the nineteenth century brass candlesticks were less of a novelty and although the production was greater than in the eighteenth century so was the demand for lighting. Relatively, brass candle-sticks were declining in popularity compared with pottery, tin, glass, Sheffield plate and Britannia metal examples.

The nineteenth century is not noted for many new designs in silver candlesticks. The classical forms such as the Adam and column designs remained popular and candlesticks were made in the Regency and Empire styles. These silver forms can help in dating brass examples.

There are few trade catalogues of the early nineteenth century extant and no major changes of technique occurred to guide us. Very few nineteenth-century candlesticks are marked and there is, as yet, no study of those maker's marks we do have.

Much more depends on style and the way candlesticks were finished. In the early nineteenth century the inside of the base of most candlesticks was turned on a lathe or labouriously chiselled away to give a smooth finish. By 1830 less care was taken to finish them and by the late nineteenth century rough cast bases appear and these were left un-polished. Examples of the finish on bases are illustrated.

In the first part of the nineteenth century the square and round based groups continued to be popular. These styles may well have remained in continuous production until 1900.

G. The Oval and Oblong Group Candlesticks with oval bases, usually with short stems first appear around 1820. Oblong examples came slightly later; perhaps in the 1830s. Both these forms were still popular in the 1890s.

H. The Round Based Group Round base candlesticks with a baluster or knopped stem first appear about 1830 and were still in production in 1900. Many have 'pushers', a form of extractor on a stem inside the bases for extracting the candle.

I. The Squared Based and Knopped Stem Group Square based candlesticks with knopped stems first enter the market in the 1830s and 1840s. Those with elaborate beehive or diamond shaped stems date from the 1870-90 period.

J. The Cast Decorated Group So far bases have provided a satisfactory method of dividing candlesticks into groups. However during the Victorian era a new group of candlesticks became popular distinguished by its elaborately cast decoration. Late eighteenth-century silver candlesticks were made with cast decorated bases

and stems, and this form of decoration was increasingly used in the nineteenth century. The degree of decoration employed grew in the 1810-15 period and gradually became more ornate by the 1840s. Brass candlesticks cast decorated with swags, flowers and classical, oriental and Egyptian motives were popular. Glick, an English maker of about 1811, illustrated several 'Egyptian' candlesticks in its catalogue, for example. Candlesticks of this style went out of fashion after the 1870s and surprisingly few examples can now be found.

Candlesticks of most seamed or hollowstemmed styles can also be found with side extractors inserted into the stem. By moving a handle up, the candle stump was forced out by a central strut. Later many candlesticks were designed with a central pusher inside their base, but such designs followed the adoption of hollow rivets in the 1830s.

Chambersticks

Lighted candlesticks were dangerous to carry about the home. They were easily spilled. A group of candleholders, with wide bases, known as chambersticks thus evolved which were safer to carry.

The earliest examples are found with a candleholder on the lid and a tinder box beneath. In this box the flint, steel and tinder were kept.

Eighteenth-century chambersticks are rare. There was usually an aperture in the stem to hold a pair of snuffers and a small hole near the handle in which a doubter rested. Some nineteenth century examples also have these features. Snuffers were used to trim the wick and doubters to put out the flame.

A group of chambersticks exists with small pins or handles at the sides, which enabled them to be placed in moveable candle arms or set in holders on the side of mirrors or pianos.

Sheet metal chambersticks are mostly nineteenth century. Fretted chamber sticks are from the period 1880-1910. Both designs were still being made in the 1920s.

Tapersticks

Another group of candlesticks which may also have been developed for carrying about the home were taper sticks. These are small candlesticks, usually about 3 to 4$\frac{1}{2}$in high, made in the popular styles of candlesticks of the period. They are made in silver, pewter, paktong (a Chinese alloy of zinc and nickel), copper and brass. The earliest examples are late seventeenth century. They were most popular in the first forty years of the eighteenth century. These miniature candlesticks were often part of desk sets and were used with a box for flint, steel and tinder.

Wall Sconces and Wall Fittings
A lighted candle could cast a subdued light in a narrow circle round where it stood. By directing this light it could be itensified. Backplates, used as reflectors, enhanced the illumination. They became known as wall sconces, which can be confusing as the same name is given to candleholders on candlesticks.

Seventeenth-century wall sconces can be beautiful: often with punched or engraved backplates. The candles were held in one or two arms coming out of the back plate. Most early wall sconces were Scandinavian or Dutch.

Later, simpler reflectors were used, often rectangular sheets of copper or brass standing vertically with the candleholder resting on a small tray at the foot of the backplate. Virtually all these sconces are Dutch though many were used in Britain. Copies of these rectangular wall-sconces, which normally date from 1720-80, were being made in the 1920s.

Some wall sconces, again usually Dutch, have a shaped backplate. This style has been widely copied and examples with seventeenth-century dates engraved on them must be treated with great caution.

An eighteenth and nineteenth century form of sconce was the 'arm', fastened to the wall. The arm was either fixed or moveable, with the candleholder situated at the end of the arm. In the late nineteenth century the candle was protected from draughts by a glass cover.

Candle Lanterns
Various forms of candle lanterns were made, mostly in tin or iron but some are in copper or brass. They usually had punched and fretted metal sides. Others had horn or glass windows set in the metal frames.

Candelabra
Candlesticks with two or more candleholders are known as candelabra. They stand on a base and might have several arms. Examples are uncommon in brass and copper but are more frequently found in Sheffield plate and in silver. Most brass examples are late Victorian or Edwardian.

Chandeliers
Where a bright light was needed and the owners could afford to burn several candles, candleholders were grouped together and hung from the ceiling in the form of chandeliers. These were costly to use and relatively few were made.

British seventeenth- and eighteenth-century chandeliers are rare, but many eighteenth- and nineteenth-century examples were made in Europe, particularly Holland, Sweden and Poland.

Chandeliers had a central baluster or circular shaped core with a section above, which was fastened to the ceiling, and another section below. A series of arms were fastened into the central core set in one, two rows or occasionally three rows. Each row might consist of between four and eight arms, although larger numbers are known. Chandeliers mostly carry between eight and twenty-four candleholders.

The three sections are usually fastened together with an iron bar running through the centre, which is screwed or soldered to the two end sections.

In early chandeliers the arms are made in several parts, pinned together. In the eighteenth century the arms were cast in one piece. The candleholder and drip trays were made separately and fastened, usually with a screw, to the arms. Each arm usually had an aperture cut in the ring around the core for it to fit easily and these were numbered as the arms would not fit if placed into the wrong hole.

Many chandeliers have been electrified but such electrification is not proof of age as chandeliers from the 1880-1900 period were also electrified for use in the 1900-20 period.

Most chandeliers on the market are not British, and most are from the late nineteenth century. Chandeliers incorporating an eagle are usually Polish.

Rush Lights

Rush lights were one of the principal sources of light over many hundreds of the years. The rushes were collected in summer, partly stripped of their skin, dried, and soaked in tallow or wax.

They offered a poorer smokier, light than did tallow candles but were cheap to make. Most families collected and made their own rush lights. Gilbert White in his *History of Shelborne* records that there were more than 1,600 individual stems in one pile of a pound of rushes. The average rush measured between 15in and 18in and burned at the rate of roughly an inch every two minutes. The cost of four hours light would have been about a farthing in old money (0.1d).

The great majority of rush light holders were made of iron but a few examples exist decorated with brass. It is hard to date rushlights because the methods by which they were made and the material used did not vary from the sixteenth to nineteenth century.

CANDLESTICKS

54 *(left)* Candles were cast in single or multiple moulds. This wooden mould stands 17³/₄in high and is 15in wide. Eight candles of varying lengths could be cast. (*R. Jorgensen Antiques*)

55 *(above)* Known as a 'trumpet base' because of its similarity with the musical instrument, this is the best known type of English seventeenth-century candlesticks. The stem can be plain or ribbed, as with this example. Candlesticks of this style were mostly made by founders and date from 1650-1700. (*Robin Bellamy Ltd*)

57 *(left)* The Dutch *Heemskeerk* style candlestick. This is one of the commonest continental candlesticks. They were made for over 300 years and several different types of stems exist, but the central drip pan and domed foot are common to all examples of this style. This candlestick is about 1600. (*Robin Bellamy Ltd*)

56 *(above)* Another example of the 'trumpet based' style. This is a slightly earlier form but less common and the base is flatter. (*Robin Bellamy Ltd*)

59 *(right)* A group 'A' candlestick with solid stem but with an unexpected 'cut' corner base, about 1700. 6in high. (*Robin Bellamy Ltd*)

60 *(below, centre)* A square-based candlestick with seamed stem, 7$^{1}/_{4}$ in high. Group 'A', about 1720-30. (*Robin Bellamy Ltd*)

58   A pair of round-based cast decorated candlesticks of Scandinavian design. This form was popular around 1680 and continued in production, with small changes of detail, into the nineteenth century. This pair is by Pearson Page (Pattern No 4020), 10$^{1}/_{2}$in high, and date from around 1930. They originally cost 54s (£2.70) each.

62 *(bottom)* Another pair of square based candlesticks with hollow seamed stems. Group 'A'. Note the similarities with Fig 65. There are many small variations which can be found. 6$^{3}/_{4}$in high. (*Lawrence Fine Art Auctioneers, Crewkerne*)

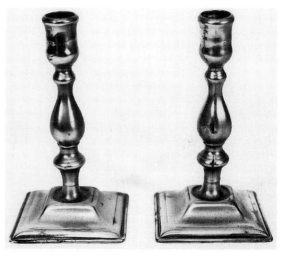

61 *(above)*   A rare form of candlestick, transitional between the trumpet-based candlesticks of the seventeenth century and the round based and knopped stem examples of the early eighteenth century. (*Robin Bellamy Ltd*)

63 *(right)* A pair of group 'A'
candlesticks with 'pear drop'
knops and hollow stems and
round bases. 6in high, about
1730. (*Private Collection*)

64 *(below)* Another seamed
round-based candlestick from
group 'A'. Note the high dome.
About 1730, 7in high. (*Duncan J.
Baggott*)

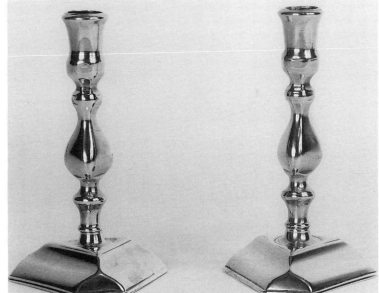

65 *(above)* A rare pair of group 'B' candlesticks with triangular bases
and hollow stems. 7$\frac{1}{4}$in high, about 1720-30. Each corner cut or in-
dented. (*Jerome Blum Antiques*)

66 *(left)* A candlestick with knopped baluster stem and octagonal base.
Group 'B'. Seamed stem. 6$\frac{1}{4}$in high, about 1710. (*Keith Hockin*)

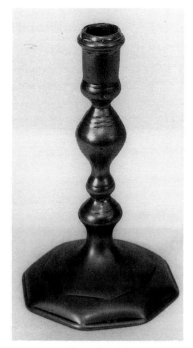

67 A candlestick with knopped seamed stem and prism base. $7^1/_2$ in high, about 1710-20. Group 'B'. (*Keith Hockin*)

68 A pair of candlesticks with six sides and high domed bases with hollow stems. $7^1/_4$in high, about 1720. Group 'B'. (*Private Collection*).

69 A pair of 'petal' based candlesticks from group 'C', with $8^1/_2$in high, hollow seamed stems, about 1750-70. (*Private Collection*)

70 A group of three candlesticks with petal or flower bases. Group 'C'. About 1750-70, $9^1/_4$in, $9^1/_4$in and 9in. (*Key Antiques*)

71 *(above)*   A 'petal-based' candlestick by Grove of Birmingham. 7³/₄in high, about 1750-70, group 'C'. (*Keith Hockin*)

72 *(above, right)*   A swirl-based candlestick with seamed stem on left (about 1750) and a fluted base example on the right (about 1740). Both are from group 'C'. 8¹/₂in and 8³/₄in high. (*Key Antiques*)

73 *(right)*   A rare candlestick with partly fluted base. This example shows that there can be many variations on the main themes. 7¹/₂in high, about 1760. Group 'C'. (*Duncan J. Baggott*)

74 *(far right)*   A most unusual candlestick with swirl base and rope twist stem. 9¹/₂in high, about 1760-70. Group 'C'. (*Duncan J. Baggott*)

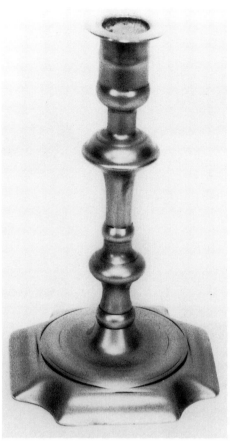

75 (*far left*) A candlestick with an almost square base but with slight indentations to the corners, perhaps an early example of group 'D'. Hollow seamed stem, 7½in high, about 1720-30. (*Duncan J. Baggott*)

76 (*left*) A more traditional form of group 'D' with fixed sconce. 7in high, about 1740-60. (*Duncan J. Baggott*)

77 A group of three candlesticks with cut corner bases, group 'D', about 1740-70, 7¾in, 7½in and 8½ in high. All with seamed stems and fixed sconces. (*Key Antiques*)

78 Square-based candlestick with cut corners and acorn knop. 6¾in high, about 1740 (*Keith Hockin*)

79 *(right)* An almost round based candlestick with 'cut' corners! Like all examples of this form it has a hollow seamed stem and as with most candlesticks, after 1780, a fixed sconce or bobeche. 7in high, about 1760. (*Duncan J. Baggott*)

80 *(far right)* A square-based candlestick with knopped stem and dished base. Group 'E', about 1770-1800. 9in high. (*Peter Norden Antiques*)

81 Six candlesticks from group 'E' with square bases and columnar stems. These candlesticks are from 11in to 11⁷/₈in high. The example on the left is seamed, but has a dished base and dates from around 1760. The next example has a domed base and there are traces of original silvering. It is the subject of a patent, No 771 controlling the grip on the candles (about 1780). There are also traces of silvering on candlestick No 3. Nos 4 and 5 both have seamed stems (nos 3, 4 and 5 are about 1760). No 6 dates from around 1770. All six examples have separate sconces. (*Jack Casimir Ltd*)

82 Square-based candlesticks with high domed bases but standing on four small feet. This is an Italian late eighteenth-century style. 11in high. British examples do not appear before the 1930s and then usually have six-sided bases. (*Duncan J. Baggott*)

83 A pair of Barlow patent round-based candlesticks of about 1840. The small knob in the front turns a patent grip which holds the candle firmly into place and dislodges it when turned. 9in high. (*Key Antiques*)

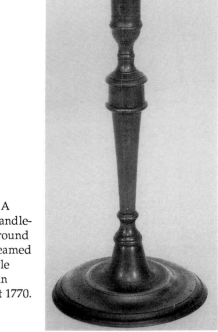

84 A pair of round-based candlesticks from group 'F' with fixed sconces and unseamed stems. They date from around 1770. 8$^1/_2$in high. (*Private Collection*)

85 (*right*) A group 'F' candlestick with round base and seamed 'Adam' style stem. 10$^1/_2$in high, about 1770. (*Duncan J. Baggott*)

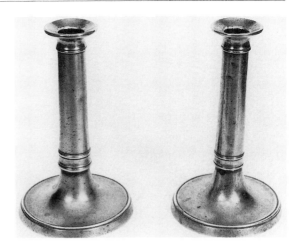

86 *(left)*   A similar candlestick from the same group, but note the unseamed stem and rounded candleholder. About 1790-1800, 8¹/₂in high. (*Duncan J. Baggott*)

87 *(above right)*   A pair of straight-sided and round-based candlesticks with slightly dished bases, 6in high. It is hard to date such examples but the features suggest a date of around 1800-20. (*R. Jorgensen Antiques*)

88 *(right)*   An example from group 'G'. This candlestick is 6in high and has a separate sconce. About 1830. (*Duncan J. Baggott*)

89 *(left)*   A taller example of group 'F' but with knopped stem and slightly domed base. 11in high, about 1790-1820. (*Peter Norden Antiques*)

90 *(right)*   A pair of telescopic candlesticks with oval bases, shown extended on the left. Group 'G'. About 1850. (*Robin Bellamy Ltd*)

91 *(left)* A group of three candlesticks. The example in the middle is from group 'G' and has an ejector or pusher inside the base to remove the candle. 12$\frac{3}{4}$in high and about 1840-50. The candlestick on the left is from group 'H'. About 1850, 12in high. The example on the right is from group 'I' and dates from around 1860. 13in high. (*Jack Casimir Ltd*)

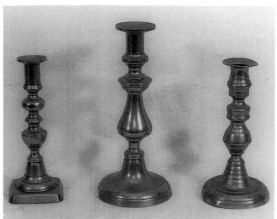

92 Another group. That on the left is from group 'I', about 1860, 8in high. The centre example is from group 'G' about 1840, 9$\frac{3}{4}$in high and that on the right is from 1870-80, group 'K', 8in high. (*Prudential Fine Art Auctions, Manchester*)

93 Three round-based candlesticks from group 'H'. Surprisingly the example on the right is seamed. Nevertheless they date from 1840-70. 8$\frac{3}{4}$in, 8$\frac{1}{4}$in, 8$\frac{1}{2}$in high. (*L. Skromme Collection*)

94 Three pairs of round-based candlesticks, those on right and left with banded baluster knops, (or beehive knops as they are sometimes called) the pair in the centre with plain knops. Group 'H' about 1860-70. (*Jerome Blum Antiques*)

95 Two candlesticks with square bases and beehive knops, that on the right being an inverted knop. Group 'H', about 1860-80. 13in and 11½in high. (*Jack Casimir Ltd*)

96 Two candlesticks, that on the left being an inverted beehive and the example on the right a multi-knopped example. 11in and 8½in. Group 'I', about 1870-80. (*Duncan J. Baggott*)

97 *(left)* A six-sided candlestick from group 'I', $11^1/_8$ in high, about 1880. (*L. Skromme Collection*)

98 *(top right)* A set of candlesticks made to commemorate the Jubilee of Queen Victoria. They are known as the Ace of Diamonds, King and Queen and the Prince and Princess. They are between 11in and 14in high. The Prince and Princess have additional blades to the stem. They bear the registration mark 385656 which dates them to after 1901. Generally group 'I'. (*Jack Casimir Ltd*)

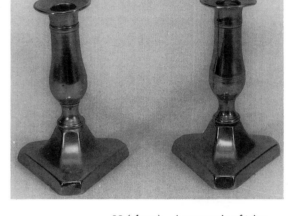

99 *(above)* A rare pair of triangular-based candlesticks from the mid-nineteenth century which do not fit exactly into any group but which have a close link with group 'F'. The method of joining the base to stem, was patented in 1839. $5^1/_2$ in high. (*Key Antiques*)

100 *(left)* A group of five twist candlesticks with round bases. The smallest example has a 1887-8 registration number. They are between 12in and $8^7/_{16}$ in high. Some of the bases are left rough cast, others have been turned off. Examples of this style were still being sold in the 1930s. (*Country Life Antiques*)

101 *(above)*   Designs for several candlesticks of Group J. presented in the *Industry of All Nations Art Union Catalogue* of 1851.

102 *(top right)*   A nineteenth-century candlestick with a bell. About 1870-90, 11$\frac{1}{4}$in high. Examples with a slightly different construction were also being sold by Pearson Page in 1927. (*L. Skromme Collection*)

103 *(below)*   Left: a small candlestick from group 'J'. The twist stem and eagle's foot base example dates from 1860-70. 5in high. Right: the round-based example with drip tray dates from 1880-1900. 6$\frac{3}{4}$in high. (*Country Life Antiques*)

104 *(right)*   A Scandinavian-style candlestick with the 'Globe and Sceptre' mark, about 1900. 9in high. (*Windrush Antiques*)

105 *(above)*   A high domed candlestick with side extractor, the stem seamed. Group 'A', about 1710-20, 7in high. (*Duncan J. Baggott*)

106 *(right)*   A round-based candlestick with side twist patented extractor by J. Barlow. 7$\frac{1}{2}$in high, about 1840-50. (*L. Skromme Collection*)

107 *(below)*   Close-up of the extractor knob on a Barlow candlestick.

108 *(above)*   The patented method of removing the used candles on a Barlow candlestick. The metal forks rise as the knob shown in the previous illustration is turned.

109 *(left)*   Another round-based candlestick with extractor, group 'A'. About 1730, 7in. (*Duncan J. Baggott*)

110 *(right)*   A rare 'hog scraper' candlestick with extractor. They are called 'hog scrapers' because the sharp base was supposedly used for scraping hair and flesh from newly-killed pork. There does seem to be some evidence for this otherwise rather fanciful name. 7$\frac{3}{4}$in high, about 1720-30. (*Jack Casimir Ltd*)

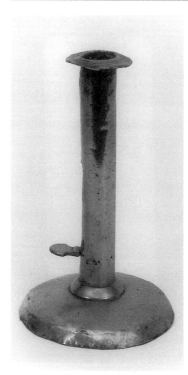  

111 An all brass hog scraper candlestick, mid-eighteenth century. (*Key Antiques*)

112 A fine cast brass hog scraper candlestick with single seam. About 1700, 8in high. (*Jack Casmir Ltd, photograph by Roy Farthing*)

113 Hog scraper candlestick with square base and typical hook for hanging on a wall. Central round knop. 8in high, about 1730. (*Duncan J. Baggott*)

114 A group of four candlesticks with extractors. The first two examples are about 1740-50, the third with a flower base is about 1750 and the last with prism base is about 1720. $6^3/_4$in to $7^1/_4$in high. (*Jack Casimir Ltd*)

115 *(above)* Two tall candlesticks with side extractors. The example on the left is of single-seamed sheet metal construction, 16in high and that on the right is cast, $12^3/_8$in high. Both date from about 1830. (*Jack Casimir Ltd*)

116 *(above right)* Close up of a round-based candlestick showing the 'pusher' which removed the used candle. (*Duncan J. Baggott*)

117 A group of reproduction candlesticks from Pearson Page & Co's 1927 catalogue, showing many of the designs from the eighteenth century still on sale. (*Photograph by Eric Adkins*)

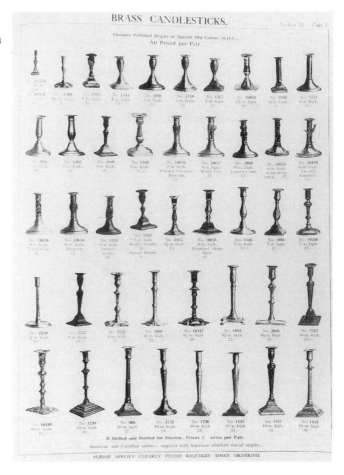

118 A group of candlesticks from the Jones catalogue, about 1930, showing some of their 'antique reproductions'. (*Photograph by Eric Adkins*)

CANDLE LAMP

CHAMBERSTICKS

119 *(left)* A student lamp of a form used in the late nineteenth century, but still available for twenty years into the twentieth century. *(Rudolph Otto Antiques)*

120 *(right)* A tinder box and chamber candlestick, this time with a side extractor. About 1730. *(Robin Bellamy Ltd)*

121 *(right)* A simple tinder box and candleholder with rounded handle, the edges of which have been turned over to thicken the handle. About 1850. *(B.I. & D.M. Howard)*

122 A tinder box with strap handle, complete with flint and steel. 4in high. 6¹/₂in wide including the handle. About 1830. *(Country Life Antiques)*

123 A chamber stick with original doubter and snuffer. 5in high and 6¹/₂in diameter. About 1750-60. *(Peter Norden Antiques)*

124 Two eighteenth-century chambersticks. Both at one time had doubters. The left example is 5$^{1}/_{2}$in wide and 2$^{1}/_{2}$in high and that on the right is 6in wide by 4$^{1}/_{4}$in high. About 1730-50. (*L. Skromme Collection*)

125 Two chambersticks with pins which were used to mount them on a mirror, candlestand or piano. About 1750-70. Most examples of this form of fitting are later. 4in by 3in and 4in by 2$^{1}/_{2}$in (*R. Jorgensen Antiques*)

126 Three chambersticks. On the left is a rare oval example, 7in by 4$^{3}/_{4}$in, the wavy example is 7in by 5in and the oblong chamberstick is 6$^{3}/_{4}$in by 5in. In each case there were originally doubters and the small apertures for them to fit into can be seen in the handles. About 1830-50. (*L. Skromme Collection*)

127 (*below*) A deep-bowled brass chamberstick of oblong form, 7in long. About 1830-50. (*B.I. & D.M. Howard*)

128 (*below right*) A similar example complete with its doubter. 5$^{1}/_{2}$in high. Mid-nineteenth century. (*R. Jorgensen Antiques*)

129 Two sheet metal chambersticks, that on the left with fretted sides and six-sided form, 9¹/₂in wide. The right-hand example is 10in wide and has lightly-cut decoration. The simple handles are rivetted into place. They date from the second half of the nineteenth century. (*L. Skromme Collection*)

130 A mid-Victorian cast-decorated chamberstick. 9in wide. (*Country Life Antiques*)

131 A pair, on left and right, of fretted chambersticks and another example in centre. Edwardian. The pair is 5¹/₄in by 3¹/₂in and the single is 2³/₄in.

132 A Pearson Page reproduction chamberstick on left of about 1930 and a late nineteenth-century example, 4¹/₂in high. (See also Fig 134)

133 A further two fretted chambersticks. The pattern on the left was still on sale in 1930, while the oval example on the right is another form also being marketed after World War II. 10¹/₄in and 9¹/₂in wide, both with handle. (See also Fig 134)

BRASS CANDLESTICKS.

Finished Polished Bright or Special Old Colour (S.O.C.).
All Priced per Pair.

No. 1702
3 in. high. Dia. of Pan, 5 in.
9/-

No. 10333
3 in. high. Dia. of Pan, 5½ in.
11/-

No. 10344
3 in. high. Dia. of Pan, 7 in.
19/-

No. 11144
6½ in. high. Dia. of Pan, 5½ in.
27/-

No. 3343
Dia. of Pan, 5⅝ in.
17/-

No. 3621
Dia. of Pan, 7½ in.
21/-

No. 2035
Dia. of Pan, 5½ in.
19/-

No. 2907
Dia. of Pan, 5½ in.
24/-

No. 2034
Dia. of Pan, 7 in.
24/-

No. 3601
Small. Dia. of Pan, 5½ in., 21/-
Large. Dia. of Pan, 7 in., 25/-

No. 2240
Dia. of Pan, 8 in. Height, 3½ in.
40/-

No. 2221
5 in. high. Pan, 7½ in. × 5½ in.
25/-

No. 2239
6½ in. high. Dia. of Pan, 7 in.
Plain, 24/- Chased, 30/-

No. 2233
7 in. high. Dia. of Pan, 7 in.
Plain, 26/- Chased, 31/-

No. 3914
Dia. of Pan, 7½ in.
23/-

No. 10944
6¾ in. × 4¾ in.
25/-

No. 1703
5 in. high. Dia. of Pan, 7 in.
33/-

No. 1704
5 in. high. Pan, 7 in. × 6 in.
33/-

No. 2244
Dia. of Pan 7 in. 8 in. 9½ in.
Height 6 in. 6½ in. 14 in.
33/- 41/- 51/-

No. 2223
Pan, 8½ in. × 5½ in.
25/-

No. 10872
4½ in. high. Pan, 7 in. × 6 in.
25/-

No. 2246
Dia. of Pan, 8½ in.
31/-

No. 2222
6½ in. high. Dia. of Pan, 8 in.
25/-

If Drilled and Bushed for Electric, Prices 5/- extra per Pair.
American and Canadian markets supplied with American standard thread nipples.

134 A page from the Pearson Page reproduction catalogue of 1927 (*Photograph by Eric Adkins*)

TAPERSTICKS

135 A pair of taper sticks and in the centre, *en suite*, a stand and snuffers. $6^5/_8$ in high. Seamed construction and octagonal base. About 1720. (*Jack Casimir Ltd*)

136 A matching set of two candlesticks, two taper sticks and a snuffer stand, (maximum 8in high). About 1725. (*Jack Casimir Ltd, photograph by Roy Farthing*)

137 (*below*) A group of fifteen miniature candlesticks from $3^1/_8$ in to 5in in height, all nineteenth century. (*L. Skromme Collection*)

138 (*above*)   A fine seventeenth-century wall sconce with *repoussé* decoration. The candleholder is probably later. (*Robin Bellamy Ltd*)

139 (*above right*)   A late eighteenth-century *repoussé*-decorated wall sconce, possibly Dutch. (*Duncan J. Baggott*)

140 (*right*)   A shaped Dutch wall sconce, about 1720-30. (*Robin Bellamy Ltd*)

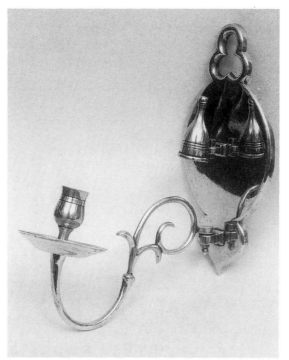

141 Cast brass wall sconce with doubter, one of pair. Mid-nineteenth century. (*Jack Casimir Ltd, photograph by Roy Farthing*)

142 Brass wall sconce, again one of a pair. Late nineteenth century. (*Jack Casimir Ltd, photograph by Roy Farthing*)

LANTERNS

143 Two lanterns, the example on the left with three candle-holders possibly English. 19in high, about 1780. The right-hand example is also probably English, about 1750, 15$\frac{1}{2}$in high. (*Robert Skinner Inc*)

145 On the left is a folding lantern, mid-eighteenth century, 5¼in high, possible British. The next two are probably French and from the first half of the eighteenth century, although similar lanterns may have been made in Britain. 7½in and 6½in high. (*Robert Skinner Inc*)

144 A fine Dutch early eight-eenth-century lantern with *repoussé*-decorated door and domed lid. 9½in high. (*Robin Bellamy Ltd*)

146(*above right*) Another group of lanterns. The first example is British, 6¾in high, about 1830. The next two are German, both nineteenth century, 7½in and 6½in high (*Robert Skinner Inc*).

147 (*right*) These two lanterns are of a form thought to have been made in Britain as well as in Europe, about 1750-70, 7½in and 5in high. (*Robert Skinner Inc*)

CANDELABRA AND STANDING LIGHTS

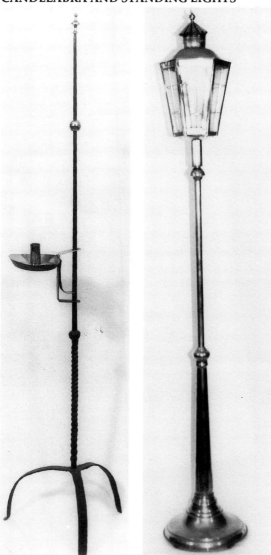

148 *(far left)*   An iron standing candleholder with moveable brass pan and candlesconce. 39½in high, late eighteenth century. (*Key Antiques*)

149 *(near left)*   Standing light, 73in high, about 1870-90. (*Windrush Antiques*)

150   A Peerage double candelabra, 15in high, about 1930.

151 *(above)* Eighteenth-century brass chandelier. Dutch, but similar examples were also made in Britain. *(Robin Bellamy Ltd)*

152 *(right)* Rare small brass chandelier with seamed stem. Early eighteenth century. *(Jack Casimir Ltd, photograph by Roy Farthing)*

153 Brass chandelier, about 1800. 24in from side to side and 21in from top to bottom. *(Jerome Blum Antiques)*

154 Almost all rushlight holders are made in iron, but this rare example has a brass foot. $9\frac{1}{2}$in high, about 1800. *(R. Jorgensen Antiques)*

OTHER FUELS FOR LIGHTING

Animal and Vegetable Oil Lamps

Since prehistoric times man has burnt natural oils in lamps to provide him with illumination.

Plants with a high oil content do not grow well in the cold climate of northern Europe, but there were other natural sources of oils, often from the more remote parts of Britain. Fish liver oil was one source, while oil from the sea bird, the fulmar (part of their defence mechanism) lit the island of St Kilda. In the nineteenth century whale oil was imported in considerable quantities.

From the earliest times through to the twentieth century animal fats like tallow were widely used. Some vegetable oils such as colza oil, made from rape seed, were imported but vegetable oils never made an impact on the British market.

Lamps burning animal and vegetable oils were not effective; they provided a poor smokey light and also gave off an offensive smell. They were not popular but the illumination they offered was cheap. Small lamps known as 'crusies' were made in Scotland and other parts of this country. Nearly all are in iron but occasional brass examples can be found. Most of the crusie lamps now to be seen are European.

Whale oil lamps form a second group. A typical example is illustrated. Whale and sperm oil provided an important new source of fuel in the nineteenth century but demand could not keep up with supply and as a consequence the price of whale oil rose more than six fold between 1832 and 1865. Most of these lamps are American or European, but it is possible that some were made here. American whale oil lamps are common in pewter; the copper alloy lamps, including highly decorated sheet metal examples, are usually European.

Other styles of oil lamps are also illustrated. A few of these small hanging lamps are to be found in brass and copper, and some may well be British.

The invention in the 1780s of the Argand Lamp, a system which was patented in 1784, increased the supply of oxygen and helped the flame burn brighter. Many variations and improvements in lamps occurred in the next four decades.

Whale and colza oil do not flow well by gravity because of their viscosity. Developments included placing the reservoir below the lamp, and in the Carcel lamp of the 1800s, by providing a clockwork feed. In 1835 further improvements were made with the Moderator Lamp, where the flow of oil was assisted by spring feeding. Gravity feed lamps continued in use throughout the mid-nineteenth century however. Lamps were made in pewter, marble, glass, porcelain, brass and copper. Most are based on an ionic column or are of rococo design. Many have square bases.

Many varieties of lamp were invented and a few examples are illustrated. In the USA alone, between 1841 and 1860, 450 lighting patents were issued. The levels of production before the discovery of petroleum can be illustrated by the 1850 census of production figures for Dietz and Co of the USA, one of many makers in the field, which showed that they made in that year some 24,000 lamp globes and 48,000 lamp chimneys. One other company was offering, about 1870, fifty-five different oil chandeliers as well as fifty-five other lamps while another company offered eighty-two types of lamps for sale.

Mineral and Refined Oil

Coal had been refined into an oil called kerosene in the 1840s and camphene, a lethal combination of kerosene and alcohol, was also used as an alternative to other oils. It was cheap at only a third of the cost of sperm oil. A Scot, James Young, refined oil from shale in 1847 to produce paraffin, and this, mostly from Roumania and Burma, was imported into Britain in the late 1850s as an alternative to kerosene. However the discovery of mineral oil in Pennsylvania in 1859 revolutionised lighting. Britain imported an average of 5.3 million gallons of petroleum products between 1863 and 1870. In 1871 £600,000 worth of petroleum products were brought into Britain and the value of imports of petroleum were to rise to £5.6 million by 1906.

The use of paraffin revolutionised British lighting. Hundreds of new designs came onto the market. One British lamp manufacturer alone made 247,000 oil lamps in 1860 and 375,000 in

1861. Some of these new lamps became known as 'Hurricane' lamps and they continued in daily use well into the twentieth century. Old lamps were converted to the new fuels and it is possible for specialists in the field to work out the changes which a lamp has undergone by examining the burners and reservoirs. Birmingham alone was making 500,000 burners a year by 1866 although cheaper American imports still dominated the market. British burners, at an average of $8^1/_2$d, were twice the cost of American imports.

Paraffin lamps were made to hang from the ceiling, to stand free on tables and to be carried about the home. They come in all sizes and are made from many materials and combinations of materials. Few are solely in brass or copper although these alloys are widely found on lamps.

Surprisingly few lamps have come down to the present in working order. Hundreds of thousands must have been thrown away with the widespread use of electricity after 1919; an indication of how speedily technological change can lead to the abandonment of a group of objects. Who wanted old paraffin lamps when clean, bright, light came at the turn of a switch? Chandeliers and candelabra were also made which used oil as the fuel.

Gas Lamps

At first gas was used for street lighting; some streets in Bath and Wells were lit from 1798 and the first London buildings were illuminated by gas in 1807. Gas was used for domestic lighting in towns from the 1840s but did not find its way into rural communities until the first two decades of this century.

By 1833 there were five firms in Birmingham making brass or copper gas fittings. By 1847 there were seventeen and by 1865 this number had swelled to twenty-five. Many other firms also made copper or brass tubes and produced lamps for use with gas; perhaps an additional 100 or more by 1865. The amount of gas used by consumers rose steadily and from 1881 to 1911 gas consumption tripled. Many improvements were made in the gas burner between 1820 and 1890 including the introduction in 1887 of a gas mantle which provided a much brighter light than the open flame. Gas fittings were made to stand, hang from ceilings or were fastened to the wall. They were made in glass, ceramics and many metals including copper and brass.

Coinciding with the development of Victorian taste, early gas lamps and fittings were elaborate. By the 1851 Exhibition a wide range of fittings were available including examples in Renaissance and Tudor style! Simpler styles of gas fittings suggest a late Victorian or twentieth-century date.

Originally the makers could only provide seamed copper tubes to supply the gas but in 1838 Charles Green invented a technique for making seamless tubes in which cylinders were elongated or extruded. From 1852 these tubes could be decorated at the same time as they were extruded. Because technical changes were so rapid, few nineteenth century gas fittings still survive.

Electric Light

Although experiments with electricity go back into the eighteenth century, our modern understanding of electricity stems from the work by Faraday in 1831. It was not however until the invention of both Swan's and Edison's incandescent filament lamps in 1878-9 however that electric lighting became a serious possibility. The early utility companies supplying electricity to towns were established in the 1880s and 1890s but progress was very slow. In spite of that, many hundreds of electric lights and lamps were on the market by 1910. One company alone, R. Williamson & Co offered 305 electric fittings, and 100 combined gas and electrical fittings of which 75 per cent were partly in brass. It was not until after World War I that any but a minority of wealthier homes had electric light.

ANIMAL AND VEGETABLE OIL LAMPS

155 *(far left)* A traditionally shaped hanging lamp, about 1800. British examples are rare and this lamp is probably German. (*R. Jorgenson Antiques*)

156 *(near left)* Brass hanging lamp, possibly European, about 1780-1800 (*R. Jorgenson Antiques*)

157 *(above)* Brass pendant lamp, with two spouts. 3in high, about 1830-40. (*B.I. & D.M. Howard*)

158 *(right)* Traditional spouted whale oil lamp of a form mostly made in Germany, Holland and the United States although some examples may have been constructed in Britain. The earliest forms are from the eighteenth century, but most are from the first 30 years of the nineteenth century. (*Robin Bellamy Ltd*)

159 A sonumbra lamp in Sheraton style made in bronze. About 1840, 16$\frac{1}{2}$in high. (*Oaks Collection*)

160 An oil lamp of hammered brass, about 1880-1900. (*Country Life Antiques*)

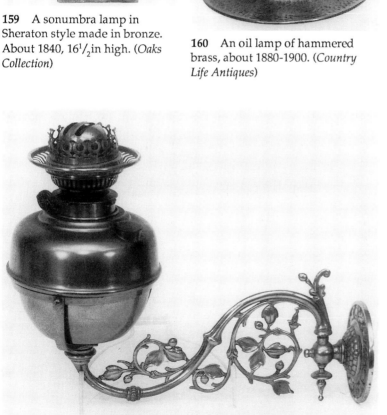

161 (*above*) An oil lamp with corinthian column and bottom reservoir by Hinks and Son, patent No 2. 13in to top of burner. About 1860. (*Duncan J. Baggott*)

162 (*left*) A wall fitting used with paraffin. 14in from wall, 8in high. Late Victorian. (*Rudolph Otto Antiques*)

163 A pair of silver-plated lamps which were also available in copper finish, 16in high. Meriden Silver Company catalogue, 1888.

GAS AND ELECTRICAL LIGHT

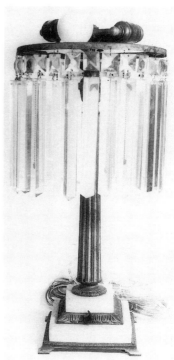

164 Design for a typical mid-nineteenth century gas Victorian Chandelier, this example is by Mr Potts of Birmingham and was part of the 1851 exhibition. (*Photograph by Eric Adkins*)

165 An American electric light of 1900 in brass and marble. 22in high. (*Oaks Collection*)

MAKING AND EXTINGUISHING LIGHT

Flint, Steel and Tinder

For hundreds of years the only practical way of obtaining a light was to use a steel, flint and tinder. This was a slow and laborious process which could take a minute to generate even a small flame. The steel, flint and tinder were kept in all kind of receptacles, wood and tin boxes, leather pouches, and in brass boxes and candle-holders. By the 1830s the use of flint steel and tinder was declining with the introduction of matches.

Matches

Early experiments with matches were based on chemical processes including sulpher tipped and self lighting matches. These were unstable and highly dangerous. By 1827 matches included the 'lucifer' and the 'prometheon'. These worked on friction and would light if rubbed against each other or against most surfaces, but eventually safety matches were developed.

Few brass containers for matches existed before 1900, when Vesta boxes appeared but there are a few match boxes combined with candle-holders of the mid to late nineteenth century.

A match receptical was incorporated in a chamber stick for the first time in 1854, when a patent was issued to J. & W. Harcourt.

Pistol Lighters

One method to obtain a light was to use a tinder pistol. These tinder pistols mechanised the use of steel and flint through the action of firing the pistol. The tinder was placed where the powder of a real pistol would have been. Tinder pistols were used from the eighteenth century and into the nineteenth century.

Spills

Spills of wood, cloth or twisted paper were employed to turn the small flame obtained via a flint and steel into a more robust flame.

Boxes of copper and brass were used to hold these spills; some free standing, others hanging from the wall. Most are nineteenth century and are made from thin sheet metal. Copies however are common and decorated examples are especially suspect.

Snuffers or Doubters

We are used to extinguishing the light by turning a switch. But with candles, the flame had to be put out manually. It was easy to burn your thumb and forefinger, while it was difficult to reach the candles set in chandeliers hung from the ceiling. One group of extinguishers, or doubters, consisted of a small cup which fitted over the top of the candle. Some of these were made with short stems; examples are often found associated with small candleholders. Others had long stems, for use with chandeliers. Another type of doubter was similar to a pair of scissors, but with flattened ends to close over the flame.

All candles need regular trimming if the light they give off is not to deteriorate. As the wax or fat burns away the exposed wick smokes, flickers and burns less brightly. Tallow candles, especially, lost their brightness quickly. A contemporary study showed that over a 30-minute period the light given off by an untrimmed tallow candle declined to 16 per cent of its original illumination. For this reason it was necessary to trim the wick by cutting away the partly burned parts, known as the 'snuff'. This was done with snuffers, but the word has aquired a different meaning today. It was only after the invention of a plaited wick in 1822 that trimming gradually became unnecessary.

Snuffers in the form of scissors, usually with a small box incorporated to hold the trimmed wick, were used from the sixteenth century to the Edwardian era. Silver, steel and silver plate examples dominate the nineteenth century but brass snuffers were in daily use in the eighteenth century and are often found with their original stands. These stands can take two main forms, one rather like a small candlestick had the snuffers set in vertically, the other form consisted of a small tray on which the snuffers rested horizontally. Keep an eye open for replacement snuffers on original eighteenth century stands since they tended to get easily separated in daily use.

SNUFFERS AND DOUBTERS

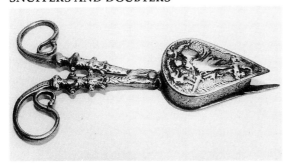

166 *(left)* A fine cast decorated pair of box snuffers from Nuremberg, about 1600. *(Robin Bellamy Ltd)*

167 *(above)* A doubter on a small tray. Used to extinguish candles. Mid nineteenth century, 2in high. *(Colin Greenway Antiques)*

168 A pair of late seventeenth-century snuffers, also probably German. Note the less elaborate style, smaller box and simpler decoration. *(Robin Bellamy Ltd)*

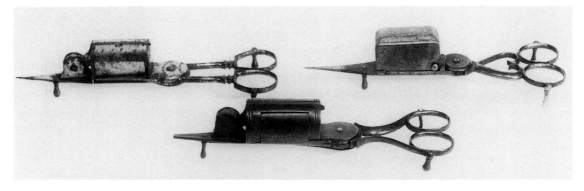

169 *(above)* A group of three snuffers, all from the early nineteenth century. *(R. Jorgensen Antiques)*

170 *(left)* A small pair of scissor-type doubters with rounded blades. Early nineteenth century, $4\frac{1}{2}$in long. *(Duncan J. Baggott)*

171 *(right)*   A tray with snuffers.
8¹/₂in overall, about 1730-40.
(Robin Bellamy Ltd)

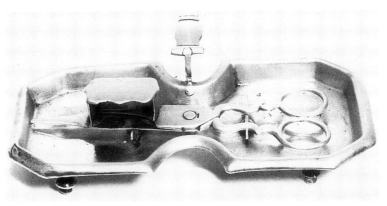

172 *(right)*
Another tray
illustrating the
variety of forms
that were used.
6¹/₄in long, mid-
eighteenth
century. (*Key
Antiques*)

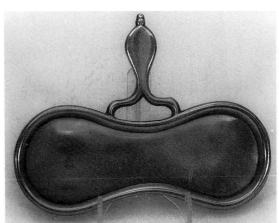

173 *(left)*   Pair
of snuffers and
stand. About
1715, 8in high.
(*J. Casimir Ltd,
photograph by
Roy Farthing*)

174 *(left)*   Two
further stands
complete with
snuffers. The
example on the
left dates from
1750, the right-
hand stand and
snuffer are a few
years earlier,
about 1730. 7¹/₂in
high. (*Duncan J.
Baggott*)

175*(right)*   A
vertical snuffer
stand and snuf-
fers. 7¹/₂in high,
about 1730.
(*Private Collection*)

LIGHTING DEVICES, MATCHBOX HOLDERS AND SPILL HOLDERS
(Some examples of tinder boxes have already been illustrated, see Figs 120-2.)

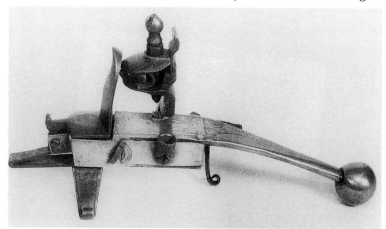

176 A pistol lighter. This rare iron and brass lighter, from the early eighteenth century is 7$^1/_2$in long overall. (*R. Jorgensen Antiques*)

177 Another candleholder and Vesta matchbox cover, again nineteenth century. 4$^1/_2$in by 4in. (*Country Life Antiques*)

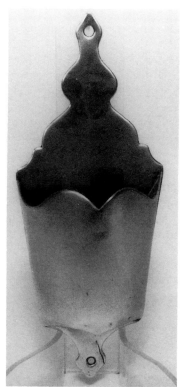

178 A spill holder. Simple brass or copper pockets such as this example were widely used for spills. They can date from 1880 to 1920. 9$^1/_2$in high. (*Duncan J. Baggott*)

6
KEEPING WARM

One of the major problems people faced was to keep warm in winter. Houses were full of draughts with plenty of crannies and cracks for the cold winds to penetrate. Prior to the mid-eighteenth century only a minority of homes had glass in their windows; the wind being excluded by wooden shutters. Until the eighteenth century, winters were colder than today. Fuel was costly and in short supply. From the middle ages into the nineteenth century there was often insufficient fuel for the poor to have a fire for more than a few hours a day. Wood was scarce and peasants had to make do with dried dung, heathers, shrubs, blackberry vines, gorse or sticks. Even in the better off homes, winter temperatures could be low. In 1784 a Swedish observer commented, ruefully, that the temperatures seldom rose above 50 degrees Farenheit in the homes he visited.

Most of the available fuels, including wood, burned best in an open fire, resting on fire dogs which helped create a draught. Peat, widely used in Somerset, Yorkshire, Ireland and Scotland, also burned best on an open hearth. Up to the Tudor period most families would, if they could afford it, keep one fire burning all the time. This served for cooking and for keeping the family warm by day and by night. It burned in the centre of the main living room and the smoke curled slowly up through a hole in the roof. At night the family would have huddled around the hearth.

Increasing prosperity meant that people could afford to build brick chimneys. In a house with a chimney it was possible to have fires in several rooms. Harrison, writing, in the sixteenth century, on those things which had changed most in his lifetime stated that 'One is the multitude of chimneys lately erected'. Progress was

gradual. In London it was not until after the rebuilding following the Great Fire in 1666 that the most homes had a chimney. The increased use of coal as a domestic fuel also encouraged the adoption of chimneys. Coal smoke was noxious, and coal fires required a greater draught than that offered by a hole in the roof.

Wood was the principal fuel for centuries in Britain. Heavy demands on timber for shipbuilding and house construction, combined with the steady rise in demand for wood as a fuel created by the growth in the population and rising living standards, led to a shortage of timber. The countryside was steadily denuded of wood, especially close to the towns.

Coal was burnt as a domestic fuel in the medieval period in London but it is mainly in the seventeenth century that its use expanded. It was shipped in barges from Newcastle to London and was known, for this reason, as sea-coal. Some idea of the increasing importance of coal as a fuel can be obtained by the production figures for the mining of coal which rose from an average of 210,000 tons in 1551-60 to 2,983,000 tons in 1681-90.

Coal does not burn well on the floor of open fireplaces. Some form of iron grate or basket was needed to provide an adequate draught. As coal slowly replaced wood so the nature of the fire changed. Hearths became smaller, with grates or baskets resting on the andirons where logs had previously burned. It did not take long for the basket to be combined with the dogs in a single fire grate. An early inventory from Ham House in 1679 records one such grate. Open wood fires continued in use throughout Britain where people had sufficient timber to hand, and among those who disliked the dirt associated with coal.

Gas and electricity did offer a late alternative, but gas was costly and electricity arrived as a heating fuel too late to have any impact on our story. Even as late as 1939 only 18.5 per cent of British homes were heated by gas and only 2.5 per cent by electricity.

Fire Dogs

Fire dogs or andirons were used to rest logs upon in the open hearth. Smaller dogs were also employed between the larger examples, called 'creepers', or 'brand dogs' to prevent logs from falling out of the fire. From the earliest days iron was the dominant metal used; hence the alternative name given to them. In the seventeenth century a few brass dogs were made. These were mostly for show as Fuller, in his *Worthies* (1662), suggests: 'The iron doggs bear the burden ... the bronze andirons stand for show'.

In the eighteenth century many were either made of brass (although the back rests usually remained of iron) or were decorated with brass. Even after the grate had replaced open wood fires, dogs were still employed as part of the hearth furniture and fire irons were rested upon them. Smaller fire dogs were either part of the much smaller fire places of the late Victorian and Edwardian period or were employed as rests for fire irons.

There are many designs for brass andirons. In the eighteenth century classical shapes, especially with baluster knops, tended to dominate, but in the Victorian period more elaborate styles briefly became popular.

Good quality brass fire dogs continued to be made into the 1930s, but genuine eighteenth-century dogs usually have extensive wear on their feet and rests where they stood in the fire, while ceremonial dogs of later periods do not have such wear. It is always possible of course that earlier dogs have had to be remounted with iron feet because of the wear, but there should be some evidence to support this possibility.

In the United States, where wood remained in easy supply, it continued as the principal fuel into the nineteenth century and as a consequence fire dogs were made in many hundreds of designs for use rather than display. Schiffer in his *Brass Book* illustrates no fewer than 150 designs of American andirons.

Grates

Once coal was established as the principal fuel, then people needed grates in which to burn it. Many fires used for cooking had cast-iron baskets and by the late eighteenth century these baskets had developed into ranges or stoves with iron sides and top.

In middle-class homes the basket or grate continued in use in the livingrooms and bedrooms and though many were in iron, examples with brass and copper are common. These grates were not simply functional but were designed to please the eye.

An antique grate will have seen substantial use and there ought to be evidence of this wear on its various parts such as the fire back, feet and fire basket. Size is not a criteria of age as there are many full sized grates made for daily use up to World War II and afterwards many were reproduced.

Bellows

Lighting a fire was never easy before the invention of the safety match. The flame had to be coaxed from steel, flint and tinder and the fire encouraged into life by providing an adequate amount of oxygen. For hundreds of years this was done with the aid of a pair of bellows.

Bellows were made from wood and leather, and usually had a brass or iron spout which was placed into the fire. Some hand bellows were decorated with sheets of repousse brass or with brass studding.

Eighteenth- and nineteenth-century bellows tend to be large, while Edwardian and reproduction bellows are smaller, and if used, are not always very servicable, being short of 'puff'.

Mechanical bellows were also used. The draft was created by turning a handle and through the use of fans, pumped the air through the spout into the fire. Bellows of this form are often known as 'Irish' or 'peat' bellows, as peat fires certainly needed all the oxygen they could get. These bellows were undoubtedly made and used in Ireland but mechanical bellows were also manufactured in mainland Britain. Most examples are nineteenth century with the height of the forms' popularity probably between 1800 and 1870.

A few 'blowing' tubes are known though most examples are from France and Flanders. These tubes were hollow and the mouth was used to blow air into the heart of the fire. Most blowing tubes are made in iron but a few examples have been found in brass. They date from the fifteenth to the seventeenth century.

Fire Irons

While it was not difficult to kick a recalcitrant log back into the fire, such activity did no good to one's boots and from the earliest times people tended to use tools to control and move logs in the hearth.

The first tools were pokers or fire hooks, made in wrought iron. Few early examples have survived. Later the hook was replaced by a pair of tongs, the design probably derived from two pokers fastened together.

The use of coal as the main fuel meant that a spade or shovel was needed to move the coals and clinkers and gradually in the eighteenth century people came to use sets of three fire irons: shovel, poker and tongs.

Most eighteenth- and early nineteenth-century examples are between 20in and 27in long although similar large sets were still on sale in 1900. The Army and Navy stores in 1907, for example, offered twenty-two different complete sets and fifteen pairs of tongs in brass or copper. Smaller sets are late Victorian or Edwardian as are sets to which a brush has also been added. Pokers normally have an iron tip. Shovels and tongs are often found in brass. Early examples tend to be plain, crude and large, while later Victorian sets are more elaborate and better balanced.

Coal Scuttles

Logs could be brought to the hearth in baskets or carried in one's arms but coal was more difficult and dirty to handle and a group of scoops or buckets were invented for this purpose. The first coal scuttles are eighteenth century but most scuttles that are now seen are from the nineteenth century.

They were also known as coal hods and examples in brass, copper, steel and laquered metal can be found. While grates remained large so did scuttles, but towards the end of the Victorian period the use of smaller grates meant that less fuel was needed at any one time and smaller scuttles became popular.

Ember Pans

Although in the seventeenth and eighteenth centuries people tried to keep their fires in overnight, the grate or hearth had to be cleaned occasionally and a group of objects now known as 'ember buckets' were designed to remove the ash and embers without spilling them on the carpet or floor. Some form of container continued to be used into the nineteenth century after coal had replaced wood. Ordinary buckets and pails were probably extensively used for this purpose. Most ember buckets now seen are Dutch. They usually stand on three feet and are slightly tapering. Many examples are in copper but with brass lids, which should closely fit the body. It is possible that some of these 'Dutch' pails were also made in Britain as in the eighteenth century many previously imported items were copied by the Birmingham makers in search of new markets.

Ember Tongs

When transferring a light from one fire to another hot coals were often used and these would have been carried in a bucket or an ember pan. Sometimes, as for example when a light was required for a pipe, a pair of tongs were used known as ember tongs. Many tongs were made in brass although iron examples are to be found. Eighteenth-century tongs are often large, a foot or two long. Later smaller tongs under 12in were made, while many small brass tongs are of recent manufacture.

Curfews

One school of thought holds that curfews, *couvre de feu* in French, were designed to keep fires in over-night. Fires were hard to light and this indeed may have been one of the functions of the hoods known as 'curfews' which were placed over the fire when the family retired for the night.

However although such a cover may have helped to restrict the flow of oxygen to the fire, there is no doubt that the curfew also provided a much needed protection against sparks leaping from the fire and starting a blaze.

Most curfews date from the late seventeenth and early eighteenth centuries. Examples are known in copper and brass, usually elaborately decorated with punch work or repouse work. Some of these are of Dutch origin, others may be English.

Later eighteenth century and nineteenth-century examples are rare. Perhaps the fender made their use redundant. However in the later Victorian period a form of curfew reappears and its manufacture continued into this century. These are small plain brass or copper ovals which may have augmented the fender overnight.

Fenders

While logs could usually be contained in the hearth by using dogs or creepers the use of coal as the main fuel increased the risk of hot coals falling out of the fire. A new form of buffer was created: the fender.

Early fenders consisted of a straight, flat piece of metal, normally brass or copper, which was often decorated by fretting. These stood in the hearth in front of the grate but they were unstable. A flat iron sheet was added at right angles to the fender to make it stand more easily and later still feet were also attached, usually in the front facing into the room. Bow-fronted fenders can be found and here their shape helped to make them stable. In due course fenders were also made with sides at right angles to the front in addition to the feet and floor plates.

Eighteenth-century fenders can be found in brass and they were also made in steel and paktong. In the nineteenth century iron fenders became popular, but fenders all or partly in copper or brass were also frequent in the nineteenth century.

Many fenders in brass or copper are decorated by fretting or cutting. This decoration provides one of the ways to help date them. Early fretting was done by hand and the result is that the cutting is often uneven. Later patterns were stamped out by machine which provided a closer neat pattern. It is useful too to check the screws employed in their construction: machine threads

must be nineteenth century or later.

Fire Screens

In the nineteenth century large fire screens were evolved to deal with sparks. Many of these are in brass or copper or have brass and copper decoration and iron or steel screens. Most of these fire screens were made with a wire mesh front and sides. Examples were still on sale in 1907 at the Army and Navy stores when there were eleven traditional designs and eight Art Nouveau designs on offer.

Foot Warmers

It was difficult to heat rooms before the introduction of central heating and people venturing out into public places suffered considerably from the cold.

Portable heaters were used to alleviate some of the rigours of winter. People took these with them on coach journeys, visits to the theatre or attendance at church. A servant would accompany the lady or gentleman of the house, set the warmer by them, or for the ladies, even under their skirts and retire until the event was over.

Some foot warmers consisted of a tin box in which hot charcoal or coals were put, encased in a decorated wooden outer cover. These wooden boxes were usually fretted and carved to make them attractive and to allow the heat to escape. Other foot warmers were of sheet iron or tin. Foot warmers are also found in brass and copper and are usually fretted. All foot warmers had a small door through which the hot coals or charcoal could be inserted. Most examples that are to be found are Dutch although English foot warmers were made. Round, rectangular, square and octagonal brass and copper foot warmers all exist. When trying to date examples look for signs of wear; hot coals damaged the metal very quickly.

In the nineteenth century coach travellers also needed warmth and this was provided by a number of different designs of copper hot water bottles. Some were placed under rugs near the feet of travellers, other were shaped to match the body's contours.

Warming Pans

Keeping warm in bed was a problem. Until the

eighteenth century bedroom fires were uncommon and where they did exist, the cost of fuel made it expensive to keep them in overnight. People tried to keep the cold out with curtains or tapestries hung round the bed and they wore bed socks and nightcaps, but perhaps the most popular form of heat was that offered by the warming pan.

These metal pans, filled with hot coals, charcoal or ash would be placed between the sheets before retirement for the night and could be moved round to heat all the corners of the bed. Hot bricks were also used for this purpose but were dirty and inefficient.

Most warming pans have long handles and were made in copper or brass. Initially handles were in iron although early brass handles are found, especially on Dutch pans. In the eighteenth century handles were also made of wood, often lacquered black.

Seventeenth and early eighteenth century pans were large, and there are two schools of thought about these early examples. One states that the lid ought to fit tightly over the base to keep the hot embers, sparks and ash within the pan. If this is true then large lids belong to large pans. Another view discounts this and says that

large lids on small pans were also common. Few pans with close fitting lids can be found and most early pans do have smaller bottoms. However with nearly all pans with larger tops, there is some evidence that the lid has been, at least, rejoined to the body. Early pan lids were decorated with punched or fretted patterns. Some may have had an inner sheet iron or tin liner.

Around 1720 warming pans were made with inset lids and after about 1740 the pans became smaller and brass or iron handles less frequent. Many were still decorated with engraving or fretting, but by the nineteenth century most pans were plain and made from copper. They were gradually replaced, first by copper containers, without handles, and then by pottery or stoneware bottles, all of which were filled with hot water. Later still, of course, came the rubber hot water bottle.

At some time in the late nineteenth century, after warming pans had been driven out of our beds by stoneware bottles, they became a decorative feature in parlours and sitting rooms, finding a place of honour by the fire, and for this reason they continued in production into the 1920s. These small round copper pans with wooden handles seldom show any signs of use.

ANDIRONS

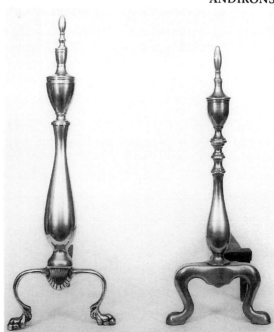

179 Two andirons in brass in the Adam style. The example on the left is 22$\frac{1}{2}$in high by 13in deep and that on the right is 20in high by 18in deep. Both styles were made in the eighteenth century but these examples are nineteenth century. (*Rudolph Otto Antiques*)

180 *(left)*   A brass and iron fire dog, 14in by 14in.
Nineteenth century. (*Country Life Antiques*)

181 *(above)*   An 'all brass' fire dog 11in high and 8$\frac{1}{4}$
in deep. May have been used as a creeper to rest fire
irons upon. An eighteenth-century style, but this
example dates from the late nineteenth century. (*Jack
Casimir Ltd*)

182   A late nineteenth-century iron and copper creeper, 10in high and
6$\frac{1}{2}$in deep. Note the Art Nouveau features of the design. (*Country Life
Antiques*)

Plate 1 *(right)* A Hungarian eighteenth-century gilt copper work of art. It represents a copper mine with miners exiting from the adit and men breaking lumps of ore. Above is a smelting oven of typical form. *(Sotheby's)*

Plate 2 *(below)* Hand embossing was widely used to decorate brass and copper. This is a seventeenth-century Dutch wall sconce. The rim is embossed and the central decoration, of a tulip, is punched. *(Robin Bellamy Ltd)*

Plate 3 *(right)* A fifteenth-century English candlestick of simple form, 5in high. *(Robin Bellamy Ltd)*

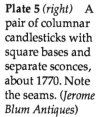

Plate 4 *(left)* A rare brass 'hog-scraper' candle-stick with side candle ejector, central ball knop and high domed, octagonal foot. About 1710-20, 9½in high. *(Key Antiques)*

Plate 5 *(right)* A pair of columnar candlesticks with square bases and separate sconces, about 1770. Note the seams. *(Jerome Blum Antiques)*

Plate 6 *(left)* Fluted or petal-based candlestick, 8½in high, about 1770. *(Key Antiques)*

Plate 7 *(above)* A pair of Adam style candlesticks with square bases and fixed sconces, about 1820-30. *(Jerome Blum Antiques)*

Plate 8 A fine double-candle-holder of rectangular form, both candlesticks with extractors. About 1790-1820. (*Jerome Blum Antiques*)

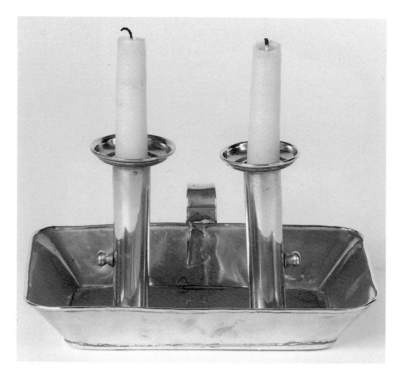

Plate 9 Tinderbox and chamber candlestick 7in long including the handle and $3\frac{1}{2}$ in high. The lid and candleholder lift off. About 1700-20. (*Key Antiques*)

Plate 10 A taper candlestick $4\frac{3}{4}$ in high, a snuffer tray and doubters $6\frac{1}{2}$ in long and a snuffer stand with doubters $7\frac{1}{2}$ in high, all mid-eighteenth century. (*Key Antiques*)

Plate 11 *(left)*
Bronze oil lamp
on a brass stem,
about 1820.
Similar stems are
found with
candleholders.
This rare
example of a
lamp mounted
on a candlestick
stem is in a style
typical of the
Regency period.
(Jerome Blum)

Plate 12 *(above right)*   Fine brass chandelier with seamed brass central
section and nine arms. 39in high, about 1745. *(Jack Casimir Ltd, photograph
by Tony McConnell)*

Plate 13 *(below)*   A tinder pistol with brass mounts from the mid-
eighteenth century. 7in long. *(Key Antiques)*

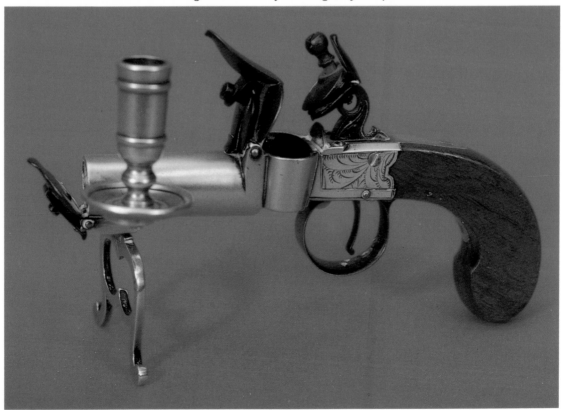

183 A griffin creeper or fire dog in the Regency manner. A fine quality casting, 10in high and 7in deep. First half of the nineteenth century. (*Colin Greenway Antiques*)

184 (*below right*) Two creepers or fire iron rests. The larger is 6in high and the smaller 3½in high. Probably early Victorian. (*Duncan J. Baggott*)

185 (*below*) A group of three creepers. The centre example has a cast iron base made to simulate marble. 6in, 8½in and 7½in high. Late Victorian, but andirons and creepers of similar form were still being offered in the Edwardian era. (*Rudolph Otto Antiques*)

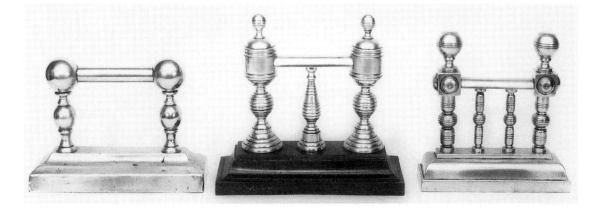

GRATES

186   A fine iron and brass grate. The fire back and fire bars are in iron, the rest is mounted in brass. 36in by 36in, 1800-30. (*Duncan J. Baggott*)

187   Brass and steel fire grate with original brass and tile surrounds, about 1870. (*Jack Casimir Ltd, photograph by Roy Farthing*)

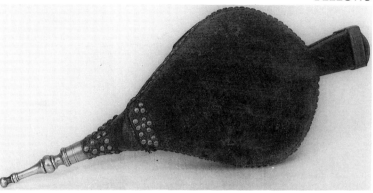

188 *(left)*   A fine decorated pair of bellows, probably Dutch, about 1680-1700. (*Robin Bellamy Ltd*)

189 *(above)*   A typical eighteenth-century wood and leather bellows with brass spout and brass studs. 25in overall. (*Key Antiques*)

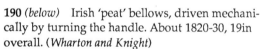

190 *(below)*   Irish 'peat' bellows, driven mechanically by turning the handle. About 1820-30, 19in overall. (*Wharton and Knight*)

191 *(right)*   A brass blowing tool, possibly French but similar examples were used in Britain, but most are made in iron. About 1680-1720. (*Robin Bellamy Ltd*)

FIRE IRONS

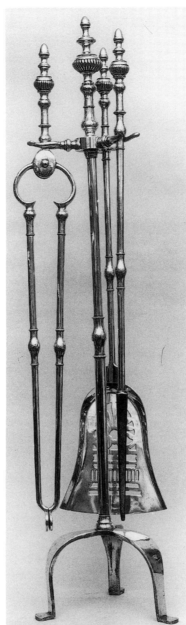

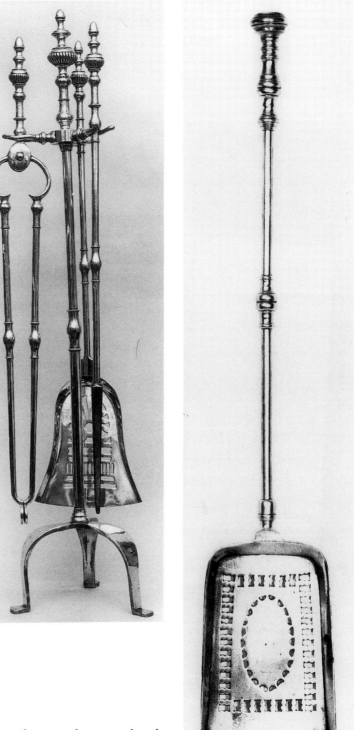

192 Most fire tools were made with iron handles and brass knops, up to the nineteenth century. This pair of fine early eighteenth-century fire irons are 40in overall. The handles finely cast. (*Duncan J. Baggott*)

193 Brass companion stand and fire tools. The surface has been engraved and chased. 33in high, early nineteenth century. (*Jack Casimir Ltd, photograph by Roy Farthing*)

194 A brass shovel. Probably late eighteenth century but examples of this form were still popular in the nineteenth century. 36in overall. (*Robin Bellamy Ltd*)

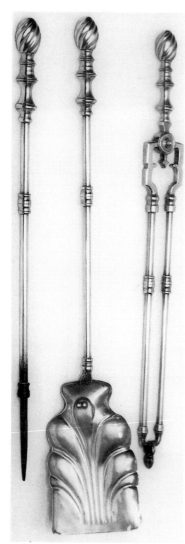

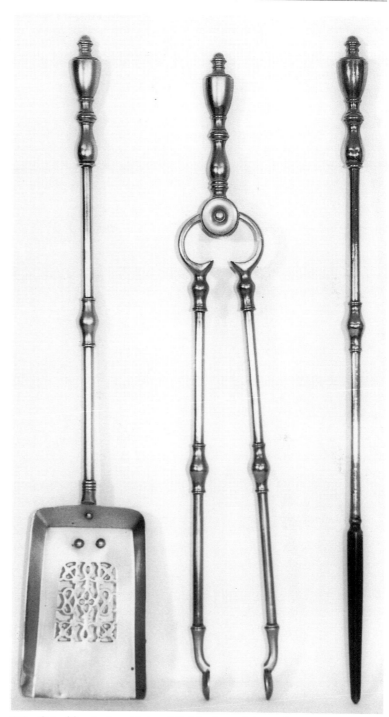

195 A set of three brass fire tools. The decorative shovel indicates a later construction. This set has the registered number 127,273 stamped on them and thus dates from 1889. (*Rudolph Otto Antiques*)

196 Set of fire tools with 'urn' finials. Late eighteenth century, 39in overall. (*Duncan J. Baggott*)

197 (*left*) Dutch fire tongs and shovel. 22in and 19in, eighteenth century. (*Duncan J. Baggott*)

198 (*right*) A pair of fire tongs. About 1800, 25in overall. (*Duncan J. Baggott*)

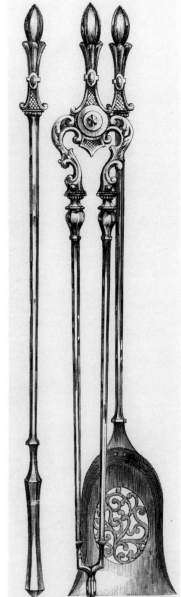

199 (*above right*) Many mid-Victorian fire tools were elaborately decorated as this set exhibited at the 1851 Exhibition by H. & W. Turner of Sheffield indicates. Simpler tools returned towards the end of the century.

200 (*far left*) Sets of fire side companions that include a brush are late Victorian or Edwardian. 19in overall, about 1880-1900. (*Country Life Antiques*)

201 (*left*) Another companion set 21$\frac{1}{2}$ins high, about 1900. (*Rudolph Otto Antiques*)

202 A good copper coal scuttle with seamed hollow handle. Probably about 1840 although the design remained popular for some time. 17in overall. (*Windrush Antiques*)

203 A copper scuttle, 18in overall. Note the similar handle and fastening. Again early Victorian. (*Duncan J. Baggott*)

204 (*left*) A copper coal hod, 23in high. Late Victorian. (*Rudolph Otto Antiques*)

205 A Victorian helmet scuttle, so called because of its supposed similarity with a cavalry trooper's helmet. 19in high. Die stamped brass handle and copper body. (*Prudential Fine Art Auctioneers, Manchester*)

206   A Victorian brass coal scuttle, 16in long. (*W. Jones Roberts*)

207 *(above right)*   Brass scuttle with decorated cover and handle, with the registered mark for 1872. 21in high including shovel. (*Rudolph Otto Antiques*)

EMBER PAN

208 *(right)*   A very decorative scuttle in brass. 18in overall, about 1850-80. (*Windrush Antiques*)

209   An ember pan. Containers of this form could also have been used for storing logs and coal. Copper box with brass handles. 12in high, about 1800-20. (*Windrush Antiques*)

210 Three pairs of ember tongs. On the left is a pair with simple ring handle, 9in long. The middle pair are 12³/₄in long, again with ring handle and the pair on the right have shaped handles, 12in long. All about 1740-50. (*Christopher Sykes Antiques*)

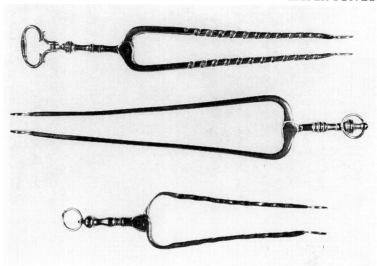

211 Another pair of brass tongs, 10in long, mid-eighteenth century. Tongs of this style and of similar form were also made in smaller sizes into the twentieth century. (*Duncan J. Baggott*

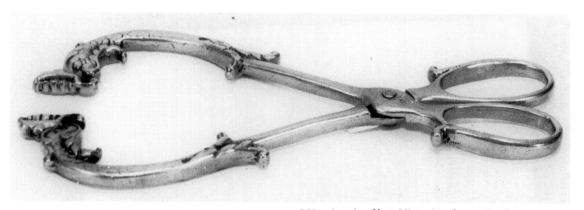

212 A pair of late Victorian decorative brass tongs, 10in long. Examples of this style continued to be made into the 1930s. (*Windrush Antiques*)

CURFEWS

213 *(left)*   Fine late seventeenth-century brass curfew or fire cover with *repoussé* decoration. (*Robin Bellamy Ltd*)

214 *(above)*   A Dutch curfew with iron handle, the body decorated with a coat of arms and with brass embossed studs. About 1700-30. (*Robin Bellamy Ltd*)

215   A curfew or hastener. This example is Dutch but examples were probably also made in Birmingham. It rests in an iron stand and there is an iron grating at the back on which food or dishes could stand while cooking or keeping warm. Mid-eighteenth century. (*Robin Bellamy Ltd*)

216 A mid-nineteenth-century copper curfew or fire cover. 11in high. (*Ian Savage Antiques*)

217 Another similar curfew in brass, 11in high. Similar curfews were still being made in the 1930s. (*Ian Savage*)

FENDERS

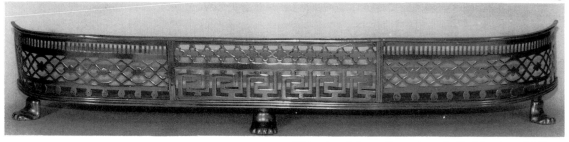

218 An eighteenth-century fretted fender with bow front. The feet are not original. 41in overall and 6in high. (*Duncan J. Baggott*)

219 A fine brass fender, 46in long, about 1820. (*Witney Antiques*)

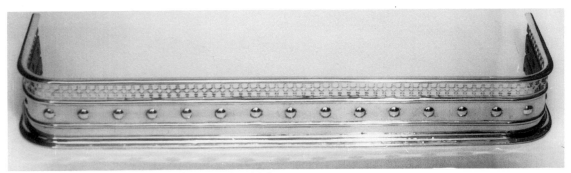

220 A Victorian brass fender 41½in long. (*Rudolph Otto Antiques*)

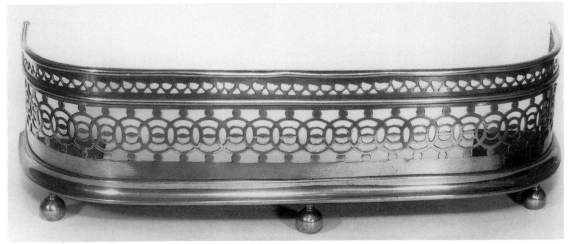

221 (*above*) A fretted fender with feet. Cast manufacture. 32in wide, about 1780. (*Jack Casimir Ltd*)

222 (*below*) A late Victorian wire-mesh fender with brass feet, 33½in wide. Note the iron sheet base. (*Duncan J. Baggott*)

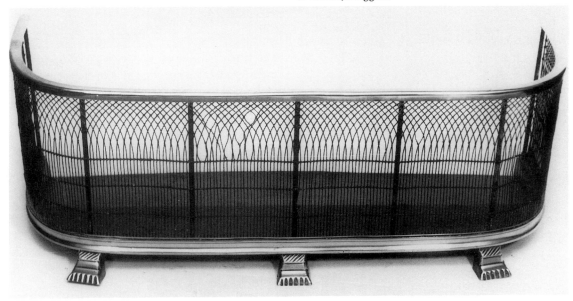

223 A cast iron fender with brass mounts. 17½in wide, about 1850. (*Colin Greenway Antiques*)

224 A brass fire canopy, 16in wide and 10in high. About 1880. (*Country Life Antiques*)

FIRE GUARDS

225 (*above*) A fan-shaped brass wire guard with iron mesh. Late Victorian, but guards of this style were still being sold in 1907. (*Windrush Antiques*)

226 (*left*) A plain late Victorian brass guard with wire mesh. 23in high and 20in wide. (*Duncan J. Baggott*)

FOOT WARMERS

227 A typical late seventeenth-century octagonal foot warmer. You can see the door which was used to put coals or charcoal inside. The date of 1776 engraved on the top is later. Dutch. (*Robin Bellamy Ltd*)

228 Another octagonal foot warmer in brass with fretted lid and *repoussé* body. Dutch or possibly English, about 1700-20. (*Robin Bellamy Ltd*)

229 (*left*) An oval foot warmer which was filled with hot water. Copper, $11\frac{1}{2}$in maximum diameter. 1840-80. (*Prudential Fine Art Auctioneers, Manchester*)

230 (*below*) A copper foot warmer, again used with hot water and probably used in a coach. The plug is now missing. 27in long, about 1850-80. (*Windrush Antiques*)

231 A late Victorian body warmer, shaped to go under clothes or a blanket. (*Robin Bellamy Ltd*)

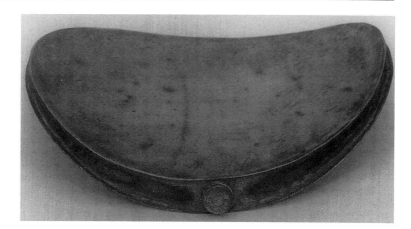

232 An Edwardian round hot water bottle in copper. (*Robin Bellamy Ltd*)

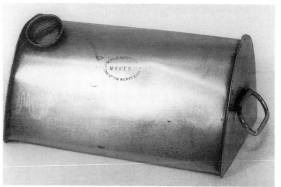

233 An oblong, rounded hot water copper bottle by 'Joesph R. Hudders and Son, Oak Street Tin Works, Shaw'. 9in long, about 1880. (*Robin Bellamy Ltd*)

234 A carriage seat warmer. Made of copper with a brass plug and used with hot water. 11$\frac{1}{2}$in wide, about 1880. Marked 'T. Beckett Preston'. (*Blacklock Antiques*)

WARMING PANS

235 *(above)*   A full-length illustration of a late seven-teenth-century English warming pan. Handles were in iron, wood or brass, this example being of iron. 47in overall. (*Key Antiques*)

236 *(above right)*   A close-up of the previous warm-ing pan. The pan is 12in diameter, and is riveted to the handle and body with three copper rivets. Stamped with 'CAP', the work of Charles Appleby of London. About 1690. (*Key Antiques*)

237 *(right)*   A warming pan with inset reeded lid and wooden handle. By the same London maker 'CAP' (Charles Appleby, see Chapter 10), about 1720. 11in diameter. (*Key Antiques*)

238 *(above)* A late seventeenth-century brass warming pan with iron handle. 44in overall. (*Keith Hockin Antiques*)

239 *(above right)* A close up of the front of the previous warming pan, inscribed 'GOD SAVE THE KING' and with a primitive engraving of a pig. 13in diameter. (*Keith Hockin Antiques*)

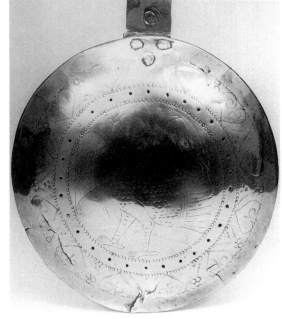

240 *(right)* A decorated warming pan with brass front, copper pan and iron handle. Engraved with a cock. Mid-eighteenth century. (*Peter Norden Antiques*)

241 *(left)*   A typical Dutch fretted and engraved warming pan with iron handle 51in long, about 1700. (*Lawrence Fine Art Auctioneers of Crewkerne*)

242 *(below left)*   A warming pan with inset lid and engraved decoration. The pan has a diameter of 13in and the wooden handle fits into a brass mount. About 1750-70. (*Prudential Fine Art Auctioneers, Manchester*)

243 *(below)*   An early nine-teenth-century copper warming pan with worn decoration, 12in diameter. (*Prudential Fine Art Auctioneers, Manchester*)

7

EQUIPMENT USED FOR COOKING AND SERVING FOOD AND DRINK

COOKING

For the hundreds of years that the open fire dominated our hearths, food was mostly boiled in pots in or over the flames, or was roasted before the fire. Oven roasting was uncommon. Some fireplaces did have bread ovens set in the wall besides them but these ovens could not achieve the high temperatures needed and had to be heated separately. Food was roasted on a spit before the flames or on a hook hung over the fire. Frying was popular, but the heat of an open fire was hard to control and people found it hot cooking close to the flames.

In the seventeenth and much of the eighteenth century cooking pots were hung over the fire or stood within it. The whole meal was cooked in one large pot. Fish, game, pork or salt meat were boiled in a pottery pot inside a bronze cauldron. Vegetables would be cooked in the pot while a pudding could be boiled, wrapped in a cloth.

With the gradual adoption of coal open hearths were replaced with a coal basket, usually resting on fire dogs but the methods of cooking were unchanged. In the late eighteenth century kitchen ranges with iron top and open front were developed. Flat bottomed saucepans, pots and frying pans replaced rounded pots. Trivets were fixed onto the bars of the open fire or stood in front of the hearth. Dutch ovens, using reflected heat to roast or bake food were also employed.

In the 1800s ovens with doors were built into one side of the range and people could now roast in an oven. By 1830 oven ranges were commonplace, but the large majority of stoves, ranges and ovens were made from cast iron.

Cooking Pots

Rounded cooking pots, with and without feet, remained in daily use for as long as open fires were employed for cooking. Cauldrons with three feet proved stable in the embers or in the hearth but these feet were slowly burned away until there are often only short stubby legs remaining and the pot rests on its belly. It is a good idea to look for signs of genuine wear on the feet of cooking pots.

Cast cooking pots have the marks of the mould on their surface. Look for evidence of these joints. The casting of large vessels was difficult and there were usually small imperfections which were filed to form square holes and then filled with bronze plugs which were hammered out to fill the gap. In the eighteenth century cast iron pots were increasingly used

Posnets and Skillets

One specialised group of pots were the posnets and skillets. Posnets have the same rounded form and feet as cauldrons but in addition they have a handle; few posnets were made after 1700. Skillets, are similar in style but have straight sides. They remained popular into the late nineteenth century. Skillets and posnets were made in a lead bronze which is often erroneously called bell metal.

A number of skillet makers have been identified through signed examples. The Palmers of Canterbury, Clement Tosier of Salisbury and John Fathers, whose origins are not yet known, worked in the seventeenth century. Eighteenth-century skillet makers include Street of Bridgewater, Bayley of Bridgewater, and Rice of Bristol. Street and Bayley, and later Street and Pyke, also worked together in partnership. In the nineteenth century leading makers included 'T.P.' of

Bridgewater, now identified as Thomas Pyke, Cox of Taunton, Wasborough of Bristol and Warner of London. Wasborough worked with several partners between 1775 and 1846 but only operated briefly on his own. Most Wasborough skillets have a number cast on the handle to indicate the capacity in Imperial pints which confirms that they are after 1826. More skillets by Warner survive than for any other maker but as he was active in London after 1850 that is, perhaps, not surprising.

Seventeenth-century skillets are found with inscriptions such as 'Pity the Poor', 'Honour thy God', 'Love thy neighbour' or 'God Bless His Magister' and the like, but eighteenth-century skillets do not have these admonishing inscriptions.

Saucepans

With the development of the stove several types of flat bottom pans came into popularity; some for general use, others with a specialised purpose.

Most pots were made from seamed sheet metal with the bases dovetailed into place. The sides of early pans are made from thick, often uneven, sheets. Few eighteenth-century pots and pans have survived. Later machine-rolled brass sheet could be made thinner and more even and its use is an indication of later manufacture. Seamed pots were still being made in the twentieth century however.

Substantial saucepans with brass or copper handles, the handle fastened with three brass rivets, are probably from the first half of the nineteenth century. Towards the end of the nineteenth century pots were stamped out from copper and brass sheet.

Saucepans with hollow iron handles are from the second half of the nineteenth century, while saucepans of rounded form are generally of an earlier design than those with straight sides.

Some pots and pans have maker's marks or stock numbers struck under the base and these indicate a late nineteenth-century manufacture.

As we have noted copper pots were usually tinned inside, as copper was toxic if acidic substances came into contact with it. Many pots originally had lids. Lids that fit neatly into or over the pan are from the first half of the nineteenth century, while lids that rest on the top of pots are late nineteenth century.

Fish Kettles

This small distinct group of cooking pans were designed solely for cooking fish. There are two main forms; the long pan for boiling salmon and other similar fishes and the specially wide pans for cooking large flat fish like turbot and brill.

Originally they all had a special tray with handles set within, on which the fish was set, which enabled it to be removed from the water when cooked, without breaking up. Fish kettles were nearly always in copper, and were tinned. They formed part of the large *'Batteries de cuisines'* found in major houses from the 1800s onwards and their popularity reached its apex in the 1850s, although they were still being made for the middle-class Edwardian housewife.

Frying Pans

In the seventeenth century frying pans had long iron handles, to make it easier for the housewife to use over an open fire. In the eighteenth century pans with short handles appear and continue in use in the nineteenth century. Few seventeenth- and eighteenth-century frying pans survive.

Early nineteenth century frying pans are of sturdy construction, with a solid iron or copper handle riveted to the body. Later pans have hollow or flat iron handles. Late nineteenth-century frying pans tend to be made in standard sizes, from 6in to 12in diameter and there were special pans made for cutlets, omelets and for general frying.

Boilers and Jam Pans

Many kinds of pots were used for boiling water. In the seventeenth century the rounded cauldron was popular but flat-bottom round pots, known as 'cettles' were also used, usually of rivetted copper construction.

In the late eighteenth century the present form of kettle was invented to supply hot water especially for tea making. Urns for boiling water also appeared and both are discussed later. Large containers in copper or brass, used for heating water were common in the late eighteenth and nineteenth centuries. There are many variations but all are large, robust and have lids to speed up heating the water. Most examples of this form are from the first half of the nineteenth century.

One of the most prolific forms is that known as the 'jam pan'. These are found mostly in brass, either with a moveable iron or brass handle or with a fixed handle. Most are from the second half of the nineteenth century. Pans were still being stamped out of sheet metal in considerable numbers near Bristol in the 1870s. Boilers and jam pans were also spun and cast.

SUPPORTING EQUIPMENT

Chaffing Dishes

A small group of pans was used for drying sweet-meats or candies near the fire or for keeping food, such as sauces, hot while they are being served. Some of these small pans had fixed legs, others rested in a separate stand or metal ring. The heat was provided by the kitchen fire or by a small container of hot charcoal placed in a receptacle beneath the chaffing dish. Most examples to be seen are from the 1750-1850 period.

Jelly Moulds

Jellies made in elaborate moulds such as castles and in the shape of beasts and birds were popular in medieval times, often garnished with gold or silver leaf. These were based on calf's foot jelly and were savoury rather than sweet. Charles II, for example, ate 'Jellys made from juices of fat capons, rich wines and ye finest herbs'.

In the early 1800s a method was found to make gelatine, an animal protein which set firm-ly, and from this time on sweet jellies and deserts such as blancmange were made in moulds of pottery, glass, tin, pewter, copper and brass. The manufacture of custard powder in the 1840s increased the popularity of this type of dessert.

Hundreds of different shapes of moulds were made. Many have a simple fluted style but there are elaborate moulds in the style of animals, birds and buildings. All-copper examples would have been tinned. Early nineteenth-century moulds are large and substantial, made from thick sheet metal, while late Victorian and Edwardian moulds are thinner.

Many have stock numbers stamped on them, and these are mostly from the late nineteenth century. A few are known with full maker's marks and these might be dated through trade directories. The Army and Navy stores were offering twenty-two types of moulds in fifty-three sizes in copper and brass in 1907.

Pastry Jiggers or Wheels

Pies were a popular form of food from medieval times onwards. Cooks often decorated them with patterns cut into the pastry. Small wheels were used to cut the pastry and to decorate it. Brass pastry wheels which have a shaped cutting device at the other end are nineteenth century.

Cullenders

From Roman times onwards cooks needed a way to separate liquid from solid. A variety of devices were made for this purpose including the sieve, made from wire or cloth, the strainer, a small bowl with a handle with holes punched in the base, and the collander (or cullender). It is not clear when the large cullender was first used; probably in the late seventeenth century. Most are made of iron or tin but a few, usually nineteenth century, are of copper or brass. It is hard to tell British from European cullenders.

Mortars

Lead bronze mortars were made from the middle ages into the nineteenth century for domestic use, for pharmaceutical purposes and for use in industry. At home, mortars were used for grind-ing up ingredients for cooking. Small mortars were used for herbs and spices, while larger mortars were used for meat, fish or grain. In the seventeenth century many mortars were deco-rated with patterns and symbols. A few were dated and signed, and although in the eighteenth century most mortars were plain and undeco-rated, the occasional dated mortar can be found.

During the eighteenth century the shape of mortars underwent a change. The earlier forms, such as the examples illustrated here gave way to two new types. The first was a simple straight sided mortar, the second group had a similar outline but in addition has two handles set at right angles to the body. Nineteenth-century

244 A sixteenth-century cooking scene showing the use of the open fire and a spit for roasting. From a Dutch painting by Pieter Van der Borcht. (*BBC Hulton Picture Library*)

mortars were made in brass rather than in the earlier lead bronze alloy. During the nineteenth century cast iron mortars became cheap and generally replaced brass mortars.

Cooking utensils

Many other utensils were used in the kitchen such as apple-corers, choppers, graters, knives, ladles, skimmers, skewers, sugar nips, strainers, rolling pins and the like. Few of these objects other than strainers and ladles are found in brass but they may well have been made and a rare example may be found.

Ladles

From medieval times to today various forms of ladles have been used. Many of these were made in copper or brass. Early examples are usually deep bowled with an iron handle riveted to the bowl. Later the ladles are flatter and have brass handles. Ladles were still being made in the 1920s and many modern copies exist.

Skimmers

Skimmers have been in service from Roman times to take cream from the top of vats or food from pans. Seventeenth- and early eighteenth-century skimmers are usually large, round and slightly concave with iron handles rivetted to the bowl. Flat, elaborately shaped skimmers, with iron or brass handles, are more likely to be decorative rather than serviceable and date from the late nineteenth century.

COOKING EQUIPMENT USED IN THE FIRE OR GRATE

Cranes, Pot Hooks and Hangers

While cooking was done over an open fire, the pots either had to be stood in the hearth or suspended over the heat. A variety of hooks for this latter purpose were employed. Many were designed to be extended or contracted. The most simple was a chain and hook, hung from a bar above the fire, the more elaborate being a chimney crane which turned on an upright axis and could either rest against the wall or be moved out over the flames. Most hooks and cranes were made in iron but a few from the late seventeenth century through to the early nineteenth century were decorated with brass or copper. Some extending hangers were made of brass.

Spits

Before the development of ovens for roasting meat was cooked over an open fire. If the meat was not to be cooked on one side and raw on the

245 Another early kitchen setting with two open fire places and a dog and a clock spit. This kitchen is at St Fagans Castle near Cardiff. (*National Museum of Wales; Welsh Folk Museum*)

other, it had to be regularly turned. Spits were made to present the meat to the fire. The simplest consisted of a spike which was driven through the joint and which rested on the andirons. These spits were turned by hand. Hence the phrase 'done to a turn'. Large free standing spits were turned by hand using a wheel.

Mechanical spits operated by dog power and smoke jacks, driven by convection heat, replaced the manual forms in the eighteenth century. Dog spits were hard to control, as the animals became tired or moved too slowly, while smoke spits needed a very hot fire to drive the fans or paddles, often too hot to be used for cooking.

Weight driven spits first appeared in the late sixteenth century; there is a reference in 1612 to a weight spit at Bishopsgate Tavern, London. Weights drove the spit round and when they reached the ground they were wound up and the process repeated.

In the eighteenth century the clockmaker came to the aid of the cook and clockwork spits were made using a very similar mechanism to the grandfather clock. The last form to be designed was the bottle spit, a clockwork vertical spit in which the meat was revolved round by clockwork, rather than turned horizontally. Bottle spits are nineteenth century, usually made with sheet copper or brass bodies and they continued to be used in the Edwardian era.

Dutch Ovens or Hasteners
In the eighteenth century Dutch ovens became popular. These stood before the open hearth and meat was roasted or pies baked utilising both the heat from the fire and the heat reflected from the rounded backplate. In the mid-eighteenth century Birmingham braziers were also making these 'Dutch' ovens. Most were in tin and iron but examples with copper backplates or with

brass decoration are to be found.

Trivets, Plate and Hearth Stands

Early trivets were fastened to the bars of ranges or stoves so that pots could be boiled or food cooked before the fire. Most trivets of this style were made of iron although brass examples are known.

In the late eighteenth century four-footed trivets appear. They rested in the hearth, and were used to boil a kettle, heat a stewpot or to rest plates upon. Initially many of these trivets were made with iron feet and with decorative brass tops. In early trivets the sheet metal used is thick, and the cutting of the fretting clearly uneven. Later in the nineteenth century 'all brass' trivets appeared. The brass tops were by now thinner, and the fretting was machine cut or stamped out. The decoration became more elaborate and patterns included beasts, birds, coasts of arms and other insignia.

Trivets were still being made in brass in 1907 and the Army and Navy stores were offering nine designs. In the 1930s C. Jones of Birmingham was making copies of older patterns and had fifteen designs for sale.

Toasters

Closely connected to the early form of trivet are a group of utensils which were fastened onto the bars of the open fire, but which had spikes facing the fire on which small birds, pieces of meat or even bread could be placed, to toast or grill before the flames. Most toasters are in iron but occasionally examples appear with brass or copper decoration. They are difficult to date but most of those with brass decoration will be nineteenth century. Some toasters are free standing, again, mostly in iron.

Chestnut Roasters

A wide range of chestnut roasters can be seen in antique shops, fairs, markets and auction sale rooms. Few of these have any evidence of use but it is possible that some examples may be Victorian and have actually been employed for preparing chestnuts. Most are late Victorian, Edwardian or of a more recent date and were made for display only. Those with elaborate shapes are not serviceable.

SERVING FOOD AND DRINK

Brass, copper and bronze were widely used in the kitchen in cooking and preparing food but they never made a similar impact on the serving of food or drink at the table. This may have been a matter of taste. Brass came into large scale production in the 1750s, the time that pottery and porcelain were increasing in popularity. In a few decades silver plate dominated the market and silver remained important for the well-to-do.

Brass faced heavy competition and succeeded where it had most natural advantages. On the table it offered little in terms of 'show' that silver and silver plate objects did not provide, while it was unable to compete in price with porcelain and pottery. Few dishes, chargers, tureens, sauce boats, salts, spoons, forks, knives, or mustard pots were made in these alloys. Some examples are illustrated, but they are the exception rather than the rule.

Plates, Dishes and Chargers

People ate off plates of wood, tin, pewter, pottery, porcelain and silver; they helped themselves from dishes made of the same materials. Brass and copper played only a minor role in the service of food.

Initially brass and copper was needed to fill other more important demands and by the time copper production was large enough, people were turning to other materials for their tableware.

Plates, dishes and chargers (as dishes over 18in diameter are known) were used domestically and occasional examples can be found. Perhaps surprisingly, few plates and dishes have much sign of the kind of wear on their surface which we would expect if they have been used for any length of time in the home. Some may also have been used in church for the collecting of alms. Brass plates were on sale as late as 1900.

Brass dishes and chargers were popular from the earliest times. Fine fifteenth- and sixteenth-century Nuremberg bowls and dishes are to be seen in museums and in specialised dealer's displays. Chargers from Scandinavia and Holland too were popular in the seventeenth and eighteenth centuries, many cast decorated or engraved. These dishes and chargers were hung on walls and also used for the washing of hands at the table. Some eighteenth-century brass chargers may also have played these roles. Others may have been used to serve food at the table. By the late Victorian period chargers were being stamped out with elaborate historic portraits and scenes embossed upon their surfaces.

On the basis of silver and pewter forms a chronology of plate and dish designs has been established; the broad rimmed and multiple reeded rishes of the seventeenth century were replaced by single reeded and plain rimmed plates in the eighteenth century. Wavy-edged plates are from the mid-eighteenth century onwards.

Bowls
A large variety of brass and copper bowls were made for domestic use. Some of these would have been kept in the kitchen, others were used to bring food to the table. The thickness of the metal, the type of rim and the degree of wear are the best indicators of age.

Trays
In the eighteenth century what became known as 'trays' began to replace the role of the traditional dish or charger for serving food and drink at the table.

Trays can be found in many shapes. Common are rectangular and round examples. Copper and brass trays are often found. Those with galleried and fretted sides are likely to be late nineteenth century. Brass and copper trays were still being made in the 1920s, but few eighteenth-century trays survive.

Some small trays or salvers, as they were called, were used for the receiving of calling cards from visitors or for serving drinks.

Plate Stands
Food kept warm if served on hot plates. A variety of plate stands were made, some in brass, on which plates could be stood before the fire to keep hot. 'Cats' were the first plate stands used in

the seventeenth century but the form continued in use into the nineteenth century. In the nineteenth century other forms of stands evolved but they were never very popular. Trivets were also used for this purpose and plates could be heated in the oven.

Ale Mullers
Stuart and Georgian gentlemen liked their alcoholic drinks hot and spiced: ginger, cinnamon, all-spice and nutmeg were widely used. Two methods of heating ale were adopted. The first was to put a red hot poker into the filled mug but there was always the danger that this would melt the pewter or crack the pottery tankard. So special ale mullers were made to sit in the fire. The upright form, known sometimes as the 'asses ear' because of its appearance, stood in the embers, but it was easy to knock over and would not stand on the table. The other form, the 'slipper', so termed because it looked like a shoe, was more stable. Most copper or brass ale mullers are from the nineteenth century.

Coffee Pots
Coffee had reached the shores of Britain by 1650, the first coffee houses being opened in London and Oxford in that decade. By 1690 coffee was extensively drunk amongst wealthy city people.

Because coffee was a luxury, most early coffee pots were in silver. You will be very lucky indeed to find an English brass or copper coffee pot made before the mid-eighteenth century. The first coffee pot had a tapering shape, and this style was copied in the nineteenth century. Some nineteenth-century tapering pots have a straight, almost horizontal, wooden handle set at right angles to the body and a domed lid; this form was still in use in 1900.

Bulbous and urn shaped coffee pots became popular in the mid to late eighteenth century and continued in manufacture over several generations. Late coffee pots usually have thin strap handles, rather thinner than is easy to use but this is because they were originally covered with a plaited rafia cover. Thin sheet metal examples with straight seams are mostly late nineteenth century.

Chocolate Pots

Never to gain the favour associated with tea and coffee, nevertheless chocolate was a popular drink in the late seventeenth and early eighteenth century. Chocolate pots were used in the nineteenth century but many that are now found have been imported in recent years from Spain and North Africa.

Chocolate pots reflect many of the styles found with coffee pots, but can normally be distinguished by a small round hole in the lid, often with a swing cover, which made it easier to stir the sticky mixture. Most chocolate pots are in copper.

Tea Pots

Initially a rich man's drink, costly, heavily taxed and widely smuggled, tea had become, by the 1750s, the universal drink of all classes. The tea drunk at the various levels of society was very different; the rich used the prime black or green leaves, the poor made do with the rejected dust or dried used tea bought from the servants of larger homes.

The universal popularity of tea lead to the creation of a range of utensils: the cup, tea bowl, saucer, kettle, tea pot, sugar bowl, cream jug, tea urn and samovar. Most tea pots were made of pottery, porcelain, silver and pewter but a few tea pots are known in brass or copper.

Tea Caddies

Because tea was costly the first tea caddies were provided with locks and were made in silver or other valuable materials. Few copper or brass caddies are to be found and those that do exist are mostly from the late nineteenth century.

Kettles

Kettles in copper and brass were made in many dozens of designs. The earliest forms had a wooden or bone handle to help dissipate the heat. Eighteenth-century kettles were generally of bulbous shape but later round, square, oblong and oval kettles were used.

Kettles with fixed strap handles are probably later than those with moveable handles, while the use of glass or other materials in the handle suggests a later date although coloured glass was popular in the 1840s. Copper kettles are much more common than brass examples. In the nineteenth century kettles can be found with capacity marks: one, two or three pints for example. They come in many shapes and styles.

Most kettles were stood on trivets or hung above the fire but some came with their own heaters. Small charcoal burners or spirit lamps were incorporated in the stands. These 'kettles on stand' are highly prized and care must be taken to see that the stand and kettle did start life together, as there are marriages of nineteenth-century kettles with twentieth-century stands.

Urns and Samovars

Urns were used to boil water at the table and date from the 1760s. Initially all urns were of classical style. Early examples were heated by charcoal burners but after 1790 small spirit lamps were employed. Hollow iron cores or containers into which a hot iron could be set were also used. Urns continued in widespread use into this century and many copper and brass examples may originally have been electro-plated. Urns should be examined with care although it is hard to detect where the electrolitic process has been reversed. This method removes the original silvering.

Most urns have a tap or spigot set at the front. Those with glass taps or fittings are probably after 1850. Bone, wood and ivory fittings were popular at all periods. Urns were also used for making the tea, not just boiling the water and examples of this sort are known as 'Samovars' from the Russian.

Porringers

Some confusion exists about porringers. Silver collectors call them 'bleeding bowls' and reserve the term 'porringer' for a two handled cup. Contemporary evidence is against them however, and the porringer was a one- or two-eared vessel used for porridge, soups, stews and other 'slops'. Pewter porringers are not uncommon and were made from the 1500s into the eighteenth century. Brass or copper examples are exceptionally rare; perhaps because porringers were going out of fashion at the time when brass and copper domestic objects were coming into their own.

One-and two-eared brass porringers with a cast Tudor rose in the base, although well made and carefully finished, are all modern.

Castors and Peppers

A range of containers used to sprinkle sugar, spices and pepper on food were made in brass and copper. The purpose of castors can sometimes be distinguished by the size and nature of the holes set in the tops. Sugar was cut from blocks and large holes were needed for the roughly ground grains of sugar to pass through. Spices and pepper would run smoothly through small holes. Pepper was costly and was usually served from small castors while spices like ginger and cinnamon were offered in larger ones.

Most castors are made in two separate parts. In castors made before 1720, the top fastens with a bayonet fitting. Many early castors are octagonal. The holes were hand cut and are uneven. Few of these fine castors are English.

In the eighteenth century castors and peppers were made with screw lids and later in the nineteenth century castors have a small hole in the base, through which they were filled, and which was closed with a cork.

Most eighteenth-century and early nineteenth-century castors are of baluster shape, while more elaborate styles such as birds and animals date from the later nineteenth century. Another form which can be found is the straight sided 'flour shaker' with its slightly rounded top and flat circular handle. Care must be taken as many modern copies have found their way on to the market.

Knives, Forks and Spoons

The occasional brass or bronze handled knife and fork may be found and most date from the late nineteenth century. Early spoons in a brass alloy known as latten are not so rare. The heydays of the latten spoon were the sixteenth and seventeenth centuries.

A few eighteenth- and nineteenth-century spoons are known, of which many are French. Many spoons were at one time electroplated. It is as well to examine copper and brass spoons and forks of the nineteenth century carefully for signs of this plating.

Tankards and Mugs

Brass and copper tankards and mugs were used for drinking ale, cider and wine. Only a very few lidded tankards are recorded and most of these were originally silvered. Early eighteenth-century tandards generally follow the silver designs. Lidless mugs from before 1826 are uncommon.

Many mugs and tankards were electro-plated and these now appear without their original coating. The letters EPNS, for electro-plated nickel silver are an indication of plating on copper and brass mugs.

In the nineteenth century there are three main styles of copper and brass mugs. The first is a series of concave tavern mugs. In Scotland there are the thistle and baluster measures which often have weights and measures capacity marks. The last group of mugs are rounded or baluster shaped and are in brass or a 'bell' metal. All three groups were normally used in taverns and have weights and measures marks on their rims. Some unmarked examples may have been used at home.

Measures

Most 'capacity' marked copper and brass measures were used in the market place. They were stamped by the weights and measures authorities and these stamps can help to date them. Where capacity marks have been erased or rubbed out, this is often an indication that they are of late construction.

The straight sided style of brass mug with a thick wide lip was for dry measure and was used in the market place. Large copper and brass ale, cider, spirits or wine measures were also popular. This unique form was made in capacities of several gallons down to a gill. The earliest examples are probably late eighteenth century and they continued in production until the 1910 period. Brass measures are rarer and generally earlier than copper examples. Several other forms of standard liquid measure were used by the authorities.

Serving Wine

The British are becoming one of the principal wine drinking nations and we are inclined to think that previously wine was relatively unimportant, but this is not so. From medieval times wines have been imported from Europe, from Spain, Portugal, France and Germany especially, in large quantities.

Harrison writing in the sixteenth century gives us some idea of how important wine imports were. Speaking of wine he says 'Neither do I mean this of small wines only as claret, white, red, French etc which amount to 56 sorts ... but also of the thirty kinds of Italian, Grecian, Spanish, Canarian etc ....'

On the whole wine did not keep well in tapped casks and this is indicated by the prices charged. New wine was eight times the cost of old in 1500, for example! Rather different from the high prices now paid for vintage wines compared with the new year's growths.

Until the mid-seventeenth century wines were stored in casks and tapped when needed, the wine being poured into pewter or silver flagons. In the seventeenth century glass bottles were available and owners began to decant their wine, generally still only when needed, corking the bottles to keep them fresh. Wine was still bought in casks and it is not until much later, probably in the nineteenth century that wine in bottles was widely for sale.

The corks in wine bottles had to be removed before the wine could be decanted or drunk and various types of corkscrews were designed. Eighteenth-century corkscrews are rare. Most early nineteenth-century corkscrews are of simple form with the screw set at right angles to a bone, ivory or wooden handle. Corkscrews also often have brushes for cleaning the neck of the bottle before pouring. A classification of cork screws can be made based on the nature of the screw and other factors, and readers with an interest in this field are referred to Robin Butler's *The Book of Wine*. Many nineteenth-century corkscrews have patented features and can be dated as a consequence. One of the first patents was issued to Thomason of Birmingham in 1802. There are hundreds of different forms. One maker, about 1800, for example, illustrated seventeen designs. Examples mounted with brass or copper are not uncommon but other materials were also popular.

Wine was frequently served spiced and hot, but by the early eighteenth century white wines were drunk chilled as is done today. Wine cisterns or coolers were used and the bottles stood in the ice to chill. Silver and wooden wine coolers were most popular but a few brass and copper examples exist. The style most frequently found is similar in form to the oval jardinieres of a later period. Most of these are Dutch, the earliest examples occur from about 1680 and they continued in use into the nineteenth century. Larger more elaborate wine coolers, of classical form, are also known.

From the eighteenth century most wine was drunk at the table after it had been transferred into decanters of glass or silver. Use was made of wine coasters to prevent spillage on polished tables. Silver and Sheffield plate examples are well known and a few brass and copper coasters were probably made. However currently there is an influx of brass coasters which have been recently imported.

CAULDRONS POSNETS AND SKILLETS

246 A typical mid-European cooking pot of bulbous form, about 1500. (*Robin Bellamy Ltd*)

247 *(below)*   A sixteenth-century posnet of rounded form and long handle. Note the tall feet and the clear sand mould marks on the body. (*Robin Bellamy Ltd*)

248 An eighteenth-century skillet with straight sides and handle. The feet are slightly worn down. (*Bradbury Collection, photograph by Peter Hooper*)

249 A typical eighteenth-century skillet by Robert Street of Bridgewater. 16$\frac{1}{2}$in maximum width, about 1770. (*Duncan J. Baggott*)

250 The handle of the previous skillet by Street. (*Duncan J. Baggot*)

251 *(above)* The handle of a seventeenth-century skillet by Thomas Palmer (or Palmar) of Canterbury. (*Robin Bellamy Ltd*)

252 *(right)* A seventeenth-century skillet handle by Clement Tozier (or Tosear) of Salisbury. (*Key Antiques*)

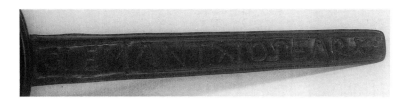

253 *(above)* A nineteenth-century skillet by the Bristol maker Wasborough. About 1830, 13$\frac{1}{2}$in wide. (*Lawrence Fine Art Auctioneers of Crewkerne*)

254 *(below)* A brass bowl riveted into a wrought iron stand and handle. Welsh borders, early eighteenth century. (*I.V. Jones Roberts*)

255 A rare brass pot in an iron stand. Mid-eighteenth century. (*Robin Bellamy Ltd*)

POTS, PANS AND SAUCEPANS

256 (*left*)   A small rounded saucepan with a lip rolled over a wire form. Wood and copper handle. 11½in maximum width, about 1800. (*Colin Greenway Antiques*)

257 (*below*)   A set of three Victorian copper saucepans of rounded form. The centre one has a rolled seam around the base, the other two are dovetailed. In each the upper rim is turned back over a wire. The first two have copper handles, the last of iron. 12in, 11½ and 8in high. (*Duncan J. Baggott*)

258 Nineteenth-century copper saucepan with straight sided body and pouring lip. Max width 14in. (*Colin Greenway Antiques*)

259 A similar copper saucepan with deeper lip. Max length 13¹/₂in. Unrecorded maker's mark on base. About 1870. (*Colin Greenway Antiques*)

260 Straight-sided brass saucepan with hollow iron handle. The pan has a diameter of 6¹/₂in. Late nineteenth century. (*I.V. Jones Roberts*)

261 A similar brass saucepan with a solid iron handle. The rivets joining the handle to the body are copper. Pan diameter 4in, about 1880. (*Windrush Antiques*)

262 A copper saucepan with inset lid, the body and lid each with an iron handle. Unknown maker's mark. 14in long, including the handle. About 1880-1900. (*Duncan J. Baggott*)

263 (*above*) A copper fish kettle for cooking flat fish such as turbot. 27in by 18½in and 8in deep. About 1830-50. (*Rudolph Otto Antiques*)

264 (right) A copper fish kettle for salmon and other large fish. 37½ long. Marked 'Langham Hotel 2'. About 1860. (*Jack Casimir Ltd*)

265 (*above*) A brass frying pan with iron handle. 10in wide, about 1840-60. (*Peter Norden*

266 (*right*) A copper frying pan with the globe mark and an iron handle. 6½in maximum width. About 1870-90. (*Rudolph Otto Antiques*)

BOILERS AND JAM PANS

267   An oval copper stock pot, 21in long with close fitting lid. About 1830-50. (*Windrush Antiques*)

268   A copper stock pot or soup urn with tap and close fitting lid. 18in wide, about 1830-50. (*Prudential Fine Art Auctioneers, Manchester*)

269 (*below*)   Another copper stock pot or soup urn with brass tap. 13$^1/_2$in high. Mid-Victorian. (*Ian Savage*)

270 (*below*)   A boiler or stock pot in copper, with rolled seam at base. 12$^1/_2$in wide and 9in high. About 1860-80. (*Duncan J. Baggott*)

271   Copper stock pot. 10in high, about 1860-80. (*Jack Casimir Ltd*)

272 (*right*)   A copper stock pot with iron handle, the pot also has a lid. 9in high to top of handle. About 1840-50. (*Jack Casimir Ltd*)

273   A typical Victorian jam pan in a hard brass, often called 'bell metal', with fixed iron handle 11$\frac{1}{2}$ in high. Similar pans were being stamped out near Bristol in 1880. (*Duncan J. Baggott*)

274   A Victorian spun brass boiling pan with fixed iron handle, the lip turned over a wire former. 7$\frac{1}{2}$in high. (*Peter Norden Antiques*)

275 A copper boiler with dove-tailed seamed base and folded rim. 18in diameter, about 1840-60. (*Duncan J. Baggott*)

276 *(left)* A copper steamer, the top half forming the lid. Oval, 10³/₄in wide, about 1860-70. (*Jack Casimir Ltd*)

277 *(below)* A copper cooking pan. Dovetailed seams, sturdy construction. 24in long, 19in wide, about 1820-40. (*Duncan J. Baggott*)

CHAFING DISHES

278 A brass chafing dish in brass on castors. The decorated top can be opened and extended and the fuel inset in a holder beneath. Probably English, about 1700. 10in when closed, 13in when open. (*Duncan J. Baggott*)

279 (*below*) The same chafing dish when opened and extended.

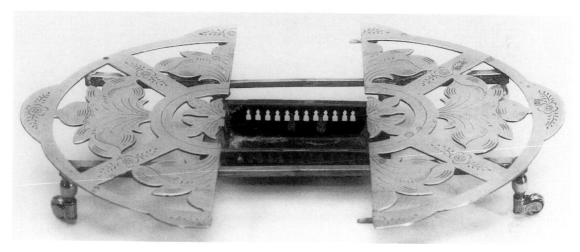

280 A fine brass folding cross or chafing dish, 13in long. Mid-eighteenth century. Traces of original silvering. (*Jack Casimir Ltd, photograph by Roy Farthing*)

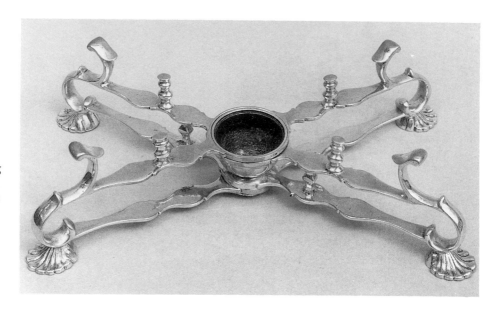

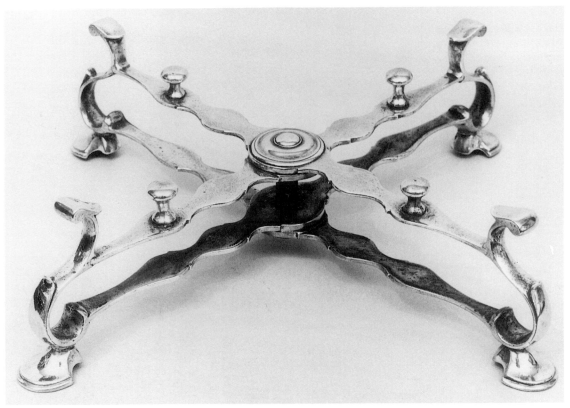

281 Another chafing dish, also with traces of silvering. 12in long. Mid-eighteenth century. (*Jack Casimir Ltd, photograph by Roy Farthing*)

282 A chafing dish with adjustable feet. Mid-eighteenth century. (*Jack Casimir Ltd, photograph by Roy Farthing*)

283 An early eighteenth-century brass brazier with yew wood handle. The plate stood on top of the three shell-shaped rests. 6½in high. (*Robin Bellamy Ltd*)

284 An early nineteenth-century sweetmeat dish or chafing dish. 4in high. (*Lawrence Fine Art Auctioneers of Crewkerne*)

JELLY MOULDS

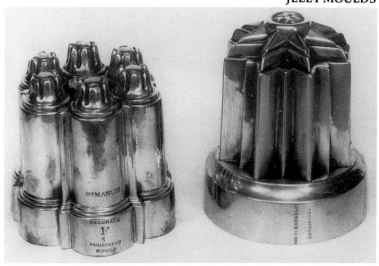

285 Two jelly moulds, the example on the left has a kite mark on the top and is also marked 'McManus, Belgrave F4, Registered Mould', about 1850. The right-hand mould has 'Registered September 1864'. 6½in high. (*Jack Casimir Ltd*)

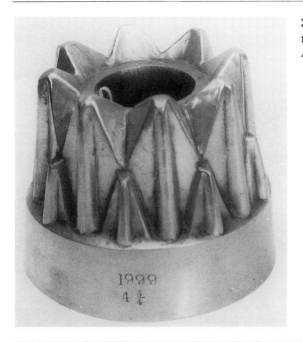

286 A copper mould marked 'RMSP' and the numbers 1999 and $4^3/_4$. Late Victorian. (*Country Life Antiques*)

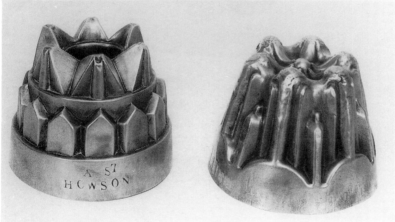

287 Two copper jelly moulds. The left example is marked 'A St Howson' and is $4^1/_2$in high. About 1860-80. (*Duncan J. Baggott*)

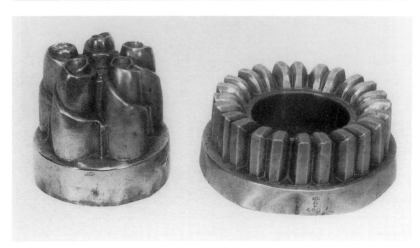

288 Two moulds, the left-hand example is $4^1/_4$in high. The ring mould is $2^1/_2$in high, marked no 490 and has the orb mark. About 1870-90. (*Duncan J. Baggott*)

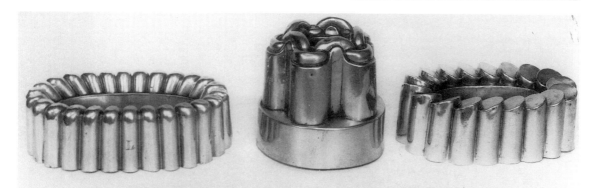

289 (*above*) Three moulds, 2$\frac{1}{2}$in, 4$\frac{3}{4}$in and 2$\frac{1}{2}$in high. The centre example represents a linked chain. All three are Victorian. (*Jack Casimir Ltd*)

290 (right) A copper ring mould marked 'Lofthouse', about 1880-1900. (*Windrush Antiques*)

291 (*right*) Four Victorian copper moulds, From 5$\frac{1}{2}$in downwards. (*Ian Savage*)

292 (*below*) Three lion moulds. The example on left is marked 'no 82' and has the orb mark. The centre example is 'The Florence' and that on the right is marked 'No 82'. The largest is 7in high. (*Jack Casimir Ltd*)

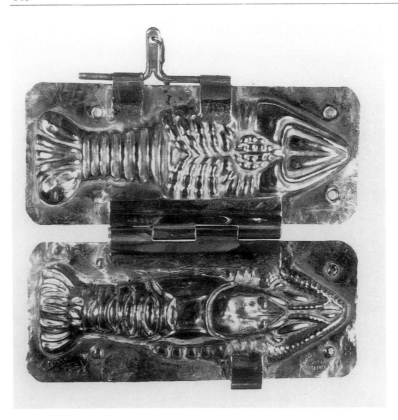

293 A lobster or crayfish mould marked 'No 85' and 'Handle and Smith, Birmingham', 6½ wide. About 1870. (*Christopher Sykes Antiques*)

PASTRY WHEELS

294 A group of five pastry wheels. Left to right: brass wheel and leaf shaped cutter, about 1800, 4¼in; brass wheel and crescent cutter, about 1800, 4¼ wooden handled cutter with three crimpers, about 1820-30; wheel with pinch crimper, 5½in about 1800; and brass wheel with star-shaped cutter, 4in, about 1800-20. (*Christopher Sykes Antiques*)

295 *(above)*   A brass bowl-
shaped cullender with copper
handle. Maximum length 15$^1/_2$in,
about 1830-50. (*Key Antiques*)

296 *(right)*   A two-handled
brass cullender with copper
rivets. 12in diameter, about
1840-60. (*Country Life Antiques*)

297   The bowl in which the above cullender stands.
(*Country Life Antiques*)

MORTARS

298 A typical late seventeenth-century mortar dated 1685, 4¹/₂in high. (*Robin Bellamy Ltd*)

299 A decorated late seventeenth-century mortar with crown motif. 4³/₄in high, about 1680. Mortars of this form continued in use into the 1720s and 1730s. (*Robin Bellamy Ltd*)

300 Three mortars. Left: Whitechapel mortar, cast in London about 1700; the stylised bands of flowers round the middle are typical of this foundry. Centre: two-handled mortar with portcullis and crowned Tudor rose decoration, about 1680. Right: mortar with a stamped date of 1708. (*Robin Bellamy Ltd*)

301 Two-handled mortar with cast date of 1705. 7in high. Made by 'HR'. (*Key Antiques*)

302 A plain early eighteenth-century spice mortar 5in high. (*Duncan J. Baggott*)

303 A two-handled mortar marked 'W Ely', late eighteenth century. 5½in high. (*Duncan J. Baggott*)

304 A spice mortar of cup form, 3½in high. About 1800. (*Peter Norden Antiques*)

305 A group of brass pestles, about 1680-1720. (*Robin Bellamy Ltd*)

SKIMMERS AND LADLES

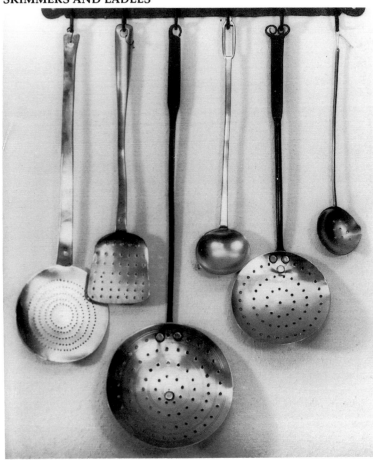

306 *(left)* A group of skimmers and ladles. Some are in brass, others in copper and some have iron handles. From 13in to 26in. About 1750-1820. (*Key Antiques*)

307 *(below)* Three more kitchen tools, about 1800-20. (*Key Antiques*)

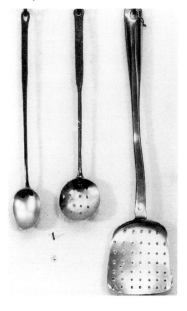

308 Four further cooking tools. The skimmer second from left, is later than the others which date from about 1840. (*Key Antiques*)

CRANES AND SPITS

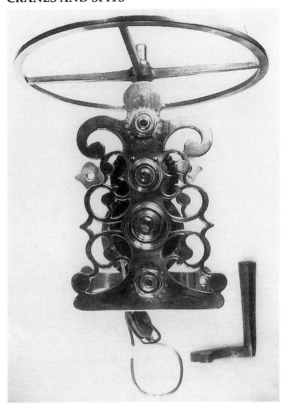

309 A clock-faced spit jack marked 'R Pearson'. Height 10in, about 1720. Driven by weights. Most of this type were made by clockmakers, and like clocks were often marked with the maker's name. (*Christopher Sykes Antiques*)

310 A spit engine faced with brass and engraved 'G. Pardon 1747'. (*Robin Bellamy Ltd*)

311 *(left)* A simple brass extending hook. Mid-eighteenth century. Note the bird shaped terminal to the locking device. (*Bradbury Collection, photograph by Peter Hooper*)

312 *(right)* A clockwork bottle spit, made by Salters. Length 13in, about 1870. (*Christopher Sykes Antiques*)

313 *(below)* A fine brass crane arm for a spit, with movable hook and swinging arm. Eighteenth century. 16$\frac{1}{2}$in when fully extended. (*Duncan J. Baggott*)

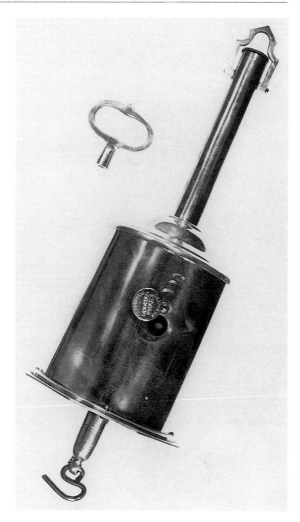

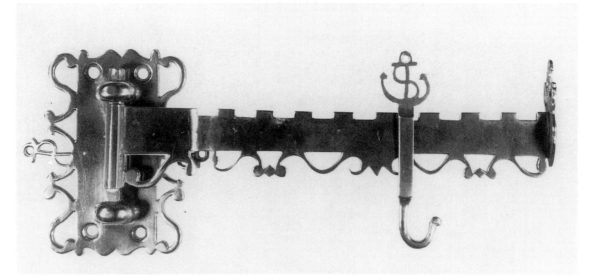

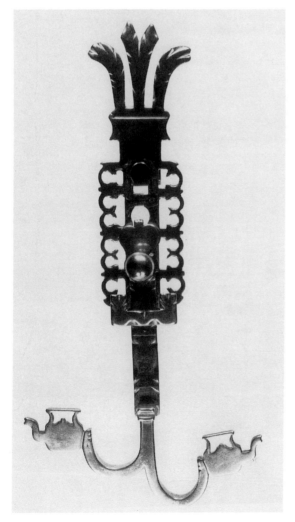

314 *(above)*   An elaborate crane with movable hook. Note the two anchor motifs. 4¹/₂in high and 11¹/₂in long, about 1820. (*Christopher Sykes Antiques*)

315 *(left)*   A trammel or extending hook for suspending cooking pots or kettles. Stylised Prince of Wales feathers at the top and kettles at the bottom. 13in overall, about 1860. (*Christopher Sykes Antiques*)

316 *(below)*   A plain example. Arms like these were screwed to the side of the fire place. 10in long, about 1870. (*Christopher Sykes Antiques*)

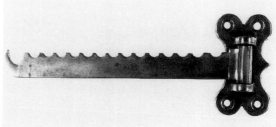

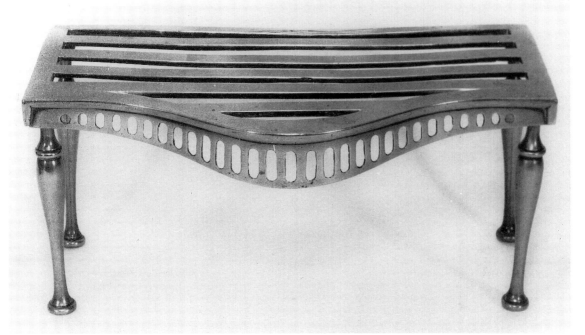

317 (above)   A brass serpentine-fronted footman in Regency style. Screwed construction, rather than riveted. 14in long, about 1820-50. (*Windrush Antiques*)

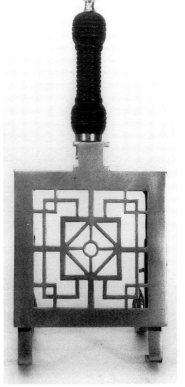

318 (*left*)   A trivet with attachments for fastening to the bars of the fire. Wooden handle, brass front and iron back. 13in overall, about 1800-30. This trivet is adjustable and can be moved away from the fire while still fastened. (*Windrush Antiques*)

319 (*below*)   A large brass footman 20in wide and 9in high. Used to stand plates on near the fire or to warm food before the blaze. Note the robust construction. About 1830-50. (*Rudolph Otto Antiques*)

320   A folding trivet of kidney shape. About 1780, 9in wide and 6¼in high. (*Country Life Antiques*)

321 *(right)*   A trivet in brass and iron for fastening to the bars of a grate. 13in, about 1840. (*Windrush Antiques*)

322   A similar trivet. The brass is cut to form a crownand the letters 'VR'. About 1840-70. (*Windrush Antiques*)

323 *(left)* A brass-topped trivet with wooden handle and iron fastenings for fixing to the bars of the fire. 11½in high, about 1830-50 (*Private Collection*)

324 *(right)* A standing trivet of similar form. George IV. (*Lawrence Fine Art Auctioneers of Crewkerne*)

325 *(right)* Oval brass trivet, 9¼in by 6in. Worn registration number. About 1850-70. (*Country Life Antiques*)

326 *(below)* Three round brass trivets. Left to right: 5in, 6¾in and 5½in diameter. Late Victorian but some similar examples were being reproduced in the 1930s. (*Country Life Antiques*)

327 *(above)*   Two tall Victorian trivets in brass, both 12in high. Sometimes called 'table' trivets because they look like small tilt tables. (*Country Life Antiques*)

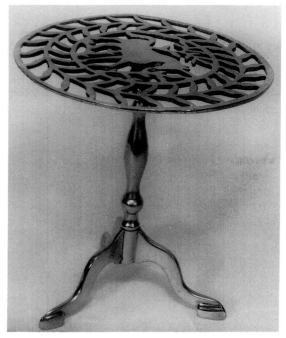

328 *(left)*   A similar trivet, $8^1/_2$in high, about 1850. (*Country Life Antiques*)

329 *(above)* Two oblong trivets by 'Peerage'.

330 *(right)* Another similar trivet with registered number 728032 stamped on it. Edwardian. (*Country Life Antiques*)

TOASTER

331 A brass and iron toaster. It was fastened to the grate front and small birds could be cooked or toast could be made before the flames. About 1800. (*Bradbury Collection, photograph by Peter Hooper*)

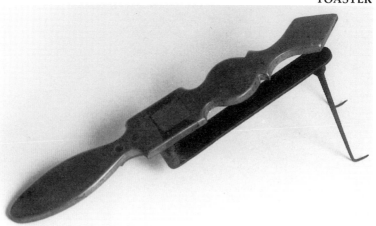

CHESTNUT ROASTERS

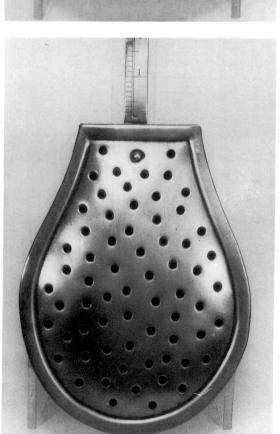

332 A round brass chestnut roaster with overlap seams, 20in long. Late Victorian. (*Country Life Antiques*)

333 (*above*) A square roaster with handle riveted into place. 4½in square plus handle. Late Victorian (*Country Life Antiques*)

334 (*left*) A mandolin-shaped chestnut roaster 6in long, about 1880-1900. (*Country Life Antiques*)

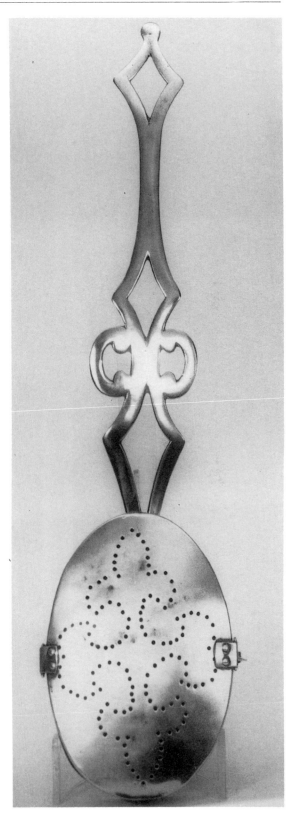

335 (left) An Edwardian brass roaster with handle. The box is 6³/₄in long. (*Windrush Antiques*)

336 An oval chestnut roaster with elaborately shaped handle. Marked 'Made in England'. 20¹/₂in long, about 1910. (*Country Life Antiques*)

49

SKIMMERS AND ROASTERS

SCALE $\frac{1}{7}$ SIZE.

PRICES

each.

No.		Price
8055	Oval	18/-
	Round	16/-
	Square	17/-
8056		18/-
8057	Oval	14/-
	Round	14/-
	Square	14/-
	Octagonal	14/-
8058		15/-

With Turned
Wood Handles.

8058A	16/-

With Brass Handles

8059	17/-

Various other patterns from
12/- upwards.

8060 Chestnut Roaster 30/-
Brazed Copper Back,
Chased Brass Lid, Iron
Handle, all hand made.

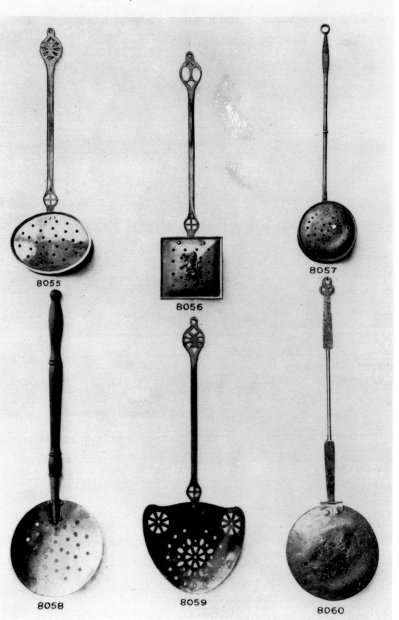

337   A page from the Pearson Page catalogue for
1927 illustrating some of the skimmers and chestnut
roasters then being offered for sale.

DISHES, PLATES, TUREENS, SERVING DISHES AND BOWLS

338 A magnificent deep
Nuremberg bowl with the Lady
and the Dove, dating from about
1450. Bowls of this style were
used as alms dishes, for display
and for washing ones hands at
table. (*Robin Bellamy Ltd*)

339 A brass plate with single
reeded rim, the edge bent back
over a wire form. 1880-1900. 10in
diameter. (*Ian Savage Antiques*)

340 (*above*)   A deep brass bowl with central boss (which, due to reflections, in the photograph appears as a hole). 15in diameter, about 1700-30. (*Robin Bellamy Ltd*)

341 (*left*)   A hammered deep bowl with everted rim. 16in diameter, about 1800. (*Windrush Antiques*)

342 Copper serving dish with lid on brass feet. 15$\frac{1}{2}$in wide, 6in deep, about 1830-40. (*Peter Norden Antiques*)

343 A mid-eighteenth-century footed brass tray or salver of typical silver style. (*Jack Casimir Ltd, photograph by Roy Farthing*)

344 Brass salver on three feet. Traces of original silvering. Mid-eighteenth century. (*Jack Casimir Ltd, photograph by Roy Farthing*)

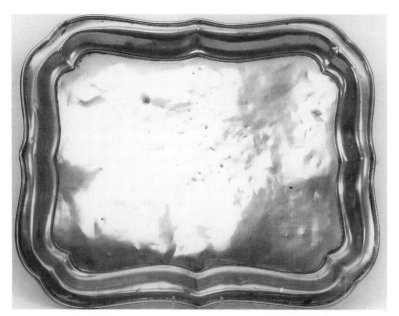

345 Brass tray with wavy edged rim. Nineteenth century. (*Key Antiques*)

346 An oblong Victorian brass tray with beaded rim 16½in by 10in. (*Country Life Antiques*)

347 (*below*) A reproduction brass tray 16in wide.

ALE MULLERS

348 *(right)*   A typical 'asses ear' copper ale muller with iron handle. Overlap seam up the muller. Mid-nineteenth century. (*Courtesy of Lawrence Fine Art*

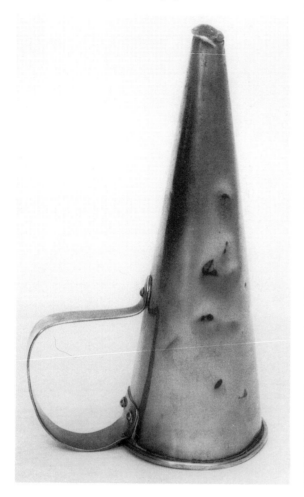

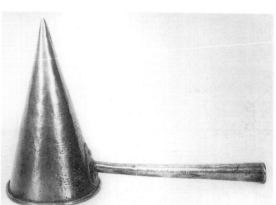

349 *(above left)*   A copper ale muller with loop handle. 10in, about 1800. (*Duncan J. Baggott*)

350 *(above right)*   A similar copper ale muller with handle. 13in overall, about 1800. (*Windrush Antiques*)

351 *(right)*   A copper slipper or shoe mull, about 1820-40. (*Lawrence Fine Art Auctioneers of Crewkerne*)

PLATE STANDS

352 *(left)* A cat or plate stand, made from three brass poles linked in the centre. Plates were stood in these cats before the fire. 19½in high, about 1880-1900. (*Duncan J. Baggott*)

353 *(right)* A folding plate stand. Nineteenth century. (*Bradbury Collection, photograph by Peter Hooper*)

COFFEE POTS

354 A copper coffee pot with brass knop and spout. 7in high, about 1710-20. (*Private Collection*)

355 Another view of the same coffee pot showing the handle and hinge.

356 A rare brass coffee pot with traces of original silvering. 10$^1/_2$in high, about 1760. (*Jack Casimir Ltd, photograph by Roy Farthing*)

357 Brass coffee pot of bulbous form with traces of original silvering and an armorial engraved on the side. 12³/₄ in high, about 1760. (*Jack Casimir Ltd, photograph by Roy Farthing*)

358 Copper coffee pot, with traces of original silvering. 8in, about 1830. (*Jack Casimir Ltd*)

359 An urn-shaped copper coffee pot, again with traces of original silvering. About 1830, 10in high. (*Jack Casimir Ltd*)

360 A brass tapering coffee pot with side handle. 8¹/₂in overall, about 1800-20. (*Duncan J. Baggott*)

361 A similar pot in copper but with narrow base. The knop is in brass. It is made with dovetailed seams and heart-shaped joint at the handle. $7\frac{1}{2}$in high, 1820-40. (*Colin Greenway Antiques*)

362 A copper coffee pot of tapering form. The double wooden handle is uncommon. 8in high, about 1780-1800. (*Duncan J. Baggott*)

393 The same coffee pot from a different angle.
Note the heavy riveted joints at base and top where
the handle joins the body, and the dovetailed seam.
(*Duncan J. Baggott*)

364 (*below*)   A tapering copper coffee pot with
overlap seam. 7$\frac{1}{2}$in high, about 1830-50. (*Duncan J.
Baggott*)

365 A similar coffee pot, 8in high, about 1780-1800. (*Duncan J. Baggott*)

366 A copper coffee pot with stepped brass knop, and wooden handle. 10$\frac{1}{2}$in, about 1820-40. (*Private Collection*)

367 *(above left)* A copper coffee pot of rounded form, with brass knop and rivets. 9in high, about 1770-1800. (*B.I. & D.M. Howard*)

368 *(above right)* A rounded coffee pot with Adam-style handle and wooden knop to lid. About 1840, 9in high. (*Jack Casimir Ltd*)

369 *(right)* A copper coffee pot with reeded handle and neck. 8in high, about 1840-50. (*Peter Norden Antiques*)

CHOCOLATE POTS

370 Two bulbous copper chocolate pots, each with brass movable knop, which was used when stirring the chocolate. 10in and 8in overall, about 1780-1800. (*Duncan J. Baggott*)

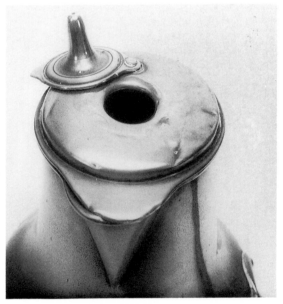

371 A close up of the lid showing the hole for stirring the chocolate.

372 A typical bulbous chocolate pot in copper with copper handle. 10in high. (*Robin Bellamy Ltd*)

373 Brass tea pot of rounded form. Nineteenth century. (*Jack Casimir Ltd, photograph by Roy Farthing*)

374 (*above*) Two copper tea pots. The left-hand example is made from sheet metal, 6in tall and dates from the late nineteenth century. The right-hand example is 6½in high and has a copper handle, about 1850-60. (*Jack Casimir Ltd*)

375 (*right*) A copper tea pot about 1820. Oval form, 7in high. (*Jack Casimir Ltd*)

376   A copper tea pot or perhaps a coffee pot from about 1840-50. Regency style, 8in high. (*Jack Casimir Ltd*)

TEA CADDIES

377   A brass tea caddy made for the Coronation of Edward VII 1902. Inscribed 'A gift from Sir Walter Gilbey Bart'. 6in high. (*Windrush Antiques*)

378 *(right)* A late Victorian seamed brass tea caddy, 6in. (*Peter Norden Antiques*)

379 Two caddies. On the left a
copper caddy, about 1870-80, 5in
high and on the right a hammered brass caddy, $4^1/_2$in high,
about 1900-10. (*Country Life
Antiques*)

KETTLES

380 Dutch copper swing-
handled kettle, 13in high. Brass
handle. This stepped style is
always Dutch and the shaped
handle is also widely found on
Dutch work. About 1800.
(*Duncan J. Baggott*)

381   A group of five Victorian kettles. The largest is
in brass, the others are in copper. 4¹/₂in to 2in high.

Possibly toys but kettles in larger sizes were common in this style. (*Duncan J. Baggott*)

382   A copper kettle of rounded form with fixed
metal handle. 9¹/₂in high. Mid-Victorian. (*Duncan J.
Baggott*)

383   A typical copper kettle. 8¹/₂in high. This
example has a bakelite handle and dates from 1900.
(*Duncan J. Baggott*)

384   Two copper kettles. The
largest is a two-pint kettle, 8in
high with brass knop, rim and
handle. Dovetailed seams.
Marked Army and Navy stores,
about 1890-1900. The smaller
kettle is 4in high, about 1880-
1900. (*Colin Greenway Antiques*)

385 *(above)* Two further late Victorian copper kettles, 13¹/₂in and 10in high. Brass knops and fixed handles of brass and copper. (*Prudential Fine Art Auctioneers, Manchester*)

386 Early nineteenth-century brass kettle on stand.(*Jack Casimir Ltd, photograph by Roy Farthing*)

387 Brass kettle and stand with original wooden handles and heating iron. 18in high, about 1825. (*Jack Casimir Ltd, photograph by Roy Farthing*)

388 Unusual brass kettle and stand with heating iron. 22in high, about 1825-30. (*Jack Casimir Ltd, photograph by Roy Farthing*)

389 A rare brass kettle on original spirit lamp stand. 11in high overall. Mid-nineteenth century. (*Duncan J. Baggott*)

390 Square copper kettle, 10in wide. Late nineteenth century. (*Jack Casimir Ltd*)

391 *(above)* Unusual Victorian rounded copper kettle with dovetailed seams. Marked 'No 4' and with the orb mark. 13½in overall width. (*Peter Norden Antiques*)

392 *(below)* Rounded Victorian brass kettle of flattened form, on four feet by 'JCB', probably Scottish, 8in high. Often termed a 'toddy' kettle. (*Peter Norden Antiques*)

394 A rare copper electric kettle with wooden handle. 11in high, about 1900. (*Duncan J. Baggott*)

393 An unusual copper kettle or jug, with overlap seam. 7in high excluding handle. Late Victorian. (*Wharton and Knight*)

395 A copper kettle or stock pot. Dovetailed seams, iron handle and brass tap. First half of the nineteenth century. (*Duncan J. Baggott*)

URNS AND SAMOVARS

396 *(above left)*   Regency coffee urn. 17¹/₂in high, about 1820. (*Jack Casimir Ltd*)

397 *(above right)*   Barrel-shaped copper samovar with brass tap and foot. 11in long and 12in high, about 1830. (*Duncan J. Baggott*)

398 *(left)*   Ball-shaped brass coffee urn, about 1820. 16¹/₂in high. (*Jack Casimir Ltd*)

400 A copper urn with brass spout and tap. About 1820-30, 17$^1/_2$in high. (*Duncan J. Baggott*)

399 Copper urn, 19$^1/_2$in. The tap is brass. About 1820-30, 17$^1/_2$in high. (*Duncan J. Baggott*)

401 *(above left)* A late Victorian copper samovar with brass handles and tap, 19$\frac{1}{2}$in high. (*Windrush Antiques*)

402 *(above right)* A mid-Victorian copper tea urn with brass lid and handles and wooden knop. (*Prudential Fine Art Auctioneers Manchester*)

403 *(right)* Typical Adam-style copper urn with reeded handles and brass lid. 19in high, Victorian. (*Prudential Fine Art Auctioneers, Manchester*)

404 A rare brass porringer $7^1/_2$in overall. The central boss and plain ear indicate a date of around 1680-1700. (*Private Collection*)

SALTS, PEPPERS AND CASTORS

405 A rare pair of engraved brass capstan salts, probably French. Early eighteenth century. (*Jack Casimir Ltd, photograph by Roy Farthing*)

406   Four brass peppers, 4in to 4¹/₂in. All eighteenth century. (*Duncan J. Baggott*)

407   An urn-shaped brass pepper, about 1780. 4¹/₂in high. (*Jack Casimir Ltd*)

408 (*above*)   Three flour sifters or dredgers, with detachable tops. The largest is 4¹/₂in high. About 1730-80. (*Christopher Sykes Antiques*)

409 A group of five flour dredgers, from 3 to 4$^1/_2$in high. First half of the eighteenth century. (*Duncan J. Baggott*)

SPOONS, FORKS AND SERVING UTENSILS

410 A fine brass sauce boat, 8$^1/_2$in long. With the maker's mark 'AC' and traces of original silvering. Mid-eighteenth century. (*Jack Casimir Ltd, photograph by Roy Farthing*)

411 A ladle and a sifter spoon, both probably at one time plated. 6$^1/_2$in, about 1800-30. (*Jack Casimir Ltd*)

412 A brass fish server, made from sheet metal and probably originally plated. Mid-nineteenth century. 11$^3/_4$in long. (*Jack Casimir Ltd*)

413   A spoon and fork in heavy cast brass. Probably silvered or gilded originally. Late eighteenth century. 7$\frac{1}{2}$in long. (*Jack Casimir Ltd*)

414(*below*)   Fine mid-Victorian steel knife and fork with bronze handles. (*Robin Bellamy Ltd*)

415(*bottom*)   A sheet metal brass cutlery tray. Late nineteenth century. 15$\frac{1}{2}$in long. (*Jack Casimir Ltd*)

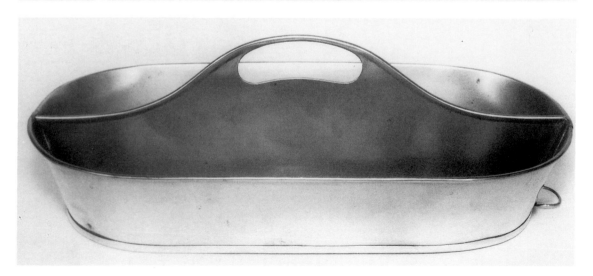

416 Two early English copper jugs, dating from about 1500. The marks of the sand mould can clearly be seen on the bodies. (*Robin Bellamy Ltd*)

417 A typical Italian copper lidded jug of the seventeenth century. 24in high. (*Robin Bellamy Ltd*)

418*(left)*   A Victorian brass jug, 9in high. Its origins are unclear, but similar jugs were used in Britain usually with basins. (*Windrush Antiques*)

419 *(above)*   A copper hot water jug with lid, 7in high, about 1830. (*Jack Casimir Ltd*)

420   A bulbous shaped brass jug with long spout, possibly Dutch, 10¹/₂ in high. Nineteenth century. (*Duncan J. Baggott*)

421   A late Victorian copper hot water jug, $6^1/_2$in high. (*Windrush Antiques*)

422   A brass 'Jersey' jug in the style popular on the island. $8^1/_2$in high. Marked 'Army and Navy Stores'. About 1890-1910. (*Blacklock Antiques*)

MISCELLANEOUS

423 *(above)*   A German seventeenth-century tureen. Few British tureens exist. (*Robin Bellamy Ltd*)

424 *(right)*   A glass biscuit barrel with brass lid and rim. Registered Number 153358 from 1890. (*Windrush Antiques*)

425 *(above)* A copper quail's egg poacher with seven small depressions for cooking the eggs. $4^1/_2$in diameter with $4^1/_2$in long handle. Part of the *batterie de cuisines* popular in the Regency period. (*Christopher Sykes Antiques*)

426 *(left)* Two late Victorian brass egg cups, 3in high. (*Duncan J. Baggott*)

427 A straight-sided brass tankard which may originally have had a lid. Traces of 'hall' marks, which indicate that it was originally silvered and marked to suggest solid silver. Quart ale standard capacity. 5$\frac{1}{2}$in high, about 1740. (*Jack Casimir Ltd*)

428 A lidded quart tankard of tulip shape. Maker's mark 'AC'. Ivory inserts in handle. About 1760. (*Jack Casimir Ltd*)

429 *(left)*   Another fine tulip-shaped lidded tankard in brass with traces of maker's marks and original silvering. Mid-eighteenth century. *(Jack Casimir Ltd, photograph by Roy Farthing)*

430 *(below left)*   A lidless brass tulip-shaped tankard. About 1740. *(Jack Casimir Ltd)*

431 *(below right)*   A brass 'belly' measure of a type widely used in taverns. This example has Edwardian capacity marks, but most measures of this form are late Victorian. $5^1/_4$ in high. *(Country Life Antiques)*

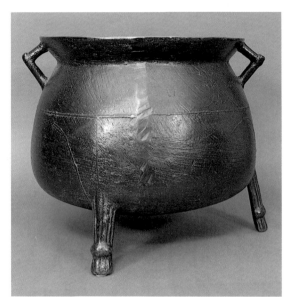

Plate 14 *(above left)* A punch-decorated and embossed Scandinavian wall light reflector or dish. Probably used for reflecting candlelight back into the room. Late seventeenth century. (*Robin Bellamy Ltd*)

Plate 15 *(above right)* A large cooking pot or cauldron with decorated feet and decoration on the body. The seams of the sand mould can clearly be seen running vertically from top to bottom of the pot. English, fifteenth century. (*Robin Bellamy Ltd*)

Plate 16 *(right)* An eighteenth-century lead bronze skillet of pint capacity. (*Robin Bellamy Ltd*)

Plate 17 *(below)* A rounded hanging pot, $5^3/_4$in diameter, about 1650. (*Robin Bellamy Ltd*)

Plate 18 *(below right)* A round Regency copper spice box with tinned inside. 8in diameter. About 1820. (*Robin Bellamy Ltd*)

Plate 19 *(left)* A copper liquid scoop or measure of half gallon capacity from the City of Bristol. It has an overlap seam and dates from the mid-eighteenth century. Possibly used for the retail sale of milk in the streets before the use of bottles. 12in high. (*Robin Bellamy Ltd*)

Plate 20 *(below)* Late nineteenth-century bell metal tankard with Victorian capacity mark. 5in high. (*Key Antiques*)

Plate 21 A group of sixteenth- and seventeenth-century spoons. From left to right: a Seal top, an Apostle, a Monk's head and a Lion Regardant. (*Robin Bellamy Ltd*)

Plate 22 Three brass castors for pepper, spices or perhaps sugar. The largest is 6in tall. About 1780-1820. (*Key Antiques*)

Plate 23 A good copper jelly mould in the form of a castle, 6in high. Nineteenth century. (*Key Antiques*)

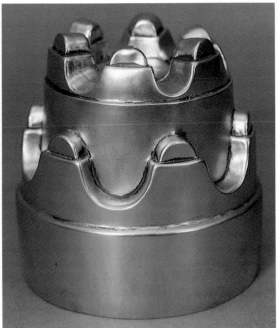

Plate 24 A bronze spoon mould for casting pewter spoons, about 1730. (*Robin Bellamy Antiques*)

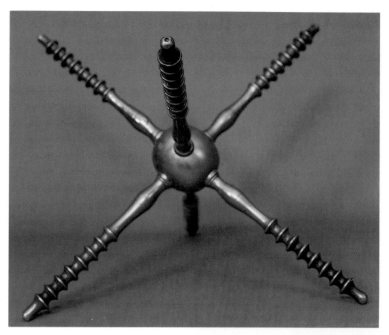

Plate 25 A three-legged 'cat', the legs fixed into position. Eighteenth century. (*Robin Bellamy Ltd*)

Plate 26 (*below*) Two snuff boxes. The example on the left is in brass and has a cast medallion of Sir Ralph Abercrombie on the lid. Sir Ralph was one of the British generals in the Penninsular War in Spain. 2⅝in diameter, about 1800. The example on the right is made of copper and is enscribed 'Thos Green, Hatter, St Clemants, Oxon'. It was made for customers' use in the shop. Mid-eighteenth century, 4in diameter. (*Robin Bellamy Ltd*)

Plate 27 (*below*) A shaped brass cribbage board engraved on a pewter plaque 'E.W. Banyard, Presented by R. Robinson'. 10in long, about 1780-1800. (*Key Antiques*)

432 *(above left)* A straight-sided brass tankard, from the early eighteenth century. *(Jack Casimir Ltd, photograph by Roy Farthing)*

433 *(above right)* A straight-sided copper mug or measure with thick brass lip. Victorian capacity marks. Measures of this style may have been used for dry measure for such substances as grain or peas. $6^{1}/_{4}$in. Late nineteenth century. *(Jack Casimir Ltd)*

434 A similar example all in brass. About 1860. *(Robin Bellamy Ltd)*

435 *(left)*   A straight sided tankard or measure by Loftus, London, about 1870. Note the typical banding. 4³/₄in high. Victorian capacity marks. (*Peter Norden Antiques*)

436 *(above right)*   A slightly tapering copper ale mug or measure with strap handle. About 1820-30. 5¹/₄in high. (*Jack Casimir Ltd*)

437 *(left)*   Two similar Regency copper tankards 4in and 3in high. (*Private Collection*)

438 *(below)*   A rare set of Victorian 'belly' measures in brass from quart down to ¹/₄ gill. Usually in a hard brass commonly known as 'bell metal'. (*Key Antiques*)

440   A Scottish half-gallon ale measure with hollow handle and spout. About 1840. (*Robin Bellamy Ltd*)

439   A copper jug with pouring lip and hollow handle. 10in high. Mid-Victorian. (*Duncan J. Baggott*)

441   Two copper Scottish 'thistle'-shaped measures. These measures in pewter, copper and brass, were found to pour badly and did not conform to the regulations, so most were destroyed. Gill and half gill, $4\frac{1}{2}$in and $3\frac{1}{2}$in high. Both have late Victorian and Edwardian capacity marks. (*Keith Hockin Antiques*)

442 *(above)*   A set of three copper baluster measures from Scotland. They have a high dome inside the base which is typical of this style. Half pint to half gill, $4^1/_2$in to $2^3/_4$in high, with Edwardian capacity marks. About 1900. (*Keith Hockin Antiques*)

443   Rare copper ale jug, with heart terminal to handle. Early nineteenth century $9^1/_2$in high. (*Jack Casimir Ltd, photograph by Roy Farthing*)

444 *(above left)* A copper bulbous jug with hollow handle and pouring spout, about 1820-30. 8in high. (*Jack Casimir Ltd*)

445 *(above right)* A straight-sided measure or jug inscribed 'Elveden' and made and marked by Jones Bros. About 1860. 10in overall. (*Jack Casimir Ltd*)

446 A mid-Victorian lidded Scottish half-gallon measure. (*Robin Bellamy Ltd*)

447 *(above left)* A copper wine or cider measure of typical 'harvester' form. One gallon capacity, 12in high. The lead seal on the top lip was restamped each time the measure passed its inspection. Victorian but examples were still in daily use in 1910. (*Windrush Antiques*)

448 *(above right)* A similar but squatter copper measure. Brass examples are usually earlier. 11in high, about 1880. (*Lawrence Fine Art Auctioneers of Crewkerne*)

449 Copper ale or water jug by W. Loftus Ltd, London. 12in high. Late Victorian. (*Lawrence Fine Art Auctioneers of Crewkerne*)

451 *(above right)*   A form of standard measure. A copper gallon measure with county mark, about 1826. Dovetailed seams. 12$^1/_2$in high. (*Jack Casimir Ltd*)

450 *(above left)*   Tall copper ale or water jug, 20in high. Victorian. (*Lawrence Fine Art Auctioneers of Crewkerne*)

452   Small brass measure, marked 'EB' on handle. 6$^1/_2$in diameter. Nineteenth century. (*Keith Hockin*)

453 *(left)* A late Victorian brass measure, from the Channel Islands or France. 7$\frac{1}{2}$in high. (*Windrush Antiques*)

454 *(right)* A brass double-ended spirit measure known as the 'double hen', 3$\frac{1}{2}$in high and serving a half or quarter gill. About 1840-60. (*Jack Casimir Ltd*)

455 A fine lidded two-handled loving cup in brass, with traces of original silvering. There is an armorial engraved on the body. 10$\frac{3}{4}$in high. Mid-eighteenth century. (*Jack Casimir Ltd, photograph by Roy Farthing*)

456 Another similar loving cup, 9in high. About 1725-50. (*Jack Casimir Ltd, photograph by Roy Farthing*)

WINE ANTIQUES

457 (*left*) Victorian wine funnel with rim turned back over a wire reinforcer. 12in high. (*Prudential Fine Art Auctioneers, Manchester*)

458 (*right*) Two copper wine funnels, 12in and 7½in high. The first is about 1850, the other is earlier perhaps around 1800. Note the dovetailed seam. (*Duncan J. Baggott*)

459 Rare Georgian copper wine cooler, with brass lion's paw feet. 21$\frac{1}{2}$in high. Regency period, about 1800-20. (*Duncan J. Baggott*)

460 Floor-standing brass oval wine cooler. Early nineteenth century. 25in long and 18$\frac{1}{2}$in high. (*Jack Casimir Ltd, photograph by Roy Farthing*)

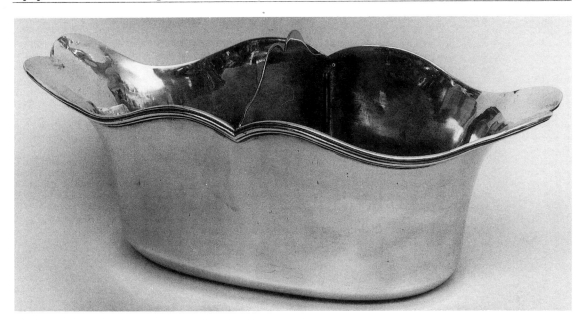

461 (*above*)   A French wine basket or bottle holder, with traces of original silvering. Late eighteenth century, 12in long. (*Jack Casimir Ltd, photograph by Roy Farthing*)

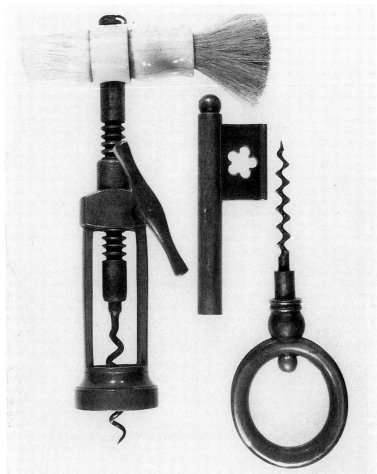

462   An unusual brass and iron 'London Rack' corkscrew fitted with dusting brush. 7^1/$_2$in long. Patented by 'Lund' about 1855. The other corkscrew consists of a ring handle and a key-shaped cover. 7in overall, Victorian. (*Christopher Sykes Antiques*)

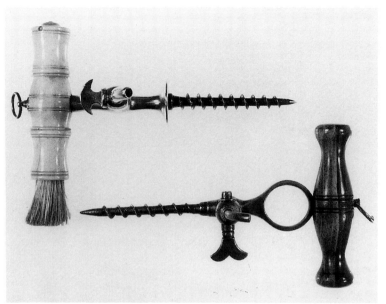

463 *(left)* Two rare Champagne taps or cork screws, which enabled the cork to be pierced without removing the wire. The champagne could then be poured a glass at a time, keeping the bottle fresh. Especially recommended for 'mothers to be' in Victorian times.

464 *(below)* Three brass roundlet combination corkscrews. Each holds additional tools including a screwdriver, gimlet, spike and tweezers. $3\frac{1}{2}$in. Victorian. (*Christopher Sykes Antiques*)

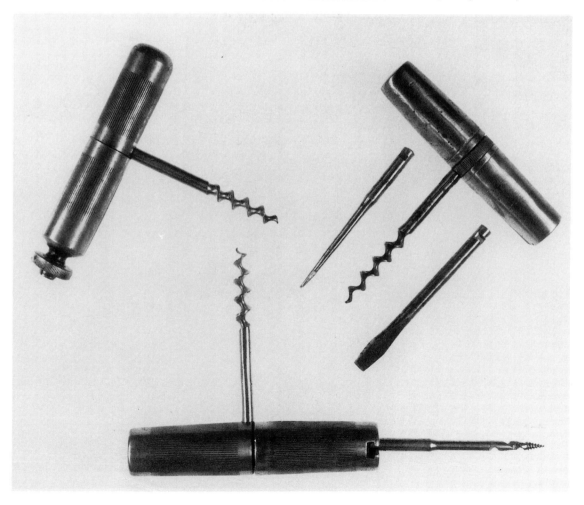

465 Three further corkscrews. The top example has a brass frame. $7^1/_2$in. The second example is by 'Farrow and Jackson Ltd, London' and is $6^1/_3$in long, while the last corkscrew is a 1904 patent by Coney and Co known as the 'King', $6^1/_2$in. About 1900. (*Christopher Sykes Antiques*)

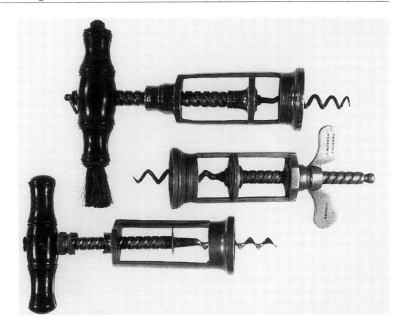

466 Three early nineteenth-century corkscrews with bone handles. The top example is marked 'Saml Cotterill Patent', the next 'Barlow Patent' and the last 'Wimot & Roberts Patent'. Their length is $7^1/_2$in, about 1820-30. (*Christopher Sykes Antiques*)

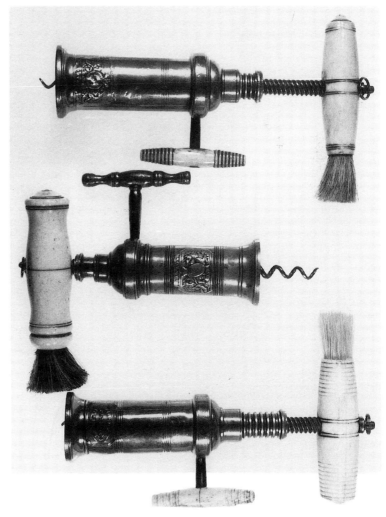

8
VARIOUS DOMESTIC ITEMS

Barber's Bowls

In the seventeenth and early eighteenth centuries barbers cut hair and acted as dentists and surgeons. It was only in the 1740s that the duties of the barber and surgeon became separated. Bowls used both in bleeding and shaving evolved. The majority are oval or round and have a cut-out which could be held round the neck while shaving. They are found in silver, pewter and pottery as well as in the copper alloys. Most barber's bowls were used in shops but some may have been employed by valets within the home. Crudely made bowls in copper and brass are generally continental.

The railway companies made widespread use of round bowls in wash-rooms and sleeping cars in the inter-war years, and many of these have had a notch cut from the rim to turn them into 'barbers' bowls. Examine the edges of barber's bowls carefully. They must not be sharp, as barbers were not well remunerated for cutting their clients' necks! Whatever form of finishing was used in the making the rim of the bowl should be continued round the notch or cut-out area.

A few bowls from the early eighteenth century can be found which have gradation marks inside the bowl. These allowed the barber-surgeon to calculate more accurately how much blood he had let. But it is easy to mark an otherwise genuine barber's bowl in this fashion to enhance its value.

Bedsteads

The nineteenth century saw the development of a demand for brass furniture, particularly brass bedsteads. Birmingham quickly became the centre of this new industry. Many beds were made in iron, but brass was used both for complete beds and for the decoration of iron beds. In some cases the beds were painted or lacquered.

The tubes from which brass bedsteads were made were initially made by seaming but after the 1840s seamless tubes were used. The tubes were extruded in a similar way to making modern plastics, and the knobs and terminals were either cast or spun. There are many varieties of beds. The earliest beds are likely to be around 1830 with most examples being made between 1860 and 1900. Brass bedsteads are still being made today.

Bells

The ringing of bells was a familiar sound to our forefathers. Peals of bells called them to worship on Sundays and the ringing of a hand bell summoned children to school. The sound of approaching carts and carriages was often heralded by the tinkling of the horse bells and cattle and sheep wore bells to help the shepherd or herdsman keep track of his charges.

Most of these bells were cast by bronze founders. A bronze alloy was ideal as it helped the metal withstand the hammering to which large bells were subjected. Cattle, sheep and horse bells were also made in sheet iron. Many animal bells were made by the Wells family of Aldbourne in Wiltshire who worked from 1760 until 1826. Bells signed 'RW' are by one of the two Robert Wells who ran the foundry between 1760 and 1799.

Within the home bells were less common, their main purpose being to call members of the family or workers in from the fields at meal times or to summon servants. In the Victorian period small hand bells became widespread for this latter purpose. Many of these domestic bells were made in brass.

Candlesticks are also known with a bell incorporated in the design but just how functional these were is not clear; perhaps they served as small gongs! Candlesticks with bells also appear in several reproduction catalogues of the 1920s.

Bird Cages

Birds have always been popular pets. An advertisement in the Flying Post in March 1704, for example, offers for sale '... singing Canary Birds mottled, white and all other sorts of colours as also Whistling Birds ....' Most cages were made in iron wire, wood or bamboo. A few examples in brass are known. It is difficult to date such examples but most will be from the second half of the nineteenth century. Cages with machine-made wire, machine-turned screws and thin even sheet metal are of late construction.

Book Covers

Brass and copper was occasionally used in the nineteenth century to cover books or to make book clasps. Copper embossed patterns in art nouveau style were especially popular around 1890-1900.

Domestic Boxes

All kinds of boxes were used in the home. Some were employed in the kitchen for salt or spices, others held matches or spills and still more were used for candles. It is often hard to know for what purpose some boxes were originally designed.

Most boxes which were hung on walls were for spills and candles. They were simple in style, with lifting lids. Boxes of this type, with engraved or stamped scenes, are likely to be nineteenth century although popular designs remained in production into the 1920s.

Larger hanging boxes may have been used for salt and kept in the kitchen or dairy. Many salt boxes were imported into Britain from Holland and Sweden. English examples after 1800 are hard to find.

Standing boxes could take many forms and served for a multitude of purposes. Robust examples can date from the eighteenth century, thin sheet embossed boxes are probably from the late nineteenth century or later.

Another group of small boxes were used to hold soap. Few British examples have been found from before 1850, but slightly larger fretted pomander boxes have been imported from the Middle East and are mistaken for soap boxes.

Pocket Boxes

A wide range of small boxes were used by men and women. They had many functions, including holding snuff and tobacco. Boxes were used for ladies' patches, for coins, as vinaigrettes or to hold visiting cards. Some small round boxes were made for love tokens, locks of hair and small amatory gifts. Few boxes of any of these types were made in copper or brass.

Buttons

Before the days of elastic, velcro and zip fasteners, everyone relied on buttons, which were made from textiles, wood, horn, ivory, pewter, silver, steel and the copper alloys.

Early metal buttons were usually cast in moulds. A button mould of the eighteenth century is illustrated. Some buttons were hand decorated by chasing or cutting. Seventeenth-century buttons tend to be round and nearly always cast decorated. Eighteenth-century buttons were usually decorated by punching a design on them with a hammer and die. Late eighteenth- and nineteenth-century buttons were often stamped out under presses. Victorian buttons became more elaborate and have a variety of shapes.

In Birmingham, the centre of the button industry, there were eighty-three makers in 1770 and this had risen to 139 by 1797.

Clocks and Watches

Clock works of all types were made in brass and there are many brass dials to clocks especially among eighteenth-century long cased examples. Brass carriage clocks were also very popular and continued to be made into this century. A few brass pocket watch cases are also known. The study of clocks is a specialised field and outside our canvas but two examples are illustrated here for the sake of completeness. There are a number of studies on clocks and clockmakers which can be consulted. One of the fascinations of clocks is that they are invariably marked with the maker's name and town, and careful study of the stylistic details can often provide a reasonably accurate date, often to within 10 years.

Dog Collars

Originally dog collars were used to help control the semi-wild hunting dogs but gradually collars carried the name and address of the owner. Most copper or brass dog collars are from the eighteenth or nineteenth centuries. A fine collection of collars is on display at Leeds Castle in Kent. Most nineteenth-century examples are plain bands with a thicker edge. Eighteenth-century collars tended to be wider than later examples. In addition to the standard band there are collars with serrated edges or spikes, to protect the dog and leather collars with metal studs.

Many are inscribed, including one famous collar which bore the following inscription:

'I am his Highness' dog at Kew
Pray tell me Sir, whose dog are you?'

Door stops

Sometimes also known as door porters they were metal objects used to hold doors open, or even to keep a banging door closed! There were probably a few cast iron door stops in the late eighteenth century but most examples, in any metal, date from the late nineteenth century onwards. Many are made to represent people: Nelson, Dickens, Punch and Judy, etc. Others, sometimes the earlier examples, are made with a shell motif, or with baskets of flowers. Common are lion's paw porters. Porters were still in production in the 1920s and 1930s and most surviving examples are from this period.

Foot Baths

We joke about enjoying a mustard bath to sooth our aches and pains but people did use foot baths. Bowls would normally have been used but in the home which had everything special foot baths were kept. A few copper or brass examples survive from the early nineteenth century.

Frames

In Georgian times people were fond of collecting small pictures, water colours, silhouettes, wax portraits and miniatures and these were occa-sionally framed in brass. Brass frames were also used in the nineteenth century for pictures and mirrors.

A frame's style is probably the best indication of its period. Elaborately decorated examples are either Regency, Victorian or Edwardian depending on the patterns adopted.

Funnels

We are all familiar with the problems of pouring a liquid from one container to another and from the earliest times people used a funnel for this purpose. Most eighteenth- and nineteenth-century funnels are in copper, a few in brass and pewter. They are often called 'wine' funnels but they were used for all kinds of liquids.

Games

A few adult games were made in brass and copper. Most frequently found are cribbage boards. Many of these would have been used in taverns but a few may have been domestic.

Irons

Flat irons for smoothing clothes date from the sixteenth century and devices for smoothing clothes were probably in use many years earlier. Initially these smoothing irons were heated on an open fire but by the late seventeenth century, box irons, in which charcoal or a heated iron bar could be inserted to keep them hot longer, were growing in popularity. Flat irons however continued in use well into this century despite the invention of the electric iron in the 1890s. Mrs Beeton records a variety of sizes in use in Victorian homes, from 4in to 10in long.

Wooden smoothing boards were also used by yesterday's housewife or servant but these were unheated and merely smoothed out the moisture and wrinkles under pressure. Closely allied with these boards are brass rolling pins used for smoothing linen sheets. Most irons are made of just that material but examples decorated in brass are occasionally to be found. Many decorated irons were made in Germany.

Goffering Irons

A specialised group of irons were used to smooth lace, pleats and ruffs. The elaborate collars of the

Elizabethan period needed to be smoothed and special tongs were invented which were heated in the fire and applied to the lace. In the nineteenth century some goffering irons were partly mechanical; a handle was turned to move ridged bars, heated by inserting a red-hot iron into their centre, over the surface of the cloth to be treated.

Another form of goffering iron was used for smoothing ribbons laces and edges where the ordinary iron could not be used. The item to be smoothed was drawn over the hot brass heated by a hot iron bar inserted in the arm.

Similar in shape to early pleating or lace tongs are crimping irons which were used to curl ladies' hair in the nineteenth century.

Iron Stands

It was easy to damage furniture by resting a hot iron on the surface and stands were designed for the iron to rest on. Many are in brass or copper and mostly date from the second half of the nineteenth century.

Jardinieres or Planters

The group of objects known today as jardinieres provide us with two problems. The first is that they are often very similar indeed to what was known in the seventeenth and early eighteenth centuries as wine coolers. The second difficulty is that while genuine Victorian examples of jardinieres do exist many now found in shops actually date from the 1920s.

The first basic question therefore is: when is a wine cooler a jardiniere? The answer probably is when it is Victorian! What occurred is that a popular and attractive design was adopted for a completely different purpose.

The Victorian era saw a vast increase in interest in flowers and all types of fauna. J.H. Plumb in his *Georgian Delights* writes of a 'rage of flowers' that swept Victorian England. This interest presents itself in many ways including the growth of gardening clubs, the appearance of many new seedsmen, and the writing of gardening guides. Cut flowers could be presented in vases but on the whole the Victorians liked a more elaborate display and turned to jardinieres to show off their plants and flowers. After the 1880s the introduction of gas lighting polluted the home atmosphere and was one of the reasons for the overwhelming popularity of the aspidistra which could survive the rigours of the home environment.

Victorian jardiniers would have been made in much the same way as later copies. The sides of jardinieres are usually stamped out of sheet metal and the bottoms are added using dovetail seams. Victorian examples were generally either oval or elongated rather than round. The decoration would mostly have been machine stamped but tended to be simple; with flutes or ribbing. Nearly all jardinieres have lion mask handles and claw or ball feet. Most elaborately decorated jardinieres are from the 1920s.

Scientific Instruments and Tools

Microscopes and scientific instruments are another field which is basically outside the terms of this study but for the sake of completeness some examples are illustrated. It was not uncommon for gentlemen to have such instruments in their home in the eighteenth and nineteenth century.

Although most hand tools were used professionally, it must be noted that most homes would have had some tools and a few of these were partly in brass or copper.

Money Boxes

In the mid-nineteenth century ordinary people were, for the first time, able to save. A 'thrift' movement developed and money boxes and money banks became popular especially with children. Hundreds of designs were introduced, many in brass. Many 'bank money boxes' are from the United States, where more than 300 types are said to have been recorded, but British boxes do exist. Many are in iron or tin but brass and copper examples are to be found.

Some money boxes are designed to represent banks; often imposing Victorian buildings, but others are simpler including a range of small post boxes in which the coins were mailed. These money boxes are all mid- to late-nineteenth century and continued to be made into the twentieth century.

Ornaments

Brass and copper were widely used as decoration. Many objects originally with a utilitarian purpose also later served as decor, but there were also brass and copper ornaments specifically made to decorate the home. Most are late nineteenth century.

Sewing Equipment
Brass and copper can be found on a few items used in sewing such as thimbles, needle cases and tape measures but their use was limited.

Spitoons
Not an elegant subject but spitoons were widely used in taverns and bars, especially during the nineteenth century when chewing tobacco was most popular.

Sundials and Hour Glasses
A few nineteenth-century hour glasses are known with brass or copper frames.

With sundials many were made in bronze or brass from the seventeenth century onwards. Larger examples were mounted in the garden. Smaller dials were fastened to window sills or to the walls of homes. Dated and signed examples can be found, but there are many modern reproductions.

Tobacco and Snuff
It is ironic that the arrival of tobacco to Britain was greeted by many as a health hazard. James I for example wrote in his work on tobacco 'there can not be a more base and harmful corruption in the country than the vile taking of tobacco'. Other commentators saw it as a marvel. Thomas Herriot wrote in 1600 of its use 'and have found many rare and wonderful experiments of the virtues thereof'. Smoking soon swept the nation and rich and poor used tobacco, mostly in clay pipes. In the 1770s it went out of fashion amongst the upper classes but revived in the form of cigarettes in the late nineteenth century. The use of tobacco, by troops especially, spread its use to all classes.

Pipe cases were occasionally made in brass, in which clay pipes could be kept. A few brass or copper pipes are also known but their use was not widespread. Pipe tampers, many in brass and copper were used from the seventeenth century onwards to push down tobacco in pipes. Those with a small foot are earlier, when clay pipes were small. Large examples are from the nineteenth century or later, made to serve larger clay pipes or modern pipes.

Tobacco boxes were frequently made in copper and brass. Earlier continental examples are long and with rounded ends. Round, square and oblong boxes are mostly nineteenth century. Dated and engraved examples were made in many designs in the 1920s and 1930s and great care must be taken with these copies.

Snuff was extensively used, especially by the upper classes, from the reign of Queen Anne. Small snuff boxes became especially popular in the late eighteenth and nineteenth centuries but most brass and copper examples are from the later period. There are many copies of snuff boxes and engraved examples are particularly suspect.

Washing Bowls and Jugs
Before the days of hot and cold running water most people went to the water barrel or well. For those with servants hot water would have been brought to them in jugs and basins. Many jugs and basins were made in pottery but a few copper and brass examples can be found. Most are Victorian.

Brass and copper jugs, were common. Eighteenth and early nineteenth century examples have tapering sides and wide flat bases or are of baluster shape. Most have dovetailed seams. Lighter jugs made from thin sheet metal with overlap joints are late nineteenth century.

Water Cisterns
People have always needed water in the home. It was not until our own times that tapped water was widely available. In the middle ages London was supplied with water via conduits but people living in small towns and in the country had to draw water from a well or local stream. Journeys of up to a quarter of a mile were common and some people had to go as much as a mile for water. The ordinary household needed many gallons a day and this meant more than one journey for the woman of the house.

Inside the home some families kept a cistern

in silver, pewter, copper or brass from which water could be drawn through a tap. However British examples are very rare.

Watering Cans

Cans for watering plants were used from the middle ages. Early watering cans were made of pottery. Watering cans in copper or brass are almost certainly from the nineteenth or twentieth centuries. Large heavy cans were used in the garden. Lighter cans were used for watering household plants and date from the mid-nineteenth century onwards, when the interest in plants was developing.

Weights and Scales

Consumer protection is not a new branch of the law. Since the middle ages the state has thought it necessary to lay down standards for weights and measures and to control the quantities by which food and drink are sold. Several different standards have existed. The troy standard exists for silver and gold, and there is the 'avoir du pois' standard, still in use in Britain, for most transactions. Most weights were either standard weights held by the authorities for checking those in public use or weights used by traders in the market.

Within the home scales and weights played little role until the nineteenth century when two social changes led to their adoption. The first change was the establishment of the Penny Post in 1840. From that time on the weight of the letter set the level of postage required so that special postal scales were evolved to weigh letters at home. Some of these have the postal rates inscribed on them and this can sometimes help to date the scales, for the postal rates have changed several times since that time.

Modern cooking recipes include the amounts of the ingredients required for a dish. By and large this was not the position until the mid-nineteenth century. Early cook books were more concerned with method and contents rather than their relationship to each other. It was not until Mrs Beeton that quantities became important and hence cooks needed to be able to measure the amounts of each ingredient. Domestic scales therefore are from the mid-nineteenth century or later. Amongst leading makers were Avery & Co, DeGrave, Doyle & Co and Bate, all primarily nineteenth-century companies. The weights used with scales were mostly of waisted form or sets of small flat weights made up into nests.

Writing Equipment

Until the nineteenth century people mostly used quill pens. With the invention of the metal nib these were quickly replaced but few pens were made in copper or brass. Before the use of the fountain pen, ink had to be carried on the person and small post, mostly of glass were used. Occasionally inkpots made or decorated with brass may be seen.

On the desk people employed standishes which are pen and ink sets made up of a small tray, an ink pot, space for quills or pens and sometimes a candleholder or small bell. British antique examples are very rare. Most standishes that are now to be seen are Spanish or from the Middle East and have been imported in the last 25 years. Few even of these are from before 1800. Many are reproductions.

A rare group of scribes' brass boxes, which held ink and pen, are known from the late-seventeenth century.

Letters were usually sealed, especially before the use of envelopes in the mid-nineteenth century. Wax was used for this purpose and sets of taper sticks and wax holders were frequently made in silver and more rarely in brass for the desk. Individual brass or copper wax jacks are also to be found. There are many copies.

In the Victorian period letter holders or large paper clips were popular in brass and elaborate examples can be found.

BEDSTEADS

467 *(left)*   Design for a mid-nineteenth century brass bed of tubular construction. Made by Winfield of Birmingham.

468 *(below)*   The head of a fine cast brass, iron and steel bed, 5ft wide. About 1865. (*David Wooley Brass Bedsteads*)

469 *(opposite top)*   The foot of a brass bedstead about 1880. The bed is 5ft wide. (*David Wooley Brass Bedsteads*)

470 *(opposite bottom)*   The head of a 4ft 6in bedstead in spun brass. About 1885. (*David Wooley Brass Bedsteads*)

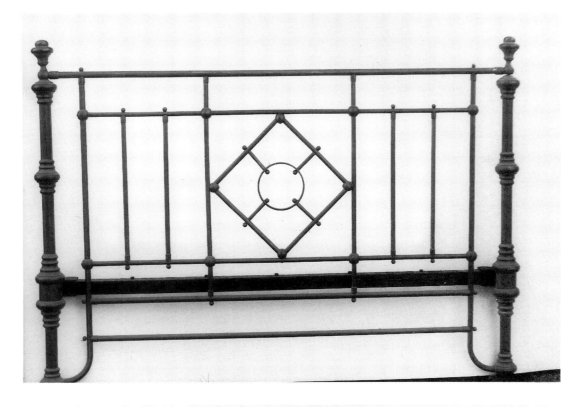

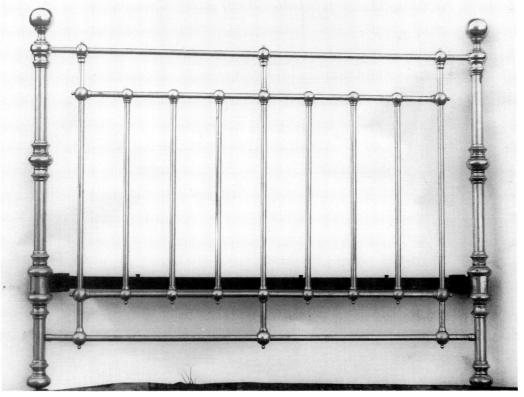

471   One of a matching pair of 3ft bedsteads with shaped back. The brass fittings are cast. About 1880. (*David Wooley Brass Bedsteads*)

472 *(below left)*   A horse or carriage bell marked RW by Robert Wells of Aldbourne, dating from the last quarter of the eighteenth century. Maximum diameter $4^1/_2$in. A packhorse collar with six identical bells can be seen at the Upper Dales Folk Museum, Hawes, North Yorkshire. (*B.I. & D.M. Howard*)

473 (below right)   A bronze bell, marked with the owner's initials 'GR' and dated 1791. 3in high. (*Duncan J. Baggott*)

BELLS

474 A table bell, late eighteenth century. 4in high. (*Duncan J. Baggott*)

475 A brass bell with turned wood handle. 6¹/₂in high. First half of nineteenth century. (*Duncan J. Baggott*)

476 Another similar bell with plain wood handle. Late nineteenth century. 9³/₄in high. (*Jack Casimir Ltd*)

477 Two call or 'punch' bells. Late nineteenth century. (*Country Life Antiques*)

478 A set of six 'lady' bells with crinoline skirts. From 3¹/₂ to 6in high. Bells of this style were still being introduced in the 1920s. (*Country Life Antiques*)

BARBER'S BOWLS

479 An oval brass barber's bowl, 11in by 9⁵/₈in, marked Geneva. Swiss, about 1880s. Barber's bowls of this style are all continental. (*Jack Casimir Ltd*)

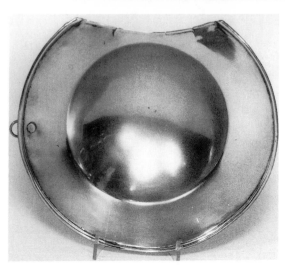

480 A brass barber's bowl, 8in diameter. Mid-eighteenth century. (*Jack Casimir Ltd*)

481 Brass parrot cage, 38in high. Mid-nineteenth century. (*Jack Casimir Ltd, photograph by Roy Farthing*)

BOOKS AND BOOK STANDS

482 A book with brass clasp. (See detail.) The clasp is engraved with the National Exhibition Hall and inscribed 'Reynolds Birmingham Almanack for 1851'. The book is 6$\frac{1}{2}$in long. (*Robin Bellamy Ltd*)

483 *(left)* Brass cover for book or blotter. 11$\frac{1}{2}$in by 9in. About 1860. (*Windrush Antiques*)

484 *(below)* Brass table stand for a bible. About 1900 (*Jack Casimir Ltd, photograph by Roy Farthing*)

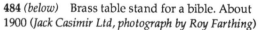

485 Most boot jacks for removing boots are in iron, but this small example from the nineteenth century is in brass. 9in overall. (*Duncan J. Baggott*)

486 A wall hanging box, possibly used for salt. Dolphin motif embossed on front and the box is also engraved. Swedish, early eighteenth century. (*Robin Bellamy Ltd*)

487 A pocket box, used on wall. This held all kinds of household requirements such as string, balls of wool, candles, etc. 12in high by 10^1/$_2$in wide. There is an Art Nouveau style to the design which suggests the box is about 1890. (*Country Life Antiques*)

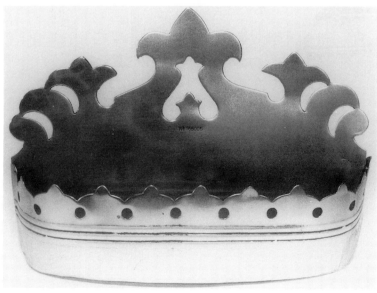

488 A brass 'crown' wall pocket, with the registered number 166005. 7^1/$_2$in wide. About 1891 (*Duncan J. Baggott*)

489 Another wall pocket possibly used for wool. Welsh. 9in long and 7in high. About 1880. (*Jack Casimir Ltd*)

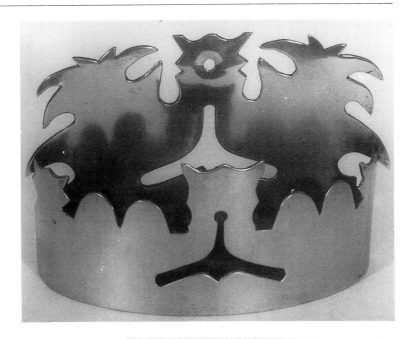

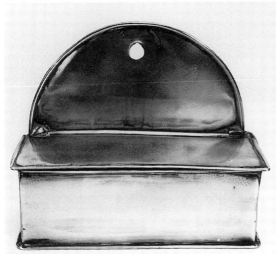

490 (*above*) A lidded wall box in brass. Mid-nineteenth century. (*Lawrence Fine Art Auctioneers of Crewkerne*)

491 (*right*) A typical reproduction wall box, this example is number 4162 of Pearson Page Ltd. 10$\frac{1}{2}$in high, about 1910-30.

492 A standing box, sometimes sold as a tea caddy
or, lined with wood, as a cigar box. 8in long.
Another Pearson Page design, although the engraving varied from box to box as it was still executed
freehand by an artist.

BUCKLE

493 Brass was widely used for
buckles. This example is from
around 1700 and is inscribed
with its owners name, Samuel
Ashton. It is for a sword belt and
was worn across the shoulders.
(*Duncan J. Baggot*)

494 *(left)* A group of ten brass buttons. Examples of this style of button were worn in Europe and Britain around 1650-1720. (*Private Collection*)

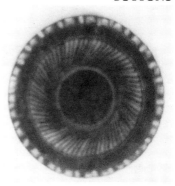

495 *(above)* A 'Colonial' copper button, late eighteenth century. (*Susan Higgins Collection*)

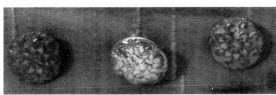

496 *(left)* Three buttons from the 'Golden Age', 1830-50. Gold was added to mercury and used for gilding buttons. The centre button is by E.W. Jackson of Gracechurch St, London. (*Susan Higgins Collection*)

497 A group of 'story' buttons, so called because the designs were related to a story, in this case St George and the Dragon, about 1900. (*Susan Higgins Collection*)

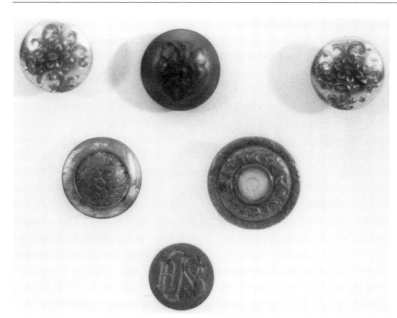

498 A group of six buttons, 1850-1907. (*Susan Higgins Collection*)

CLOCKS

499 *(above)* The brass-faced dial of a long case clock by William Grimes of London, about 1725. Most clocks before the end of the eighteenth century had brass dials. This simple, but elegant dial is typical of early eighteenth-century clocks. Later in the century provincial clocks, especially in the north, became more elaborate. (*Witney Antiques*)

500 *(right)* A long case clock movement. Most clock movements are made mainly from brass. (*Witney Antiques*)

501 *(above left)* A brass dog collar engraved 'Joseph Masters Jnr, Witney'. 6in diameter. About 1800. *(Private Collection)*

502 *(above right)* A plain brass dog collar with padlock, engraved 'William Wall, Esq, 1767'. $4^3/_4$in diameter. *(Duncan J. Baggott)*

503 *(left)* A brass dog collar with links. Engraved 'William Freer', about 1800. *(Jack Casimir Ltd)*

504 A leather dog collar set with brass studs, early nineteenth century. *(Jack Casimir Ltd)*

DOOR PORTERS

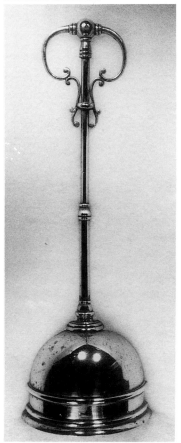

505 *(above left)* A brass door stop of plain form. 17$^1/_2$in high. Note the simplicity of design compared with later reproductions. About 1810-25. (*Christopher Sykes Antiques*)

506 *(above centre)* A brass porter of a Great Dane 9$^1/_2$in high. About 1860-70.

507 *(above)* Another porter with a fox head, the base is of lead. 15in high, mid-Victorian. (*Christopher Sykes Antiques*)

508 *(right)* A reproduction porter with lion's claw, No 1520 from Pearson Page (see also the illustration opposite, top row second from right). 15$^1/_2$in high.

509 *(opposite)* A page from the Pearson Page catalogue of reproduction brass porters, 1927. (*Photograph by Eric Adkins*)

BRASS DOOR PORTERS.

Section 33.   Page 1.

Made with or without 1¼ in. Projecting Plate at bottom to Prevent Door Sliding.

Metallic finished either Bronze, Ivory, or Verde Green.

All Priced Each.

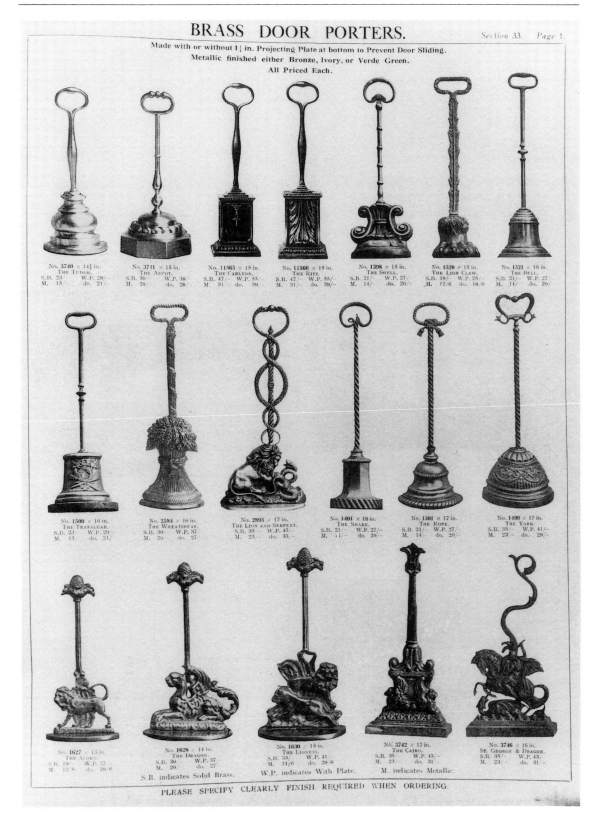

No. 3740 × 14½ in.
THE TUDOR.
S.B. 23/-   W.P. 29/-
M. 15/-   do. 21/-

No. 3711 × 15 in.
THE ASCOT.
S.B. 30/   W.P. 38/
M. 20/   do. 28/

No. 11565 × 15 in.
THE CARLTON.
S.B. 47/-   W.P. 55/
M. 31/-   do. 39/

No. 11566 × 15 in.
THE RITZ.
S.B. 47/   W.P. 55/-
M. 31/-   do. 39/-

No. 1398 × 15 in.
THE SHELL.
S.B. 21/-   W.P. 27/
M. 14/-   do. 20/-

No. 1520 × 15 in.
THE LION CLAW.
S.B. 19/-   W.P. 25/-
M. 12/6   do. 18/6

No. 1521 × 16 in.
THE BELL.
S.B. 21/-   W.P. 27/
M. 14/-   do. 20/-

No. 1500 × 16 in.
THE TRAFALGAR.
S.B. 23/   W.P. 29/
M. 15/   do. 21/

No. 2584 × 16 in.
THE WHEATSHEAF.
S.B. 30/   W.P. 37/
M. 29/   do. 27/

No. 2895 × 17 in.
THE LION AND SERPENT.
S.B. 35/   W.P. 45/-
M. 23/   do. 33/-

No. 1491 × 18 in.
THE SNAKE.
S.B. 21/-   W.P. 27/-
M. 14/-   do. 20/-

No. 1501 × 17 in.
THE ROPE.
S.B. 21/-   W.P. 27/
M. 14/   do. 20/

No. 1499 × 17 in.
THE YORK.
S.B. 35/   W.P. 41/-
M. 23/   do. 29/-

No. 1627 × 13 in.
THE ACORN.
S.B. 19/-   W.P. 27/-
M. 12/6   do. 20/6

No. 1628 × 14 in.
THE DRAGON.
S.B. 30/   W.P. 37/
M. 29/   do. 27/

No. 1630 × 15 in.
THE LIONESS.
S.B. 21/   W.P. 41/
M. 21/6   do. 29/6

No. 3742 × 17 in.
THE CAIRO.
S.B. 35/   W.P. 43/-
M. 23/   do. 31/-

No. 3746 × 16 in.
ST. GEORGE & DRAGON.
S.B. 35/   W.P. 43/-
M. 23/   do. 31/-

S.B. indicates Solid Brass.   W.P. indicates With Plate.   M. indicates Metallic.

PLEASE SPECIFY CLEARLY FINISH REQUIRED WHEN ORDERING.

FRAMES

511   A picture frame in cast brass 8$\frac{1}{2}$in high. About 1880. (*Windrush Antiques*)

510   A mirror frame, in cast brass, 17in by 10$\frac{1}{2}$in. About 1860-80. (*Rudolph Otto Antiques*)

FOOT BATH

512   An unusual copper foot bath with brass handles, 14in long by 8in high. About 1800-30. (*Duncan J. Baggott*)

GAMES

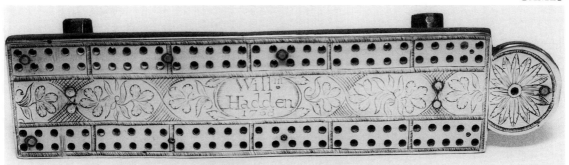

513 *(above)* An eighteenth-century brass cribbage board with engraved decoration and the inscription 'Willm. Hadden 1758'. 9^1/$_2$in long (*Duncan J. Baggott*)

514 *(right)* A brass cribbage board set on wooden base, 11^1/$_2$in Victorian. (*Country Life Antiques*)

GONG

515 A brass gong, 11^1/$_2$in high. About 1900. (*Duncan J. Baggott*)

IRONS

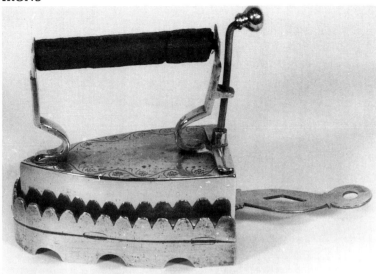

516 A rare brass iron on stand. Late eighteenth century, possibly Dutch. The stand 9$^1/_2$in long by 1$^1/_2$in high. The iron 5in high. (*B.I. & D.M. Howard*)

517 A flat iron with 'blow lamp' type heater, and a brass reservoir. Marked 'British Made', 10in long. About 1880-1900. (*Country Life Antiques*)

518 A late Victorian goffering iron stand marked 'D. Clegg, Montrose', 10$^1/_2$in high. (*Ian Savage*)

519 A goffering iron stand in brass. Rough cast base. About 1880-1900, 6in high. (*Ian Savage*)

520 A crimping machine in brass and iron. Marked 'T. & C. Clarke & Co Warranted Crimping Machine'. 17in long and 9¹/₂ in high. About 1850-70. (*B.I. & D.M. Howard*)

521(*below*) Late nineteenth-century brass 'linen' roller made, 18in long. (*Jack Casimir Ltd*)

522 (*bottom*) Another similar linen roller, 18¹/₂in long, late Victorian. (*Jack Casimir Ltd*)

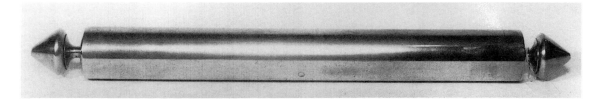

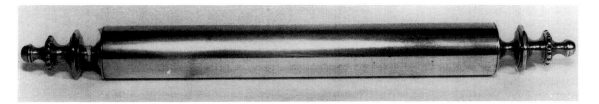

523 A brass and copper flat iron stand. The three feet are in the form of men's boots. 10¹/₂in long. About 1800-20. (*Christopher Sykes Antiques*)

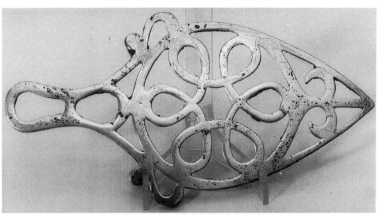

524 (*left*) A Victorian brass flat-iron stand, but with a high copper content. 10in overall. (*Country Life Antiques*)

525 (*below*) Another brass flat-iron stand, 9in long. About 1880-1900. (*Country Life Antiques*)

JARDINIERS

A group of jardinieres stamped out under pressure using dies. The bases are seamed into the body. Jardinieres of many shapes and sizes with hundreds of different embossed designs were made from the 1850s up until today. The majority of those likely to be seen are after 1900.

526 Oval jardiniere 14in long. (*Country Life Antiques*)

527 Round jardiniere, 14in. (*Duncan J. Baggott*)

528 Brass jardiniere 10¹/₂in. (*Duncan J. Baggott*)

529   Planter 11in high. (*Country Life Antiques*)

530   Larger jardiniere, 14in diameter. (*Duncan J. Baggott*)

531   Some designs are found both on British and Dutch jardinieres. Popular in the late nineteenth and early twentieth century were Dutch traditional scenes. This example is probably Dutch. 10in (*Duncan J. Baggott*)

532   A round planter $5^1/_2$in high of different style, the embossed rim seamed to the base. (*Country Life Antiques*)

533 An oval engraved jardiniere purporting to be from
1712, but actually a reproduction
of the 1930s.

534 A brass planter 12in by 8in
marked 'Made in England',
registered design number
933,307. (*Country Life Antiques*)

535 *(below)* Two pages from the
Pearson Page catalogue of
reproduction jardinieres, 1927.

TOOLS AND SCIENTIFIC INSTRUMENTS

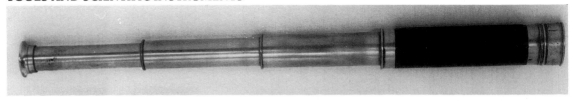

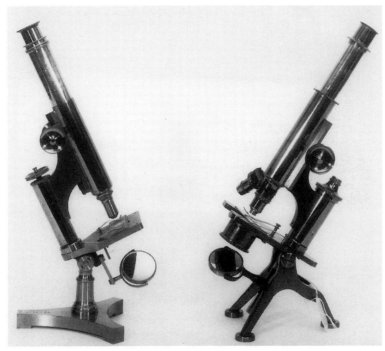

536 *(above)*   A Late Victorian ladies telescope, 16in long when extended. Brass with leather mounts. *(Country Life Antiques)*

537 *(left)*   Two brass microscopes. The example on the left is by R. & J. Beck of London, about 1860-80 and that on the right is about 1870-80. *(Country Life Antiques)*

538 *(above)*   A simple plane in brass, wood and steel. 4in long. Mid-nineteenth century. Tools of all types would have been used domestically as well as by craftsmen. *(Colin Greenway Antiques)*

539 *(right)*   Brass and wood magnifying glass, engraved and dated 1773. *(Jack Casimir Ltd, photograph by Roy Farthing)*

540 *(right)* A good brass money box mounted on a wooden base. Heavy cast brass, 5^1/$_4$in high. Late nineteenth century, 6in. *(Jack Casimir Ltd)*

541 *(below right)* A brass money box in the form of a post box. Inscribed 'Bank' on a copper plate. Late nineteenth century, 4^3/$_4$in high. *(Country Life Antiques)*

542 *(below left)* An unusual tubular money box on thin sheet metal feet. Sometimes also called a 'swear box'. Late nineteenth century, 6in *(Jack Casimir Ltd)*

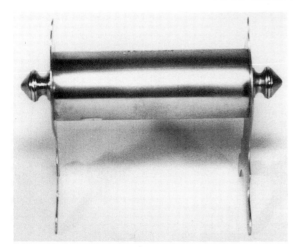

543 *(right)* A sheet metal brass money box with ten sides, top and base. 3^3/$_4$in high. Late nineteenth century. *(Jack Casimir Ltd)*

ORNAMENTS

544 *(left)*   A Victorian brass chimney ornament, 9in high. (*Colin Greenway Antiques*)

545 *(above)*   The fisherman, a registered design No 987,948. 11$\frac{1}{2}$in long. (*Windrush Antiques*)

546 *(left)*   A brass chimney ornament in the form of a horse, 7$\frac{1}{2}$ in long. Late nineteenth century. (*Duncan J. Baggott*)

547 *(right)* A late Victorian brass cannon and soldier. The cannon is 11in long and the soldier 6¹/₄in high. (*Colin Greenway Antiques*)

548 *(below)* A group of four ornaments. On the left and right two small brass tilt tables, 4in high. The tiger is 3¹/₂in high and the leopard 2¹/₂in high. All about 1880-1900. (*Colin Greenway Antiques*)

SEWING ACCESSORY

549 A rare brass thistle tape measure with pin cushion. 1¹/₂in high, Victorian. (*Colin Greenway Antiques*)

SPITOON

550   A copper spitoon probably used in a tavern. Examples with pottery bowls and copper or brass surrounds are also to be found. About 1880-1910, 8in diameter. (*Duncan J. Baggott*)

SUNDIALS

551   A sundial complete with its gnomon which casts the shadow. Eighteenth century. (*Robin Bellamy Ltd*)

552 An eighteenth-century sundial, inscribed with the names of John Owen, Hugh Owen, Edward Owen, David John and Hugh Ibotts. (*Robin Bellamy Ltd*)

553 A small window sill or wall mounted sundial. Late eighteenth century. 4in diameter. (*Keith Hockin Antiques*)

TOBACCO AND SNUFF ACCESSORIES

554 A fine cast brass tobacco box, possibly Dutch. About 1750. (*Robin Bellamy Ltd*)

555 *(below)* Three brass tobacco boxes with combination locks. 3¹⁄₂in, 3¹⁄₂in and 3¹⁄₄in long. Early nineteenth century. (*Keith Hockin Antiques*)

556 Three cast brass tobacco jars. Mid-nineteenth century. The largest is $6^1/_2$ in high. (*Jack Casimir Ltd*)

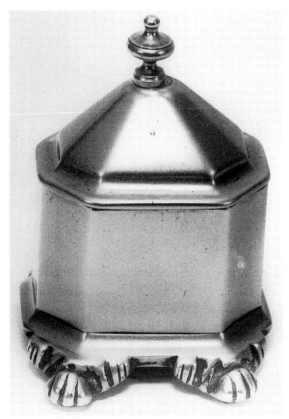

558 Edwardian brass ash tray and pipe holder. 4in high. (*Colin Greenway Antiques*)

557 A brass tobacco jar. $5^1/_4$ in high. Heavy cast brass. About 1850-70. (*Duncan J. Baggott*)

559 *(left)* Steel and brass cigar cutter on burr wood base. About 1840-50, 6³/₄in long. *(Jack Casimir Ltd)*

560 *(below)* A group of four snuff and tobacco boxes. Left and right two snuff boxes about 1820. The centre two larger boxes are for tobacco and are mid-eighteenth century. From 3¹/₄in to 5¹/₄in. *(Jack Casimir Ltd)*

561 Snuff box inscribed 'W. Baldwin', 3¹/₄in long. About 1840. *(Colin Greenway Antiques)*

562 An elongated oval box inscribed 'Samuel Baggott, Rose and Crown, Moxley'. 5in long, about 1820-40. (*Duncan J. Baggott*)

563 An oval tobacco box, engraved with a cock fighting scene. 5¹/₄in. Reproduction.

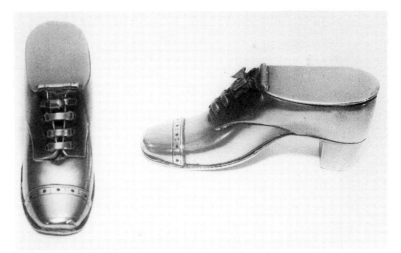

564 (*above*)   Two shoe snuffs. 3¹/₄in long, about 1850-80. (*Duncan J. Baggott*)

565 (*left*)   A pipe tamper and matchbox in the form of a wine bottle. Engraved 'Privilege, Chateau de Conde, Epernay' 1¹/₂in high, about 1890. (*Colin Greenway Antiques*)

566 *(left)* The pipe tampers on left and right represent Sam Weller, while the middle is a figure of a primitive man. 1¹/₂ to 2³/₄ in high, about 1840-60. (*Christopher Sykes Antiques*)

567 *(below)* Three smoking utensils. The top example is a pipe box with compartment for vesta matches, 5in long, about 1850. The pipe with the loop is in steel. The brass pipe case was used to protect clay pipes (1810-40). At the bottom is a tobacco box engraved with flowers and the name 'A. Walker', 7in long, early nineteenth century. (*Christopher Sykes Antiques*)

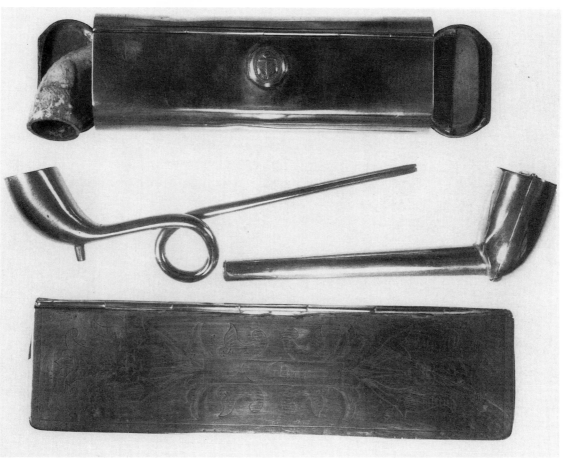

STAMP, SNUFF, & TOBACCO BOXES.

Customers' special designs can be engraved on any of the Sheet Metal Boxes excepting the embossed patterns
All Boxes Sheet Metal except where stated "Cast"

All Priced Each.

No. 2008 STAMP BOX. 1¼ in. × 1½ in. THE WINDMILL. 5/-

No. 2007 STAMP BOX. 1⅜ in. × 1⅜ in. THE SKULL AND CROSSBONES. 5/-

No. 2016 SNUFF BOX. 2¼ in. × 1¾ in. THE MASONIC. 13/-

No. 2013 SNUFF BOX. 2 in. × 2 in. THE LAST PATCH. 9/-

No. 2012 SNUFF BOX. 2⅛ in. diameter. THE TOILERS. 9/-

No. 1842 SNUFF BOX. 2¼ in. × 1¼ in. THE TULIP. 9/-

No. 1840 SNUFF BOX. 2¼ in. × 1¼ in. THE JOCKEY. 9/-

No. 1846 DOUBLE STAMP BOX. 2¾ in. × 1¾ in. THE SPORTSMAN. 10/-

No. 2392 2¾ in. × 2¾ in. THE BULL DOG. 8/-

No. 1844 TOBACCO BOX. THE WARWICK. (Cast Brass) 2½ in. dia., 11/- 3 in. dia., 17/-

No. 2394 TOBACCO BOX. 2¾ in. × 2¼ in. BLOODHOUND. 8/-

No. 1835 TINDER BOX. 3¼ in. × 2 in. THE ANCIENT LIGHTER. (Flint, Steel, and Tallow Compartments). 10/-

No. 1839 SNUFF BOX. 2¼ in. × 1¼ in. THE JUGGLER. 10/-

No. 1841 SNUFF BOX. 2¾ in. × 1¼ in. THE HERALDIC. 9/-

No. 1837 SNUFF BOX. 2¼ in. × 2 in. THE WOLSEY. 12/-

No. 2396 TOBACCO BOX. 3¼ in. × 2 in. × 1¼ in. THE DICKENS. (Cast Brass) 13/-

No. 1836 TOBACCO BOX. 3¼ in. diameter. THE DEFOE. 13/-

No. 2010 TOBACCO BOX. 3¼ in. × 3¼ in. wide. THE HUNTSMAN. 16/-

No. 2393 TOBACCO BOX. 4 in. × 2¾ in. THE RETRIEVER. 8/-

No. 2390 TOBACCO BOX. 3 in. diameter. THE SHAKESPEARE. 4/6

No. 10561 TOBACCO BOX. 3¼ in. × 3¼ in. THE UNICORN. 13/-

No. 1832 TOBACCO BOX. 3¼ in. × 3¼ in. AN EARLY VICTORIAN COACHMAN. 14/-

No. 2015 LARGE SNUFF BOX. THE EAGLE. 3¼ in. × 2¼ in. 13/-

No. 1830 TOBACCO BOX. THE GRIFFIN. Small, 5 in. × 1½ in., 14/- Large, 7 in. × 1¾ in., 17/-

No. 2009 TOBACCO BOX. THE OLD BOOT. 5½ in. long × 1¼ in. wide. 15/-

No. 1838 THE WALLET TOBACCO BOX. THE LIGHTHOUSE. 4⅞ in. × 2¼ in. 16/-

No. 1833 TOBACCO OR BISCUIT BOX. 4⅞ in. × 3⅞ in. "FISHING" 20/-

No. 1829 THE SMOKER'S FRIEND. 5 in. × 2 in. (Contains Compartments for Pipe, Tobacco and Matches). 21/-

No. 1834 LARGE TOBACCO BOX 6 in. × 3¼ in. THE POACHER. 17/-

No. 1831 TOBACCO OR BISCUIT BOX. 5 in. × 4 in. THE CAT AND MONKEY. 19/-

PLEASE SPECIFY CLEARLY FINISH REQUIRED WHEN ORDERING

568 1927 Pearson Page catalogue with reproduction snuff and tobacco boxes. (*Photograph by Eric Adkins*)

569 Tavern tobacco box. A penny inserted in the slot allowed a fill of pipe tobacco to be withdrawn. This example is Rich's Patent, about 1840. 9^3/$_4$in long. (*Christopher Sykes Antiques*)

WASHING EQUIPMENT

570 Fine brass soap box with traces of original silvering and an armorial. English or French, about 1740. (*Jack Casimir Ltd, photograph by Roy Farthing*)

571 *(above)* A round sponge or soap box, $5^1/_2$in diameter. Probably nineteenth century. (*Duncan J. Baggott*)

572 *(above)* A tapering water carrier, 19in high. The inside is tinned and it has rolled seams. Maker's mark on base. (*Duncan J. Baggott*)

573 *(left)* Copper jug with dovetailed seams and wooden handle. $12^1/_2$in high, about 1830. (*Wharton & Knight*)

574   A brass hot water can. 11$\frac{1}{2}$ in high, about 1870-1900. (*Country Life Antiques*)

575 (*below left*)   A late Victorian copper jug, 9in to lip. (*Blacklock Antiques*)

576 (*below right*)   A brass jug, 10in high. End of nineteenth century. (*Country Life Antiques*)

577 A typical Victorian brass
watering can with copper rose.
13in high and 17¹/₂in overall.
(*Key Antiques*)

578 An Art Deco watering can in copper, 17in
long, about 1900. (*Country Life Antiques*)

WEIGHTS AND SCALES

579 *(left)*   Fine Queen Anne wool weight. Used for weighing wool bales and not normally found in the home (*Jack Casimir Ltd, photograph by Roy Farthing*)

580 *(right)*   A troy weight only used for silver and gold. 200 troy ounces, with Victorian weights and measures mark. (*Jack Casimir Ltd*)

581 *(right)*   Two Victorian brass weights, each of 7lb. Worn maker's marks, 7in high. (*Country Life Antiques*)

582 *(below)*   A set of George III weights in bronze. 3in high. (*Duncan J. Baggott*)

583 *(left)* A rare 7lb brass weight of particular interest as it comes from the Borough of Birmingham and is so inscribed. Late eighteenth century. *(Duncan J. Baggott)*

584 Two sets of weights. On the left is a set of weights, late nineteenth century. The right-hand set weigh a total of 1lb and is made up of weights from $\frac{1}{2}$lb to $\frac{1}{4}$oz. 'VR' Imperial marks, about 1850. *(Jack Casimir Ltd)*

585 A pair of late Victorian postal scales for 1d post. $10\frac{1}{2}$in wide. Late Victorian. *(Country Life Antiques)*

586   Another pair of postal scales, 10¹/₂in wide.
Late Victorian. (*Country Life Antiques*)

587   A balance in brass with iron hooks. 15in
overall. Eighteenth century. (*Duncan J. Baggott*)

588 *(right)* A pair of balance scales with steel beam, brass chains and copper bowls. 7in overall, about 1830-40. (*Christopher Sykes Antiques*)

589 *(below)* Three brass sovereign or guinea scales for weighing gold coins. 4in long, about 1840-60. The top one, with its original box, is 'Harrison's Improved Sovereign Balance'. (*Christopher Sykes Antiques*)

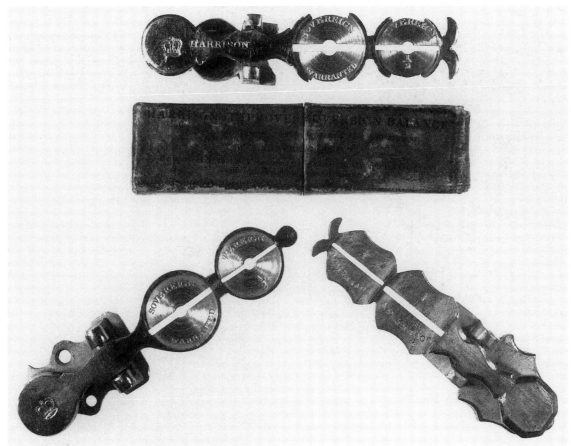

WRITING ACCESSORIES

590 *(above)*   Rare brass treasury style ink stand with two flap lids, traces of original silvering and an armorial. Made by 'AC', mid-eighteenth century. *(Jack Casimir Ltd, photograph by Roy Farthing)*

591 *(left)*   Late Victorian brass pen wiper, for cleaning knibs. 3½in high. *(Colin Greenway Antiques)*

592 *(right)*   Cast brass letter rack, 5¼in. Late nineteenth century. *(Jack Casimir Antiques)*

593 Brass ink well, 7in high. The top of the nest lifts off to reveal the ink well. About 1850-60. (*Colin Greenway Antiques*)

594 (*below*) Brass wax jack for sealing letters. This style was made from the 1820s until the turn of the century. 5$\frac{1}{2}$in, about 1850. (*Private Collection*)

595 (*left*) Another mid-Victorian wax jack. 5in high. (*Robin Bellamy Ltd*)

596 Brass horizontal wax jack with traces of
original silvering. 6^1/$_2$in high, about 1800. (*Jack
Casimir Ltd, photograph by Roy Farthing*)

597 Another wax jack, 7^1/$_4$in high. About 1800.
(*Jack Casimir Ltd, photograph by Roy Farthing*)

598   Very rare brass wax jack, about 1690-1700.
(*Jack Casimir Ltd, photograph by Roy Farthing*)

599 A group of Victorian brass paper or letter clips. The top-right example is inscribed 'Reg Oct 3 1843, No 24 by Merry Phipson & Parkers, Letter Clip'. Heights $3\frac{1}{2}$ to $5\frac{1}{2}$in. (*Christopher Sykes Antiques*)

9
COLLECTING BRASS, COPPER AND BRONZE

COLLECTING

Why do people collect? There is no final or simple answer to this question. Motives for human actions are hard to identify. For some it is the hunt, for other's the sense of ownership and a few collect as an investment. Whatever the motive, people like to surround themselves with things that they like.

If profit is what drives you into collecting then remember that values can fall as well as rise. The track record of antiques has been good since World War II, but there is no certainty that the current high level of prices will last for ever. The mood of nostalgia which exists now might disappear and people may come once more to regard antiques as just yesterdays junk!

There are many different sorts of collections. One person will try and furnish their home with the kind of things that it would have contained in the past. Such a person is a collector of antiques but does not limit himself to any one field. Other collectors seek just one type of antiques: silver, pewter, glass or pottery, for example. Some people keep to a period, others to a narrow area such as snuff boxes, buttons or candlesticks.

There are many ways in which a collection of antique copper, brass and bronze can be developed. Some collectors look to just one period such as the eighteenth century, others seek kitchen antiques, buttons, tankards or weights and so on. The choice is yours.

ACQUIRING KNOWLEDGE

Anyone setting out to collect needs some theoretical knowledge. You can start with some further reading and a few useful books are provided in the bibliography.

It is far more important to obtain a little practical experience. There is no easy way to acquire this. Regretfully, experience comes only with time, but there are several ways of gaining familiarity with antique metalware.

Many museums display some brass, copper and bronze domestic items, but there is no museum specialising in this field. In any case one is not able to handle items in museums and it is difficult to pick out construction features or signs of wear from outside a showcase.

Antique dealer's shops and market displays are one valuable source of knowledge. Things can be handled and most dealers are willing to chat about their stock. Do not feel embarrassed to ask for information nor compelled to buy, even if you have taken up a dealer's time. If he is worth his salt he will be happy to get to know you and hope that you will build up some confidence in him. Relate what he tells you to what you have learnt through this book and your other reading.

Market stalls and booths in small antique fairs are another good source of experience. Most week-ends there are several fairs, mostly held in hotels, and you will not have to travel too far to visit one. Regular antiques markets are also held in many parts of the country.

One word of caution is necessary. It is often assumed that the lower you get in the antique trade the lower will be the prices and the higher the chance of finding a bargain. This is not necessarily so. Less experienced dealers, and many start out part time in the market situation, may not have the knowledge of prices that a more experienced dealer has acquired. I have been asked in a market two or three times the going rate at Sothebys for brass and I do not recall when last I found a bargain in the same situation. What is common to the specialist may appear rare to the stallholder. But you may be lucky, and this is an excellent place to start.

Look at what is on offer. Handle the pieces. Try and see what are the good and bad features. Do you think it is as old as the dealer says or older? It is a good idea to ask other dealers who they would recommend for metalware other than themselves. You will learn something about their attitudes to their business competitors and you may also find their suggestions helpful. Often one or two names will re-occur and you can then try these dealers to see what they have to offer and how you get on.

Another excellent source of information and experience is the auction sale-room. Local sale-rooms may have interesting items from time to time but few of them specialise in metalware and few have experts able to catalogue the rarer items. It is best to go to one of the major sale rooms, in London perhaps, where the standard of writing catalogues in specialist areas is higher.

Read the catalogue descriptions carefully. 'In the style of' does not mean that this is its date. Indeed it draws attention to the doubts of the auction house. Nor does 'bearing the date 1620' mean that the auction room thinks 1620 is when it was made. Look for a clear unequivocal statement of age. If it is not there, they do not think it is old.

Examine all the items in the sale, and look for faults. By and large auction houses do not record damage. Their problem is that if they do for some items and miss the occasional repair on others they might be liable.

Sit through the sale. Try and work out why some things made more than the estimates and others less. Talk to the auctioneer or dealers after the sale about the lots you were especially interested in. In this way you will become familiar with prices and experienced at looking at antique metalware and begin to be able to exercise your own independent judgement. But you will still make mistakes. We all do!

BUYING

One day the time will come and you will cease to be a browser or looker and become a buyer. If you buy from dealers you are entitled to a fully detailed receipt. Always insist on this receipt setting out the main features of what you were told about an object. Never accept a receipt which says 'Brass Kettle' if you were told that it was an 'eighteenth century' kettle. If any repairs are mentioned then get them listed on the receipt.

Once you have this you are covered by the Trade Descriptions Act and if you ever find out that the object was not as it was described you can go back to the dealer fully armed or complain to the local Consumer Protection authorities. A false trade description is an offence, not simply a civil matter.

With a sale room you are not so well protected. Very few cases have been brought under the Trade Descriptions Act against auctioneers and it is not certain how far its terms apply. Read the small print in most catalogues and you will see that while the auction houses will, within certain time limits, accept back fakes, your rights are much less than you obtain with a purchase in a shop or market. They also do not offer a warranty of title; ie they do not guarantee that they have the right to sell the goods in the first place.

Sothebys currently state, for example, that 'All goods are sold with all faults and imperfections and errors of description .... Buyers should satisfy themselves as to the condition of each lot and should exercise and rely on their own judgement as to whether the lot accords with its description.' You can always seek advice from the auction houses, but as with a dealer this advice will be no better and no worse than the knowledge of the person you consult.

Certainly in the early days of collecting you need some guidance. This can come from a fellow collector and it is a good idea to join a local antiques club. There is, as yet, no collecting club for brass, copper and bronze. Many collectors find that they tend to rely on one or two dealers who specialise in the field, and although such advice cannot be impartial it is often the best available. Most established dealers will want you to come back and buy again. Members of the British Antique Dealers Association also offer other services including an arbitration scheme in a case of dispute.

CONDITION

One of the first decisions that a collector will have to make is about condition. Are you going to buy only items in first class un-repaired condition or will you purchase things that are damaged or repaired?

It is a matter of taste. Some collectors feel that with rarer more costly items that they will never be able to buy a fine example and will have to settle for one in less good condition. Others are simply not concerned with condition. They see the damage as part of the natural story of the object and proof of its age.

Other collectors report that repairs grate upon them after a time and that they regret buying some of the damaged things they collected in their early days. The best advice is to buy the best conditioned examples that you can find and can afford. There is no doubt that fine examples have appreciated in value faster over the last decade than repaired pieces and in a market fall would probably hold on to their value better.

You can never have perfection but there are degrees of damage. Everything used in the home over a long period will have dents, small splits and blemishes, some oxide and plenty of signs of wear. These are all acceptable, but what of replaced parts, such as new lids or handles? How do you regard major faults such as holes?

REPAIRS, CARE AND MAINTENANCE

It is hard to repair brass, copper and bronze. Most repairs involve 'brazing' with solder and need considerable skill. Any heat applied to copper and brass changes the colour and it can take many months of polishing to return the repaired parts to the same colour as the rest of the object, while too much heat can melt the item.

If new sections, such as a handle or lid, have to be added then it is important to have the original metal analysed so that the repair can be made in the same mixture. If you do not do this, after six months the colour will start to change as the sections oxide at a different rate and in a few years the new part will stand out like a sore thumb.

Unless you are a skilled metalworker, do not try and do repairs yourself. There are a few professionals in London who carry out repairs on antique metalware and you had best consult one of these people or try a local silversmith who may have the necessary skills.

Some people like a highly polished reflective surface on their brass and copper. Other collectors appreciate the softer tones of oxided metal. It is up to the individual, but remember that it is easy to remove patina, as it is termed, but impossible to replace it. So it is best to leave things alone unless you have a clear preference.

Most discolouration or light oxide can be removed with polishing with a metal polish such as Duraglit or Brasso. Rub away and polish off with a clean cloth. With heavy oxide more drastic treatment is needed including cleaning with caustics or acids and re-polishing on a buffing wheel. Do not try these yourself but go to a metal polisher. But remember that once highly polished it can take years for a surface to dull down.

If your items have the colour you like then all you have to do is polish them every few weeks and they will stay in this condition. If you cannot be bothered to polish then you can paint them with a lacquer but this will eventually wear away and show streaks and not everyone finds its hard shine attractive.

INSURANCE, RECORDS AND PHOTOGRAPHS

Most collectors insure their antiques, but insurance does have a cost. A few low priced articles will normally be covered by the ordinary domestic policy but if individual items or the total become significant then a separate insurance will be needed.

It is worth while consulting a broker as there are several ways that coverage can be obtained.

You can insure for the full cost of the goods, for their current market value or some part of either of these totals. There are other more complex deals available which can protect all your collection up to an agreed value, without 'averaging' any loss.

It is as well to record your purchases carefully, keeping all receipts and any other information you have acquired on the items. Your chance of recovering any loss is greatly enhanced too by photographs. You can take these yourself in daylight against a white cloth, or employ a photographer. Every year you should revalue the collection. Up to a certain point the insurance companies will accept a personal revaluation, but if the collection is valuable they may want an independent valuation. Specialist dealers and auctioneers offer this service.

10

BRASSMAKERS
AND THEIR MARKS

THE MARK'S BOOK OF THE ARMOURERS AND BRASIERS COMPANY

The book of maker's marks, catalogue number L37, 12090 from the collection of the Worshipful Company of Armourers and Brasiers is held at the Guildhall Library, London. Marks from this manuscript book are reproduced by kind permission of the Court of the Company, and have never appeared in print before.

Originally catalogued as a book of armourers' marks from around 1675, more recent research suggests that it comes from a later period. The style of writing employed, the types of marks used and the paper and binding all suggest an early eighteenth-century origin. After a search of the company records for the apprenticeship indentures of people listed in the book and for their admission to the Freedom of the Company it became clear that many of those included within the book did not become members of the Guild until the eighteenth century.

Not all the people whose marks are contained with the book have been identified from the records of the Company. Many of the entries in the Apprenticeship records and the Freedom admissions are very worn and faded and are unreadable. There is also some potential confusion between fathers and sons, who had the same christian names. It was normal for the eldest son to take the name of his father and to follow the same trade, so that you can often find two or three members of the same family with the same name and same ancestry in the Guild records. Over 40 years up to three different generations could be involved.

The marks book might have been compiled at one time, but some entries are in a different hand. If it was completed at one time, it could not have been before 1729 and such a late date would make the frequency with which makers within the book received their freedom in the late seventeenth century difficult to comprehend.

I suggest that it was compiled in 1708 and subsequently added to over the years. Both armourers and brasiers are included, but it does not contain all the master craftsmen who were members of the Guild at that time. Several members of the Court and some of the Masters, Under and Renter Wardens also do not appear in the book. Nor does it contain only the marks and names of armourers on the one hand or braziers on the other. Its exact purpose was has not yet been discovered but it does hold the names of many brasiers who worked in London between 1708 and 1740.

The bulk of the entries appear to have been made around 1708. Out of the seventy-two identified makers, fifty-five were either admitted to the Freedom before 1708, were already members of the Court at that date or can be assumed to have taken their Freedom before that date on the basis of their Apprenticeship records. Of these fifty-five makers, thirty-four either were Guild Members before 1700, or are likely to have been admitted to the Freedom by that date on the basis of their Apprenticeship records or membership of the Court, and twenty-one makers became members of the Guild, on the same basis, between 1700 and 1708. Only seventeen are likely to have been free of the Company between 1709 and 1729. On this basis it is likely that the lists were begun in 1708.

From other sources we know that the craftsman's life could be brief, due to the high mortality rate and frequent bankruptcies, but that successful men might work for forty years at their trade. Some members of the Court spent over 20 years as members of that body.

The street or area in London where the craftsman worked, which are recorded in the book, are indicated in the lists, but as with the names of the makers, not all can be deciphered. The lists have been put into strict alphabetical order. Fig 47 shows an example of a brass item with a mark which is clearly identifiable with one shown here, but it must be emphasised that known examples of marks on brassware are not common.

MARKS OF THE LONDON BRASIERS AND ARMOURERS

	Situated at	Apprenticed	Livery or Freeman	First recorded in Court	Office Holder	Mark
H. Alburt (?)	Aldwich					
Wm Annison	Borner Lane	1689				
Charles Appelby	New Street	1683		1720		
John Appleby (dead by 1720)	Snowshill				Master 1720	
Simon Archer	Petty Coat Lane					
John Arnold	Petty Coat Lane	1691				
M. Ashworth						
Savage Attwood (dead by 1732)	London Wall		1707 Livery 1709		Master 1726	
Abraham Badbury (dead by 1727)	Beech Lane, Barbican	1673		1708		

	Situated at	Appr-enticed	Livery or Freeman	First recorded in Court	Office Holder	Mark
John Ball	Wapping	1685				IBALL
Joseph Ballard	Southwark	1680		1708	Master 1712	
John Barnet	Turnmill Street	1695	1705			
Roger Bartlett (dead by 1728)	St Olaves St, Southwark		Livery 1691	1710	Master 1713	
William Barwell	Minories, Aldergate	1692	Livery 1710		Master 1729	
John Baybury	Southwark					IBAY BUR
Joseph Bayley	Warwick Lane					I·BA
Daniel Bentley	Bethlehem, Lambeth Road	1688				DBe
Benjamin Boss	Houndsditch	1695	1702 Livery 1714	1724	Master 1730	B BOSS
Edward Bradbury	Little Britain off Aldersgate St	1683				E·BR
E. Briggs	Shoe Lane		Livery 1710			EBR

	Situated at	Appr-enticed	Livery or Freeman	First recorded in Court	Office Holder	Mark
Robert Briggs	Church Lane	1691	1712 Livery 1720	1720		R·BR
Wm Brotherton (dead by 1738)	Shoe Lane	1694	1701 Livery 1713	1727	Master 1735	WBR
Ephraim Brown	The Mint, Southwark	1722	1729			EBR
John Brown	The Mint, Southwark	1698		1729		IBR
Joseph Brown	Fleet Lane	1701	1708			I·BR
Samuel Butler	Jew Lane					SBv
Wm Carpenter	St James Street	1709	1717			W.Ca
Godwin Conen	Houndsditch	1700	1707			G.Co
Thomas Cooper	Deadmans Place, Southwark		1710-11			TCo
Jacob Coyn(e)	Grafton Street (?) Seven Dials					I CO
I. Cripps	Panton Street in Haymarket		1711			I CR

	Situated at	Appr-enticed	Livery or Freeman	First recorded in Court	Office Holder	Mark
Nicholas Crispin	Mold Street					NCR
Robert Davidson	Turnmill Street					RDa
John Dowe	Nicholas Street (?) Spitalfield		1694			V ID
Peter Dow	Red Lion, Spitalfields					V PD
William Draycott	Huss Street, Southwark		1673			W DR
Henry Evans	Bishopsgate Street					H·EV
Leonard Fitzhugh (dead by 1719)	The corner of Harp Alley		Livery 1708	1712	Master 1715	L FI
John Francis	Clarkman Street, Southwark	1696	1703			I·FR
Joseph Gillman	East (?) Smithfield	1689 & 1693	1708			IGI
Thomas Gillman	Haymarket		1708			T GI
Thomas Haines	Houndsditch	1698		1709		THa

	Situated at	Appr-enticed	Livery or Freeman	First recorded in Court	Office Holder	Mark
Frederick Hart	Westminster					F.HA
A. Hawke (?)	Houndsditch					AH$_A$
Richard Hawkinson	Barbican	1691	1699 Livery 1708			R HA
Gabriel Holinden (dead by 1714)	Southwark			1708	Master 1710	GH$_o$
Charles Holt	St Albans St, Pall Mall	1697				C HO
Giles Hunt	Shoe Lane		1693			G.HV
John Ingram	Fleet Ditch			1708		I IH
William Jackson	Red Lion at Whitecross Street					
Mardy Jacobs	Shoe Lane					M.IA
James Jarman	Shoe Lane		Livery 1716			I I$_A$
John Johnson (dead by 1716)	Ratcliffe Cross				Master 1709	II$_o$

	Situated at	Appr-enticed	Livery or Freeman	First recorded in Court	Office Holder	Mark
William Johnson	Ratcliff	1692	1698			
William Johnson	Knightrider Street	1717	1723	1728	Master 1750	
William Kent	Harp Alley	1692	Livery 1701	1716	Master 1719	
A. Lawrence (?)	Maison St, (?) Long Arches					
Walter Lock	Holborn					
Thomas Lutwith	St Johns Lane					
Nathaniel Maccascree	Barbican	1699	Livery 1709	1724	Master 1728	
Samuel Manlove (dead by 1728)	Little Tower Street	1704	1711 Livery 1716	1725		
Robert Monk	Longditch, Westminster					
John Morris	Blackamore Street	1689		1708		
William Moss	Southwark	1682	1713			

	Situated at	Appr-enticed	Livery or Freeman	First recorded in Court	Office Holder	Mark
James Mouner	Quakers Street, Spitalfields					IMO
Andrew Niblett (dead by 1736)	Bishops Gate Street, Without	1698	1706 Livery 1711	1724	Master 1731	
Jesse Norman (dead by 1733)	Harp Alley	1697	Livery 1718			
John Oliver	Turnagain Lane	1686	1693			
(?) Orr	Fleet Lane					
Samuel Osborne	Guild Lane		Livery 1708			
Francis Pawley	London Wall, Bishopsgate	1694	1701 Livery 1708			
John Pendelton	London Stone		1693	1706		
Francis Roberts	Coleman Street					
Francis Roberts	Grub Street					
James Robertson (dead by 1713)	Whitechapel		1679			I·Ro

	Situated at	Appr- enticed	Livery or Freeman	First recorded in Court	Office Holder	Mark .
Nibr (?) Samuel	Stone Bridge					
Samuel Shad(e)	Ratcliffe					
John Sheppard	Whitechapel	1696	Livery 1710			
N. Sherwin	King St, Westminster	1690				
Nicholas Sherwin	King St, Westminster		Livery 1717			
Richard Sherman	Holborn		1693 Livery 1708			
Richard Slade	Shoe Lane		1701 Livery 1710			
Henry Smith	St Martins Lane	1703	1713			
John Smith (dead by 1725)	Longlane		1693	1708		
Thomas Smith	Ratcliffe Highway	1696	1703			
Joseph Spencer	Shoe Lane	1701				

	Situated at	Appr-enticed	Livery or Freeman	First recorded in Court	Office Holder	Mark
Wm Stevenson	Turnagain Lane		1712			
John Stilles	Ratcliffe					
Richard Skornton	Poultry Lane	1696				
John Stott	Wood Street	1694		1708		
James Tallman (dead by 1717)	London Bridge			1708	Renter Warden 1709	
Anthony Taylor	Holborn Bridge		Livery 1705	1716	Master 1722	
James Taylor (dead by 1725)	Juxon Street (?)				Master 1708	
Henry Taylor	Piccadilly	1685	Livery 1703	1708	Master 1711	
William Todd	Stowmarket (?), Blackfriars	1681				
Henry Tunis	Piccadilly					
Edward Underwood	Charing	1690				

	Situated at	Appr-enticed	Livery or Freeman	First recorded in Court	Office Holder	Mark
P. Vaughan	St John Street	1720				
Richard Walker (dead by 1742)	Barbican		Livery 1705	1718	Master 1724	
Thomas Westal (dead by 1729)	St Anne's Lane, Aldersgate Street		Livery 1715	1725		
Richard Williamson	Cow Lane	1684	1691-2			
John You	East Street, Spitalfields					
Richard Young	Grafton Passage		1709			

FOUNDERS AND BRAZIERS MARKS FOUND ON DOMESTIC WARE

Although, unfortunately for the collector, the majoriy of domestic brassware does not carry maker's names or marks, some items such as early skillets and mortars are identified with the name of the maker. The list below includes names or initials which have been identified on English domestic items, even though in some instances few details of the maker are known.

Name	Items	Town	Dates
Ashton, Luke	Mortars & bells	Wigan	1724-50
Ashtons, Ralf	Mortars & bells	Wigan	1703-20
Bayley, T. or I.	Candlesticks	Bridgewater	c1760
Bayley & Street	Skillets	Bridgewater	c1750
Barlow	Candlesticks	Birmingham	1800-20
Bartlett, Thomas	Mortars	Durham	c1600-32
Beardmore & Co	Mortars	London	mid-C18th
Beardmore & Reynolds	Mortars	London	last quarter C18th
Carter, William	Mortars & bells	London	c1615
Cors, Robert, William, Oliver & John	Bells	Aldbourne	1694-1740
Cox	Skillets	Taunton	c1870
C.I., probably John Conyers	Mortars	Hull	1616-30
Dowler, Thomas & Co	Candlesticks	Birmingham	1770-1803
Durnall, Edward	Candlesticks	Birmingham	1759-1812
Fathers or Feathers, J (also initials 'I.F.' used)	Skillets	?	c1685
Grove, George	Candlesticks	Birmingham	1748-68
Harrison, James	Candlesticks	Birmingham	1770-1797
E.K.	Candlesticks	?	c1780-1820
Knight, Henry	Mortars & bells	Reading	1587-1623
Lakin, Thomas	Candlesticks	Birmingham	1729-1760
Lee, William	Candlesticks	Birmingham	1759-17880
G.M.	Candlesticks	?	c1750
Martin, John	Mortars	Worcester	1644-93
Mears, William, Thomas & others	Bells etc	London	1784-1861
Neale, Edward Sr & Jr	Mortars	Burford	1641-c85
Palmer or Palmar, Thomas	Mortars, skillets & bells	Canterbury	c1650-1680
Palmer or Palmar, John	Mortars & bells	Canterbury	c1630-50
Pyke, Thomas (skillets marked 'T.P.B.WATER')	Skillets	Bridgwater	c1770-1810
R.A., probably Abraham Ruddall Snr & Jnr	Mortars	Gloucester	c1657-1736
W.S.	Candlesticks	?	c1800-20
Smith, Samuel Snr & Jnr	Mortars	York	c1663-1731
Street	Skillets	Bridgewater	c1775-1810
Street & Pyke (primarily bellfounders, who occasionally made clocks)	Skillets	Bridgewater	c1775
Tosier or Tosear, Clement	Mortars	Salisbury	1679-1713
Tosier or Tosear, John	Mortars & skillets	Salisbury	1684-1733
Turner & Co	Candlesticks	?	c1750
Warner	Skillets	London	c1850-1900

Washborough	Skillets	Bristol	1793-1797 & 1826
(also with various partners 1783-1825 & 1827-1846)			
Wells, Robert	Bells	Aldbourne	1770-1820
Wood & Grove	Candlesticks	Birmingham	c1748-1760
Wood, Joseph	Candlesticks	Birmingham	1735-60

BIRMINGHAM MID-NINETEENTH CENTURY MAKERS

There were many craftsmen operating in or near Birmingham throughout the nineteenth century, but most employed only a few workers. In 1861, for example, there were 216 individual brass-makers or brasiers listed in the *Birmingham Trade Directory* but only a small proportion of these would have actually made brass objects for domestic use and most would have been in business in a small way.

This list of leading domestic brass-makers in Birmingham has been compiled for the period 1875-90. Few items will be found with the marks of these makers as only a small proportion of firms used trade marks or registered designs.

Name	*Items*
James Boyce	General founders
William Bodin	Fenders, fire iron & grates
James Booth & Co	Brass tubes
Thomas Bladon	Lamps
William Blews	Bell founders and chandeliers
Bocock & Wilkinson	Oil burners & lamps
Smith & Chamberlaine	Brass founders. A long established firm.
Francis Crisp	Domestic brassware
T. Carpenter	Light fittings
I. Clements	Die sinkers, stampers and piercers. Employed seventy workers in 1888. There were at least another nine firms supplying the trade with stamps, punches and dies at that time inBirmingham.
C.F. Davis & Co	
Elliot Metal Co	
Fisher Brown & Co	Bedsteads
James Hinks	Duplex lamps
Samuel Heath	General brass ware
Hooper & Edman	Fenders, fire irons and screens
Charles Joyner	Chandeliers and gas fittings
Lawrence & Bishop	Wire workers and bird cages
T.M. Lee	Cooper ware
W. Lowe	Candlesticks and stamped goods
Martineau & Smith	General merchants and brass cocks
Donald McKenzie	Candlesticks and sconces
Samuel Mason	Pewter and brass. 120 employees.
Morris & Norton	Brass bedsteads
Joseph Nichols	Wire work and bird cages
Nash & Bond	Stamped brass foundry
F. & C. Osler	Chandeliers and electric light fittings
Albert Oldham	General founders
W. Platt & Co	Lamps

Preston & Bishop	Mill brass castings
Albert Phillips	Brass beds
Phipson & Wade	Beds
James Russell	Brass tubes
J. Saunders	Chandeliers & gas fittings
Henry Sheldon	Rolled brass
W. Henry Sheldon	Lamps and electrical fittings
Sheldon & Co	Brass founders
Thomas Smart	Fire brass
Brass Warehouse & Co	General merchants
Thomas Taylor	Old established firm
William Tonks	Long established. Made the whole range of domestic objects. Owned 15,000 casting patterns.
Townsend & Thompson	Candlesticks, washing sets, toddy kettles and general brassware. Had a London office
S.F. Turner	Bedsteads
A. & J. Vincent & Lynes	Brass founders and gas fittings
E. Wilkes	
John Wright	Beds and fire brasses
William Bros	Desk sets & fire screens
R.W. Winfields	Rolled metal and gas fittings. Lighting and brass foundry. 200 to 300 employees.

FURTHER READING

History

'Brass and Brass Making', W.C. Aitkin (in *Birmingham and Midlands Hardware Distrct*.) edited by S. Timmins (Birmingham, 1866, reprinted 1967)

Bristol Brass: The History of the Industry. Joan Day (David Charles, 1973)

Citizen and Founders. A History of the Founders 1365-1975. G.D. Hadley (London, 1971)

The English Brass and Copper Industry to 1800. Henry Hamilton (Cass, 1967)

Fodinae Regales. Sir John Pettus (London, 1670)

The Objects

Birmingham, Brass Candlesticks. J. Burke. (University of Virginia, 1986)

Collecting Copper and Brass. G. Wills (London, 1968)

English Domestic Brass 1684-1810. R. Gentle & R. Field (1964)

Old Domestic Brass Candlesticks. R. Michaelis, (Antique Collector's Club), 1978

Pewter, Copper and Brass. P. Hornsby (Hamlyn, 1981)

REFERENCE SOURCES

The following books, journals and manuscripts were consulted by the author in the preparation of this book, and the author gratefully acknowledges the help that they have provided.

General History

Citizens & Founders. A History of the Founders 1365-1975. G.D. Hadley (London, 1971)

The English Brass & Copper Industries to 1800, H. Hamilton (Cass, 1967)

A History of the Founders Company, W.N. Hibbert (London, 1925)

Masters & Men, M. Rowlands (Manchester University Press, 1975)

'Swedish Travellers', A. Woolrich, *Journal of Bristol Industrial Archaeology Society*, 4 (1971)

Wardens Accounts; The Worshipful Company of Founders of the City of London 1497-1681, G.Parslow (Ed) (University of London, 1964)

Social History

The British Consumer Society, N. McKendrick (Ed) (Indiana Univ Press, 1985)

English Social History, G.M. Trevelyan (Longmans, 1946)

Irons in the Fire, R. Field (Crowood Press, 1984)

The Kitchen in History, M. Harrison (Osprey Publishing, 1972)

The Social History of Lighting, W. O'Dea (London, 1958)

A Woman's Place, M. Filbee (London, 1980)

Regional History

Birmingham Gazette. 1744-1830. Local Studies Dept, Birmingham Central Library

Birmingham Inventors and Inventions, R. Prosser (reprinted 1970)

Bridgwater Industries, Past and Present, E. Porter (undated private publication)

Bristol Brass: The History of the Industry. Joan Day (David Charles, 1973)

The Cornish Miner A.H. Jenkin (David & Charles, 1972)

Industrial Development of Birmingham and the Black Country 1860-1927, G.C. Allen (George Allen & Unwin, 1929)

Industries of Birmingham, anon (Birmingham Industrial Pub Co, 1888)

Pearsons Trade Directory (1777)

Silk Town. Industrial and Cultural History of Macclesfield. 1750-1838, G. Malmgreen (University of Hull, 1985)

A Short History of the Brass Trade, W.J. Davis (Birmingham, 1892)

Thomas Bolton and Sons Ltd, J. Morton, (MPC 1983)

Warrington and the Mid-Mersey Valley, G. Cole (1971)

Studies of Copper, Brass and Bronze Items

Bells of England, J.J. Raven (Methuen, 1906)

Bells thru the Ages, J.R. Nichols (Chapman & Holt, 1928)

Birmingham Brass Candlesticks, J. Burke (University of Virginia, 1986)

Church Bells of Gloucestershire, H.T. Ellacombe (1881)

Collecting Antique Metalware, E. Perry (Country Life Books, 1974)

Collecting Copper and Brass, G. Wills (London, 1968)

Early Lighting, anon (Compiled and published by The Rushlight Club, 1980)

English Domestic Brass 1684-1810, R. Gentle and R. Field (1964)

Iron and Brass Implements of the English House, J. Seymour Lindsay (1927, 2nd edition 1970)

Making Fire and Light in the Home pre-1820, J. Capsall (Antique Collector's Club, 1987)

Old Domestic Brass Candlesticks, R. Michaelis (Antique Collector's Club, 1978)

Old English Pattern Books, Victoria & Albert Museum (1913)

Yesterdays Shopping, Army and Navy Stores Coop Society Catalogue 1907, anon (David & Charles, 1969)

Manuscripts

Armourers and Brasiers Company: MS 12,024; MS 12,087; MS 12,147 and MS 12,680, Guildhall Museum, London

The Founders Company: MS 6336; MS 6337; MS 6338 and MS 6340, Guildhall Museum, London

George Greenwood MS 'The Elmbridge Water Mills', Suurey Archaeological Society

Talk by J.R. Harris (MS 1358 Warrington Public Library) 'The Pattens of Warrington'

Index to Eighteenth-Century Birmingham Press. Birmingham University, Economics Faculty.

Public Records Office: Port Record Books E. 190.

INDEX

INDEX TO ILLUSTRATIONS